NATIONAL UNIVERSITY
LIBRARY SAN DIEGO

D0744385

Opening the Gates: The Rise of the Prisoners' Movement

Opening the Gates: The Rise of the Prisoners' Movement

Ronald Berkman
Brooklyn College,
City University of New York

LexingtonBooks
D.C. Heath and Company
Lexington, Massachusetts
Toronto

Library of Congress Cataloging in Publication Data

Berkman, Ronald.
Opening the gates: the rise of the prisoners' movement.

Bibliography: p.
Includes Index.
1. Prisoners—United States—Political activity. 2. Prisoners—Legal status, laws, etc.—United States. 3. Politics, Practical. 4. Prison violence—United States. I. Title.
HV9471.B44 365'.6 78-24767
ISBN 0-669-02828-2

Copyright © 1979 by D.C. Heath and Company

All rights reserved. No part of this publication may be reproduced or transmitted in any form or by any means, electronic or mechanical, including photocopy, recording, or any information storage or retrieval system, without permission in writing from the publisher.

Published simultaneously in Canada.

Printed in the United States of America.

International Standard Book Number: 0-669-02828-2

Library of Congress Catalog Card Number: 78-24767

To my father—who fought his own quiet and courageous struggle for a lifetime

Contents

Preface and Acknowledgments

In broad terms this book is concerned with the birth and maturation of a political movement—a movement that grew within the milieu of America's maximum security prisons.

Specifically, it focuses on the prisoner movements in California and New Jersey, with greater emphasis on California. California became the focus because the movement first developed there, and it has consequently evolved further there than in other states. Also, a vast amount of information was available on the history of the movement and the policy decisions made by prison administrations in that state. Even though prison is a small community with a contained environment, it was not possible to examine every effect of protest movements that developed within its walls. Therefore, it was necessary to isolate certain concerns and attempt to gather information about them.

My interest in the subject developed during a period of research in a maximum security prison in New Jersey. Although much of the data gathered in the New Jersey prison is not often mentioned in the book, the value of the experience cannot be overestimated. Much of the terrain that I explored in California prisons is closely related to the concerns that developed as a result of my experiences in New Jersey. It was this experience that prepared the agenda of concerns and interest that I brought to the study of the California prisoners' movement.

In New Jersey I encountered a political system within the prison that in many ways resembled the political system in the larger community. Prisoners were organized into pluralist interest groups, each purporting to represent the interests of a particular constituency within the prison. Each group sought to further the interests of its purported constituency by bringing the needs and desires of that constituency to the attention of institutional decision makers. Struck by the similarity between the pluralist conception of politics and the actual political structure of the prison I was curious to understand how a form of organization so similar to that in the outside community developed within the prison. This led directly to an attempt to reconstruct the political history of the prison from the early fifties until the present. It soon became evident that in order to understand the political system that prevailed in the prison, it was necessary to examine closely the period of political activity between 1964 and 1972. The bulk of the political history that follows deals directly with this period, which germinated the political system that exists within the California and New Jersey prison systems.

In the midst of this examination it became clear that in order to understand the forces which brought about the group form of politics it was necessary to understand the total political program out of which the group movement grew. In California, that included the challenges that prisoners raised concerning the system of labor within the prison, the system of individual and collective rights, and the ideology of the governing groups which supported these systems within the prison.

Consequently, the book deals with particular economic and political practices within the prison and the effect that the prisoners' movement had on prevailing policy. It is an attempt to show the continuity between the quantity and quality of the particular protests and the administration's response. Finally, there is an effort to explore the significance of the protest and the political system that now exists. This involved probing the attitudes of the prisoners and administrators concerning the new form of political organization to attempt to elicit the objectives of the system and the extent to which they have been realized.

Once having decided on the objectives of the study, it was necessary to devise a means to accomplish these ends satisfactorily. This was a difficult task. First, there was almost nothing in the literature concerning group politics within prisons. The literature on the historical period of interest was sparse and often less than comprehensive. Second, it was necessary to spend an extended period of time in the prison to observe the system and speak with prisoners, officers and administrators who could shed light on the historical period that I was concerned with. Additionally, to be sure that I spoke with a variety of prisoners who might have experienced the historical period in different ways. Finally, it was imperative to design a means to test a broad spectrum of opinion concerning the political systems of the prison.

With the objective of reconstructing a political history of the prisoners' movement, analyzing the forces within the movement, gaining personal knowledge about the operation of the political system, and testing the attitudes of those within the walls, it was quickly apparent that no one methodological approach would accomplish these ends. Consequently, the methodology that evolved had several facets, each designed to accomplish a particular end.

The first priority was to gain admittance to an institution in California and spend as much time as possible acquainting myself with the environment, prisoners, and staff. After three months of negotiations and many refusals I managed to obtain the approval of the Department of Corrections and a prison superintendent. Once admitted, I spent eight to ten hours a day at the institution for a period of three months. Much of this time was devoted to informal conversation with prisoners and staff and attending many of the functions of the prisoner groups. I was free to move about the prison at will and talk to anyone.

Much time was devoted to scrutinizing the historical records of the prison. Besides these records, I examined all the current policies and standards, memos, directives, and management reports. All communications, including the minutes of all of the Men's Advisory Council (MAC) (the organ of prisoner representation) meetings, the superintendent's responses to MAC proposals and all the superintendent's directives dating back to September 1965 were made available. Most of this work was done on weekends and was in addition to the eight hours spent within the institution daily.

Before I even entered the institution, I had spent a number of months interviewing prisoners who had directly participated in prison politics in the sixties. Many contacts with the prisoners came through community organizations involved in prison work. These interviews enabled me to begin to construct a history of the period. In addition, I spent time speaking with administrators of the state prison bureaucracy in Sacramento and examining the archives of the Department of Corrections. By the time my project was approved, I had garnered a good knowledge of many of the key events and key forces that characterized the prisoners' movement in the sixties.

The final facet of the methodological approach was conducting formal, standardized interviews with leaders of prison groups, administrators and a random sample of prisoners. A discussion of the interview techniques employed can be found in appendix A.

The problem of establishing trust and openness is always a concern when one acquires information through interviews. This problem is particularly vexing in a prison, where numerous institutional forces conspire to create an environment of apprehension and fear.

Anticipating that this veil of fear might interfere with the information-gathering process, I composed a statement of confidentiality, which stated the purposes of the study and the manner information received would be used. Furthermore, the statement was my personal assurance that no information conveyed in the interviews would be reported in a manner where statements could be traced to particular individuals. To remain true to this pledge, I have chosen to refer to the California prison as West Prison and the New Jersey institution as East Prison.

I am indebted to many individuals who helped make the book possible—most of all the prisoners who were often willing to share their private fears and talk candidly about activities which could have had profound repercussions on their lives if the information became known to institutional authorities. It was these private decisions to trust me and my mission that made everything possible.

The institutional authorities, particularly those in California, were extremely helpful and cooperative. They made no attempt to limit my activities and promptly responded to all my requests for information and access. Their cooperation made my task considerably easier.

On the academic side, I owe a special thanks to Professor Jameson Doig, who was consistently supportive and helpful. He read the entire manuscript and made many important suggestions. The Research Program in Criminal Justice at the Woodrow Wilson School at Princeton University, funded by the Guggenheim Foundation, provided financial support during the two years that I researched and wrote the book.

I am especially grateful to Professor H.H. Wilson. He has been a dear friend, a close confidant, a source of endless feedback concerning my work, but, most importantly, a human being whom I truly loved and admired.

Finally, there are many friends who provided important support in many forms. I am particularly grateful to Michael Polizzi who read the manuscript and suggested stylistic revisions and Isabelle Bedard who provided patience, understanding, and love in great quantities.

Introduction

There is little doubt that the political activity of the early sixties has affected the political and social landscape of America. It is evident that the period produced intense political energy and mass opposition to many prevailing structures and policies of American institutions. The Civil Rights Movement awakened the consciousness of America to the plight of the nation's largest minority. The antiwar movement focused attention on the objectives of American foreign policy. Additionally, the social protest of the sixties had implications for people and institutions outside the core of the movement. The effects of the movement on these institutions and constituencies has yet to receive much careful attention.

Constituencies intimately affected by the movements of the sixties were those in the clientist spheres. A client is an individual who maintains a dependent relation with an organ of the state, who depends on the state for some form of income or service. These can include direct cash payments, food stamps or social services. Client groups include welfare recipients, the handicapped, social security recipients, prisoners, juvenile delinquents, and mental patients.

As a general rule, those who maintain this sort of relationship with the state are required to forfeit certain citizenship protections afforded the general population. The types of protections the individual is required to forfeit seem directly related to the degree of dependency that he or she maintains with the state. For example, social security recipients are unable to secure employment that would allow them to expand their total incomes beyond certain levels. Welfare recipients have historically been forced to forfeit their rights of privacy so that inspectors could, at will, examine the conditions of life within a recipient's home.[1]

At the bottom is the prisoner, who is totally dependent on the state for basic sustenance. The degree of dependence is almost total and the rights retained by the prisoner are few. The loss of citizenship rights, a condition which accompanies the client status, was an issue that strongly emerged during the ferment of the sixties. Out of the political programs of the sixties emerged organizations seeking to restore the prisoner and other client groups to full citizenship status. The National Welfare Rights Organization is an example of one such organization.

This study focuses on the political activity that developed among prisoners as a result of the broad social movements of the sixties and the policies adopted by the prison administration to deal with the new political challenge. Because the prison is a contained institution, directly governed by a small ruling group, it provides an excellent opportunity to examine a political movement and a government response to that movement. The prison is one of the more unlikely places for political activity to emerge. It is a totalitarian institution, governed by ruling strata whose power exceeds almost all other governing bodies in the nation. The prisoners are subjects, as opposed to citizens. They retain few of the rights of the citizen in the outside community. Few of the normal checks and balances to guard against the abuse of discretionary power operate within the prison. In this environment any form of organized political activity among prisoners must be regarded as extraordinary.

Historically, the rise of the prisoners' movement can be traced to a variety of ideologies, movements and national occurrences coming together in the 1960s. However, some elements are particularly important in explaining the rise of the movement. These include the activism of the federal courts, the formation of the Black Muslim movement and the civil rights and antiwar movements.

Each of these events or movements significantly contributed to the prisoners' movement's birth. The activism of the courts allowed prisoners to seek redress for institutional conditions that courts had traditionally regarded as outside their jurisdiction. The Black Muslim movement provided a paradigm for strong organizational forms and replaced the ideology of "pathological disorder," in which prisoners identified themselves as suffering from organic or behavioral deficiencies, with an ideology of "collective oppression," which opened new political vistas. Finally, the antiwar and civil rights movements revealed much about American society, particularly in relation to the position of poor and minority groups. Also, these movements created vast political energy in the populace and supplied strategies for resistance.

Programmatically, the prisoners' movement had wide interests. However, the greatest emphasis was put on issues concerning individual and collective rights and the conditions of labor within the institutions. These issues dominated the demands of prisoners, who in the early seventies engaged in organized open insurrection in California and New Jersey.

The demands concerning individual and collective rights had several facets. The demand for the expansion of collective rights was essentially a demand to legalize group meeting and activities, through which particular constituencies could create political or educational organizations to deal with institutional problems. The demands centered on individual rights sought to bring citizenship protections, such as freedom of speech and due process to the prisoner. Through this expansion of rights the chasm between citizens and prisoners would narrow.

Prisoners had never addressed the issues of prison labor before the insurrections of the early seventies. At that time, prisoners adopted programs aimed at totally restructuring the system of prisoner labor. Some of the modifications contained in the program included provisions allowing prisoners to join labor unions, receive vocational training and generally receive the protections afforded workers in the outside community.

No political movement can be effectively understood without closely examining the context in which it operates. The history of the prisoners' movement, the decisions concerning the issues to be pursued and the paths to follow were, in part, conditioned by the nature of the prison and the policies adopted by administrative officials.

The actions of the prisoners' movement and the administration were much like a chess match—a series of attacks, the erection of a defense, a counterattack, a new defense. In the midst of these battles between prisoners and administrators, the political system that had dominated prison governance for centuries, a system characterized by strong authoritarian rule, was beginning to undergo subtle but perceivable change.

In the later stages of development (middle game) a new system of prison rule was being slowly inaugurated. The new system was characterized by more open, formal, and representative political associations. This new system was fashioned from the ideological material of pluralist democracy. It permitted the birth of formal interest group association among the prison population, in effect, conceding some alterations demanded by the prisoners' movement. The political system that arose within the prison is examined through the eyes of the prisoners and administrators. Thus, it is possible to understand the political objectives, policies and opinions embedded in the structure.

Although the major emphasis of the book is on the political saga occasioned by the rise of the prisoner's movement there are many connections between this movement and government structures and movements throughout the United States. The theories developed as a result of this microcosmic study will, it is hoped, contribute to a broader understanding of movements for change in the United States and other countries and the institutional structures and officials confronted by these movements.

Note

1. For a complete historical survey of the relationship between welfare recipients and the state, see Frances Fox Piven and Richard A. Cloward, *Regulating The Poor*.

1 The Prison Governance System

As you approach the interior of a maximum security prison the feeling that something enigmatic awaits you beyond those doors descends quickly and strongly. Once inside, it is clear that no experience in the outside world has prepared you for the dimensions of the world inside.

As you walk through the heavy metal doors your senses are bombarded by persistent noise, ringing from every corner. The architecture is foreign and the sight of so many men seemingly huddled together in a steel-cased box is overpowering. Sensually the experience is shrill and traumatic. But the visual confrontation is only a small part of a larger society, "a society of captives" as Gresham Sykes has aptly called it. This chapter provides an elemental map to help discern some of the dynamics of this society.

From the Inside

Once incarcerated, the individual is forced to adjust to a world different from the one that ejected him or her. The perceptual, objective and subjective worlds of the individual are dramatically transformed. Connections are broken, communications among friends and family are interrupted, familiar patterns of daily life are rudely interrupted.

There is no one major deprivation produced by the prison environment. Particular prisoners find different features of the social system more oppressive. But there is no one condition that can be singled out and labeled "most oppressive." It is a system, a series of rules, constraints and expectations, rather than a particular policy, which conspires to create the oppressive nuance of institutions. The alleviation of any one irritant brings only temporary relief for the prisoners—alleviating one irritant will usually in the long term increase the effect or visibility of the many remaining irritants.

A distinguishing characteristic of institutional life is the intense similarity of everyday experience. Anything that breaks the never-ending pattern and rhythm of life is desirable. Incidents that would be a source of pity, concern, or unhappiness in the outside world are sometimes a source of exhilaration within the prison. A prisoner at East Prison recounted how a fellow prisoner fell down a flight of stairs, bloodied his nose, knocked out some teeth, and cut his face. The prisoners who witnessed the incident all found it hilarious. Although the prisoner who told the story shared in the laughter, he also experienced waves of fear—fear that the prison world was turning his sensibilities upside-down, causing him to lose touch with normal modes of perceiving events.

The laughter was not a reaction to the prisoner's fall itself, but a reaction to how that event related to all other events in the prison. The fall was unexpected, it broke with the prisoner's expectations of what would occur that day. The fact that something spontaneous occurred, no matter who might have been harmed by it, was enough to generate emotion. Here, the relationship between structure and perception is vividly demonstrated.

Almost every aspect of prison life is subject to close regulation and continuous routine. Magnifying the intensity of the routine is the closed space of the institution. The prisoner experiences the same perceptual world as long as he is incarcerated. And where the perceptual world of the subject is essentially one of steel and concrete, the fact assumes an order of importance transcending the particulars of its shape.[1]

The confined space of the community, even without the complex set of prohibitions, would severely limit the normal movement of individuals. With this set of prohibitions the world of the prisoner becomes even more confined, since rules determine if he can be in a particular place at a particular time. The prisoner can make very few choices in determining where he would like to spend his time. Possible alternatives and variations are quickly exhausted so that after a short time all areas of the prison take on similar features and meaning.

Prohibitions on movement also severely limit the already constricted possibilities for human interaction. For example, in West Prison, prisoners are not allowed to enter other quadrants (housing units), limiting the possibility of carrying on friendships with prisoners in other quadrants. Friendships usually extend no further than those who are "locked" nearby, or those who work or attend school together. Of course, the lack of female relationships intensifies the pressures of carrying out successful and satisfying relationships with other prisoners.

Restrictions on movement and the similarity of the environments accessible to prisoners tend to structure the communications which can and do occur. On the outside there is usually a fairly important relationship between environment and communication. Different sorts of environments seem to engender both different levels and different topics of communications. When accessibility to new environments is limited, communication tends to stay within familiar boundaries. As a result, dialogue between prisoners is somewhat standardized, tending to be frequently repeated.

A prison argot, familiar to those who have studied or spent time in institutions, is a common feature of the inmate social system. This argot, or special language, is thought to embody or reflect important aspects of the inmate social system. For instance, "rat," "stool pigeon," "center-man" are commonly used terms which describe prisoners who collude with the captors. This alternative language, it is suggested, is a means used by prisoners to drive a wedge between the social system (values) of the captives and that of the captors.[2]

Alternatively, this prison argot might be seen as a measure of the way communication between prisoners is standardized. If the scope of communication is narrow, consisting of regularly recurring themes, standardization through an argot or shorthand almost inevitably occurs. The argot is not unlike the vocabulary developed by bartenders and taxi drivers, for instance. The argot is an indication of some unified understanding of particular experiences. The size or scope of the argot seems to be related to the degree of commonly shared experiences. If there is a small range of experience, or the experience itself only comprises a portion of an individual's life, the argot is limited and generally employed with those who share that experience. If the range of experience that the argot defines is wide, the lexicon is expanded.

As a result, in the prison where the common experience is wide and pierces all aspects of community life the argot is quite extensive. The limitation of the perceptual, objective, and subjective fields corresponds to the limitations on communication expressed through the use of prison argot.

The regularization of experiences and communications reflected in the use of prison argot is attributable to restrictions on movement and communications and the breakdown of normal categories of time and space. As Goffman has noted, total institutions provide no means to separate what are usually distinct functions of life carried out in distinct environments. In the prison, work, sleep, study, eating, sexual activity, are all conducted in the same environment.[3]

This contraction of time and space has the effect of turning normal modes or relations and activities inside out. So, "[If] friendship is a symptom of mental health in the outside world, it is viewed as a symptom of pending deviance inside the walls."[4]

Structure and official policy collude in creating an environment characterized by a high degree of atomization. An excerpt from a pamphlet called "Facts about the Adjustment Center" will illustrate the degree to which atomization is officially encouraged.

> We wish to encourage you to do your own time and mind your own business. Don't be concerned about what other inmates are doing, what they have to say to you, and what they might think about you. Don't allow anyone to persuade you to get into trouble, start fires, create disturbances, etc. Make up your own mind.[5]

Administration

The superintendent and his associates compose the local administration of the prison. Their superiors are members of the state's correctional bureaucracy, organized at a departmental or cabinet level in the state government. (Unless otherwise specified, the term "administration" will apply to the local prison administration.)

The superintendent and his associates form the corpus of official decision making in the institution. Structurally, the administrative organization varies from institution to institution. For example, at West Prison, administrative decision making is spread widely. A superintendent charged with the overall operation of the institution is assisted by four associate superintendents who administer different aspects of institutional life (custody, inmate affairs, business manager, treatment, and classification). Below this level are program administrators, who are technically supposed to govern their particular quadrant autonomously, but who in reality are far from autonomous. The next level of power is held by the correctional hierarchy—captains, lieutenants, and sergeants.

At East Prison, the superintendent and one associate, illustratively referred to as P.K. (principal keeper) form the top layer of administration power. Below them is a deputy chief, the highest ranking correction officer in the institution. Because there are fewer levels, the relationship between the administration and correctional staff at East Prison is more direct than it is at West Prison.

The administration depends on the correctional establishment to implement its policies and secure compliance to institutional rules and regulations. Because of the hierarchical organization of the administration and enforcement branches the distance between the superintendent and the line officer is vast. Within a bureaucratic organization like the prison, information tends to flow faster from the top down than from the bottom up.[6] Thus, it is difficult for the administration to determine whether policy is being carried out in the way intended.

This form of organization means that the line officer charged with the daily responsibility of handling large groups of prisoners exercises a considerable amount of discretion. Rule enforcement, according to prisoners interviewed, varies from officer to officer. Some officers enforce certain rules that others choose to ignore. There is a sizable gap between what is written in the formal policies of the institution and what is actually enforced.

Correction officers use their discretion to accomplish varied objectives, which vary from officer to officer. Some use their discretion to lessen the rigors attached to enforcing a vast body of rules. In this instance discretion makes the job of the officer less burdensome. Discretion can also be used to increase an officer's control by punishing select prisoners for offenses usually not subject to disciplinary write-ups. This sort of discretion allows the officer to find a way to control disruptive elements.

There are also collective displays of discretion by large numbers of correction officers. Lacking formal mechanisms to effect the decision-making process, the correction officers use discretion to signal dissatisfaction with policy decisions. Discretion compensates for the lack of a formal policy role. For example, the superintendent of West Prison told me that although mail censorship was supposedly confined to select items for select prisoners, he knew that censorship was a widespread practice among the correction staff. This was a means, according to the superintendent, for correction officers to register their dissatisfaction with administrative policy and attempt to influence a restoration of censorship. For if "illegal" communications between prisoners and outsiders was uncovered, even though the means were illegal, the correctional staff believed that the administration would have to "see the light." These are some of the ways that the correctional establishment exercises influence in policy decisions. But the administration is subject to other influences as well. To some degree, the public, the courts, the state bureaucracy, budgetary considerations, the legislature, and prisoner groups all exert some influence in policy decisions. In the end the administrator must fashion a governing policy that at least in part reflects the interests of these groups.

The foremost concern of the administration, the objective that takes precedence over all others, is the smooth functioning of the institution. Smooth functioning occurs when escapes are avoided, violence between prisoners and staff is minimized, political activity is controlled, and prisoners are adhering to the rules of the institution. Escapes and violence tend to attract the attention of outside forces and produce demands for more effective control. Political activity tends to undermine the formal system of rules and regulations upon which the strength of the governance system rests. To avoid malfunctions the administration depends on a sophisticated system of social control embodied in the rules, policies, and procedures of the institution.

Rules cover every aspect of prison life. There are rules about when an inmate may wake up, when he may eat, what he may eat, what he may wear. There is no aspect of institutional life that is not covered by some rule. Rule systems within institutions are almost always expanding. Even when a particular rule is changed or abandoned other rules grow up to regulate the area of activity formally covered by the rule, or other contingencies produced by change.

This tendency of rule systems to grow is exemplified in the regulations regarding what prisoners may wear. In West Prison, most prisoners are still required to wear clothing issued by the institution, although there are some exceptions. This was also the policy at East Prison until a few years ago, when the rule requiring prisoners to wear clothes issued by the institution was abandoned, and prisoners were permitted to don street clothing. Instead of the rule which required prisoners to wear clothes issued by the institution there came a plethora of rules regarding the type of street clothes that could or could not be worn. This included regulations concerning type of clothes, color and styles; for example, no dashikis were allowed.

Other examples of this sort abound. There seems to be a natural and immutable tendency for rule systems to expand. When a conflict arises, this natural tendency requires a rearrangement or expansion of rules to cover the area in which the crisis occurred. The logic is that further crises can be avoided if rules are strengthened or expanded. The lament runs, "if there was only a rule the crisis could have been avoided."

Rule systems are passed from one administration to the next and for the most part are unquestioningly accepted. But there are assumptions behind the rule system—assumptions about the individual who is being governed and about means to secure his compliance. Accepting the rules means, at least in part, accepting the assumptions about the governed clothed in the rules.

Rules are an effective means of limiting the freedom of the incarcerated and cutting off outlets for autonomous activity. The compulsion is to get the prisoner to obey, to submit to legally constituted authority without questions. Excess or improperly used freedom is thought to have played a major role in the commission of the crime which led to incarceration. Consequently, to limit freedom is to increase the probability that the individual will learn to respect freedom and use it properly. This sort of explanation is implicit in theories which elevate rules to the category of "therapeutic devices."

The centrality of the rule system in the system of governance tends to immunize it from scrutiny.

> Rules remain the singularly most important regulatory factor within the institution. Rules serve to both generate and rationalize behavior in all segments of prison society.[7]

Eliot Studt headed a group of researchers who attempted to establish an alternative community in one California prison. The community was an attempt to remold the system of rules into a system of mutual obligations and respect. Studt immediately comprehended the rigidity built into the present system of rules: ". . . rule violation did not provide an occasion for examination of the rules themselves—the rules were taken as given."[8]

The rule system is designed to increase the predictability of the system—predictability being the hallmark of efficient bureaucratic governance. Predictability, the ability to anticipate events, is closely related to power within the administrative structure. "Each group held power in its own sphere by virtue of its ability to predict events, and each was able to extend its power by communication."[9]

Of course the bureaucratic goal of predictability is best achieved when automonous thought is contained. Prisoners come to understand that autonomous thought and action are in themselves considered indexes of unsatisfactory adjustment to institutional life. This premise is nicely stated by a prisoner who took part in Studt's (C-Unit) experiment.

> When I was on the mainline before I was in C-Unit it was as though I had no voice. Life was like a movie. I watched it but didn't take part. Other people told me what to do but I was never asked what I thought.[10]

This antipathy between the bureaucratic end of predictability (rationality) and autonomous thought appears not only in the prison, but in all spheres of activity governed by bureaucratic structures. Max Weber recognized this antagonism. Bureaucratic organization routinizes the world by routinizing thought and action. The system of rules in the prison is both the concrete and philosophical embodiment of Weber's "iron cage."

Enforcement

The mere existence of a rule system does not imply compliance with the rules. And, of course, the rule system is of little utility without compliance. The administration hence must devise strategies to secure the compliance of the exiled.

Feeling that prisoners as a group are more easily influenced to adopt deviant modes of behavior, the administration believes that rule infractions by any substantial group of prisoners will lead to more rule infractions.[11] Consequently, the administration must quickly demonstrate the perils involved in breaking the rules.

Sykes and other prison researchers have noted a phenomenon which Sykes in a chapter title refers to as "The Defects of Total Power."[12] In essence, these authors claim that the administration faces great difficulties in securing the compliance of prisoners. This difficulty is caused by a lack of effective tools through which the administration might fashion strategies to promote compliance. Without comparing the type and availability of mechanisms within the prison to those utilized by other administrators in pursuit of conformity, it can be said that the prison administration manipulates the tools at its disposal with considerable facility. Sykes and others have, to some degree, underestimated the resourcefulness of the system in gaining compliance.

According to Sykes, the concept of authority is closely linked to forms of compliance. Authority, according to Sykes, has two basic elements. First, there must be a rightful and legitimate effort to exercise control, and second, there must be a moral compulsion to obey by those controlled. Sykes argues that in the prison there is the first without the second.[13] The prisoners acknowledge the legitimate authority of the keepers but possess no moral compulsion to obey. This seems rather simplistic. If prisoners actually acknowledge the legitimate rule of the custodians, only a theory of opportunism or character deficiency could explain their lack of compliance.

It is true that there are prisoners who accept the right of the custodians to govern, although their number is diminishing. But accepting the right of the custodians to make decisions in an environment which provides few alternative adaptations is not the same as accepting their rightful and legitimate role in the exercise of total power.

In relation to the problem of compliance, Sykes argues that administrators cannot depend on force to maintain the routine of the institution. Sykes contends that force will not bring about step-by-step compliance to rules. Here again, the utility of force is somewhat underestimated. Prisoners believe, and the evidence seems to be on their side, that the administration will resort to force if it is necessary to insure compliance. Although it is difficult to measure how widespread the actual use of force is, the belief that the administration will use it if necessary is enough to promote quietism and a degree of adherence.

Customarily, compliance to rule systems is promoted through a set of punishments and rewards, which, to paraphrase Gompers, "punishes its enemies and rewards its friends." Sykes argues that administrators possess neither sufficient rewards nor punishments to secure compliance. Custodians grant prisoners almost all the available rewards and benefits upon their entrance, leaving administrators virtually no cake to offer later.[14] Although the rewards are not as powerful as they could be, they still seem to have sufficient force not only to promote compliance but to encourage collusion.

In New Jersey and California the administration possesses some leverage in deciding how long particular prisoners will serve, the most powerful of rewards to the prisoner. Messinger has noted that prison administrators have historically attempted to broaden the range of influence in this area.[15] But the actual power available to administrators in influencing release is considerably overestimated by the prisoners, who generally feel, especially in New Jersey, that if administrators want to, they can get them out. So the power of the administration is considerably enhanced by the belief among prisoners that they have much influence in deciding who is to be paroled. Administrative ideology does nothing to close the chasm between appearance and reality.

Although the rewards are not grandiose, they can make institutional life less fatiguing. Classification in minimum custody status makes prisoners eligible for such programs as work release, furlough, work study, and in California, conjugal visits. Minimum custody status allows the prisoner greater freedom of movement and possibilities for employment in more desirable jobs within the institution. These rewards are not minor when viewed in the context of the rigidity and regimentation of institutional life.

Although the administration has a considerable array of rewards at its disposal they are often utilized in a curious fashion. For example, the addition of conjugal visits at West Prison was a means to increase the rewards associated with compliance. In fact, statistics show that the strategy significantly lowered the number of disciplinary charges per month. However, the strategy was unable to promote long-term compliance.

This consequent rise in disciplinary charges speaks to the nature of this particular reward as well as to the reward system in general. The reward was only available to a portion of the prisoners, since only married prisoners were entitled to conjugal visits. Thus, for a large percentage the reward was inaccessible no matter how they performed. The fact that some prisoners could qualify for conjugal visits, while others could not, increased the resentment of the excluded. To a great degree the resentment was aimed at the system that promulgated what single prisoners felt was a discriminatory policy. The example of conjugal visiting is indicative of the general tendency of the institutional reward system. Generally, the rewards apply only to a segment of the population, or else the process for attaining the reward is complex and uncertain. The power of the reward is diminished by uncertainty—that prescribed forms of conduct will not automatically result in the prisoner attaining the reward. Added to this uncertainty is the fact that any member of the correctional staff can conceivably thwart the prisoner's attempt to gain the reward by exercising his power to file disciplinary charges against the prisoner.

Yet, by using rewards in this fashion, the reward system has the additional feature of undermining solidarity among the prisoners. It creates numerous categories of prisoners—categories based on rewards the particular groups have attained or are capable of attaining. Simply, it creates groups of people who tend to have much more to lose by engaging in collective political activity than other groups have.

The system of rewards does seem to create incentives for compliance, although these incentives might be more efficiently employed if they were more widely applicable. However, making the rewards automatic, or extending them to a greater percentage of the prisoners, would on the other hand seem to decrease stratification and increase the potential for solidarity among prisoners. Because of this inherent duality, then, the rule system is able to divide at the same time as it rewards.

Punishments

Withholding many of the rewards mentioned above is itself a form of punishment. For example, the administration can withhold access to custody levels which would enable the prisoner to participate in numerous programs.

Aside from withholding access to desirable custody status, the administration has other punishments in its repertoire. None of the punishments available to the administration is as harsh as the prisoner's initial punishment (incarceration), but that is not to say that they cannot be effective. The administration can have an influence in extending the prisoner's sentence, strip him of even those minimal privileges he receives upon admission, such as access to television, movies, visits, and the like, or lock him away in segregation.

The strategy of segregation is most often the one chosen to deal with frequent rule-breakers, because like the reward system it accomplishes a dual function.

> The logic of the strategy of segregation is fairly simple . . . identify potential troublemakers as early as possible, try to get them to comply with institutional rules, failing that, segregate them.
>
> The justification is twofold: segregation will, at a minimum, limit the unwanted socialization of otherwise relatively docile inmates, minimizing disruption of routine; further, it will provide an opportunity to develop "special programs" for the troublemakers themselves.[16]

The likelihood that those who are involved in rule infraction will significantly influence the conformists prompts the widespread use of segregation as a disciplinary strategy. The conception of discipline, seeing rule infraction as the unwillingness to submit to duly constituted authority, makes rule infraction a political act. Today, discipline is acclaimed as an integral part of the reform process, "augmenting the rehabilitative influences of inmate-staff relationships."[17]

The Manual of Correction Standards of the American Correctional Association explains the universality of disciplinary procedures within prisons:

> Discipline . . . looks beyond the limits of the inmate's term of confinement. It must seek to insure carry-over values by inculcating standards which the inmates will maintain after release. It is not merely the prisoner's ability to conform to institutional rules and regulations, but his ability and desire to conform to accepted standards for individual and community life in free society. Discipline must . . . develop in the inmate personal responsibility to which he will return.[18]

Another major punishment available to the administration is transfer. At West Prison, almost all inmates volunteered the information that prisoners who were involved in persistent rule violation or insurgent political activity were routinely transferred to other prisons. The prisoners refer to the practice as "bus therapy." Since the transfer is always to a prison with a more restrictive environment, it is a sanction widely feared by prisoners. Going to another institution requires the prisoner to repeat the adaptative process, getting to know fellow prisoners, correction officers, administrators, and the institutional system. The prisoner becomes a rookie in the new institution, forced to learn the ropes and assert himself to gain a respected position in the prison social system.

In addition, the prisoner comes to his new institution with the reputation of having been unmanageable. This inspires the administration and correctional staff to pay special attention to ensure that the prisoner does not disrupt the routine of the institution. Although the administration generally presumes that the common characteristic of all the exiled is a "readiness to exploit each other in defiance of duly constituted authority,"[19] the prisoner transferred from another institution is thought to be especially ready.

Besides the problem of institutional dislocation and labeling, a transfer may result in decreasing the prisoner's access to family and friends. In California, a vast state, institutional transfer often means a virtual end to family visits. Because of the distance that separates institutions in California, transfer is a somewhat more powerful sanction than in a densely populated state like New Jersey. In New Jersey, or a state of comparable density, the likelihood that transfer would result in a complete break of family ties is diminished, but the other deprivations associated with transfer still pertain.

Administrators in states where transfer is not a viable option are more dependent on internal segregation as a means of isolation. The courts, however, have applied restrictions on the time prisoners can be kept in segregation facilities.

> . . . the staff feels that such pressure from court is a usurpation of traditional roles in the prison and thus have resorted to other mechanisms to exile "the exiled." One of the usual means is to send the inmate to the state mental hospital.
>
> In 1972, 6,190 inmates in the various penitentiaries in America were transferred to state mental hospitals. This represents roughly 6 percent of the total inmate population and three times the national average for psychiatric admissions for that year.[20]

This sanction has a severe limitation. The administration cannot control the time that the prisoners will be kept in the mental facility.

These sorts of sanctions are undoubtedly important factors in promoting compliance. Alone, they will not promote complete adherence to institutional rules, because there are many countervailing forces which mitigate their effectiveness. Yet, they play an unmistakably important role.

Since Sykes, Messinger and Robert Reich all seem to undervalue both the reward and punishment system within the institution they must look to other factors to explain why prisoners obey institutional rules. All three of these writers, who are certainly among the most perceptive in the field, turn to the concept of bargaining to explain why compliance occurs.

These authors argue that the inability to insure compliance necessitates widespread bargaining between "kept" and keeper.[21] This argument seems to imply that it is the bargaining system, not the rule system, which stabilizes the institution. The essentials of this bargaining system are outlined by Reich in a well-argued paper published in the *Yale Law Review*:

> In return for the toleration of a degree of low-visibility violation under the "surface" the inmates agree to avoid larger and more visible violations which would necessitate the use of force. The bargain may be as casual as a mere tacit understanding, "You play ball with me, and I'll play with you," or it may be highly structured and selective. Whatever its character, correctional officers and inmates become mutually dependent. The inmates maintain surface order for the correctional officer and the correctional officer turns his back on minor violations.[22]

Bargaining does occur within the institutions where I spent time. But the existence of bargaining is not a prior indication that the bargaining reflects a failure of the system of rewards and punishments. Rather, it may reflect an expedient decision on the part of the correction officer, a decision that is designed to make his job easier to perform. In grade school, teachers chose class monitors to check on the behavior of their peers when no teacher was in the room and report those who were disorderly. The monitor often received special considerations and was afforded a certain status in performing the surrogate duties of teacher. Recruiting monitors is not an indication that the rule system is completely ineffective, it simply allows the teacher more freedom.

The same principle applies in prison. The correction officers recruit certain prisoners to monitor the behavior of the others. The prisoner performing the task receives special considerations from the officers. Sometimes, the prisoner chooses to distribute these rewards among his constituency, often he chooses not to. Whether the prisoner in the bargaining relationship chooses to distribute the rewards depends in large part on what he feels is necessary to retain the position of dominance.

It would seem the social control system would continue to function without the bargaining system. That is to say, a breakdown in the bargaining relationship would not lead to total anarchy. In fact, during the height of politization movement among prisoners the bargaining relationship was significantly altered.

While the system would not break down, an alteration in the bargaining relationship would make the job of both the correction officer and administrator more difficult, for the system of bargaining is first and foremost a system of collusion between captives and captors. It develops informers, creates animosities, heightens suspicions, and divides the body of prisoners. It adds to the power of the captors at the direct expense of the power of the captives. In this sense, bargaining is a zero-sum game.

Because bargaining creates another division among prisoners, it is certainly a useful implement in the administration's arsenal. With the rise of the prisoners' movement, institutional bargaining declined, indicating that prisoners recognized the cooptative effects of the process. The rule system must be considered as an extremely important mechanism for the preservation of social control.

Labor

It is difficult to find much in the prison literature concerning work within prison. While many researchers may have underestimated the importance of the labor system in prison, the political activities of prisoners in the 1970s made it eminently clear that labor was one of the most important facets of prison life. Consequently, the system of labor and production in the prison must receive extensive attention. Through their activities the prisoners have clearly established labor as a high priority on their agenda—a priority that no student of the prison can rightfully ignore.

Early forms of prison labor usually involved the intervention of outside economic forces. Under the lease system, care and custody of prisoners were given to outside entrepreneurs in exchange for a stipulated fee.[23] Here, the state acted merely as an agent in bartering both the lives and labor of those incarcerated.

The contract system of labor also involved the use of economic resources outside the prison community. However, under the contract system of labor, the state retained control of inmates, but sold their labor to an entrepreneur at a daily per capita fee.[24] In many ways, the present practice called "work release" resembles this form of labor. The state permits outside economic interests to use the labor power of the prisoners. In return, the prisoner must agree to relinquish a percentage of his wages to the state as payment for room and board. In New Jersey the state usually garnishes about 60 percent of the prisoner's wage.[25] The results of the contract system and work release system are essentially the same for the state; in each case it recovers a percentage of the prisoner's wage.

Another form of prison labor is referred to as the "state account system." This system maintains the state's hegemony over both custody and labor-power. The state becomes the manager of production and sells the commodities produced on the open market. This system met with stiff opposition from manufacturers, and by 1900, they had succeeded in securing legislation to block the sale of prison-produced commodities on the free market, making this system obsolete.[26] For the most part, the earlier systems (lease, contract, state account) were abandoned because of stiff resistance from business and organized labor. Myriad expositions documenting massive exploitation, corruption and medieval abuses of prisoners also helped speed the demise of these forms of labor-power.

Today, almost all prison systems use prison labor in state-use industries and public works systems or both. The state-use industries programs in California and New Jersey restrict the economic activity of the prison to producing goods and services for agencies of the state and their political subdivisions. The public works system, also used in California and New Jersey, allows prison labor to be employed in government projects like road construction and repair, institutional maintenance, reforestation, soil erosion and the like.[27] Under both systems the state maintains authority over labor-power and custody.

Wage systems and rates vary from one jurisdiction to another. In a national survey, twenty states, the District of Columbia and the Federal system reported paying wages to 90-100 percent of their inmates. In five states no more than 10 percent earn money.[28] Six states do not permit inmates to earn anything. Of thirty-three states supplying such information in another survey, wages ranged from 4 cents a day to a high of $1.30 a day.

Wages and conditions of labor are subject to several broad regulatory principles. With the growth of prison labor in the nineteenth and twentieth centuries, debates about prison labor and its relationship to outside labor became prominent. Several defining notions arose during the period. One such principle, coined the principle of "less eligibility," argued that prisoners should be considered less worthy of satisfactory employment and training than the worst paid noncriminal. Later this principle was supplanted by what Mannhein called the "principle of nonsuperiority." Simply, the earlier principle was liberalized to mandate that the conditions of the prisoner should not be superior to that of the worst-paid noncriminal.[29]

These two principles still regulate wage and work conditions of prison labor. Rather than being assigned to the shelves of history, the principles of "less eligibility" and "nonsuperiority" are the fulcrum for those who argue that prisoners should not be eligible for the benefits bestowed on the "law-abiding."

For those who argue that prisons should perform a rehabilitative function, the principles of less eligibility and nonsuperiority are somewhat of a barrier. Consequently, it would be expected that the doctrine of rehabilitation should at least partially rupture these two principles. In fact, the doctrine of rehabilitation has occasioned an amendment to both principles. Whether the amendment was in the name of rehabilitation or efficiency is questionable. Further examinations of the contemporary system of prison labor should yield an answer.

The Philosophy of Labor-Power

As the modes of prison labor change so do the arguments about the justification for the use of the prisoner's labor-power, and the goals of prison labor in general. Customarily there are at least two sorts of explanations to justify the use of inmate labor. Particular prison systems often justify prisoner labor by invoking a combination of these.

First, there are utility arguments. One refers to the utility of labor for the prison system in general; the other, the utility of labor for the particular inmate. The first assumes that the state has the right, if not the obligation, to transfer some cost of incarceration onto the incarcerated.[30] This assumes that incarceration entitles the state to assume total control over the labor-power of the individual without the individual's consent. It also seems to assume that the incarcerated has not paid a proportional share of the costs of his incarceration through taxes. When this argument is applied without qualification the prisoner would have little choice over the type of labor performed. The claim that prisoners should be compelled to submit to work as a means of deferring costs has historically been a sufficient justification for prison labor. Even today the claim carries much force. Forced labor seems acceptable when prisoners are viewed as a class of people existing outside the normal community and who have forfeited the protection of the community. Prisoners are thought of as members of an abnormal world, a world where many assumptions about life are turned upside-down. The reversal of tasks and expectations, so prevalent in institutional life, works to justify the system of prison labor. "The prisoner's forced labor is deprived of the dignity and incentives of labor in general. His work becomes an activity which isolates him from the rest of society."[31]

Although it is entirely plausible that the community would accept prison labor strictly as a means to defer cost, the official doctrine concerning prison labor is more expansive. In California and New Jersey, deferring the costs of incarceration is cited as a secondary goal of prison labor. Labor is primarily designed to be a part of the rehabilitative process, eradicating "bad" habits and developing "good" ones. This forms the basis for the individual utility argument.

Prison labor, according to official doctrine, increases the chances for successful reentry into the community by promoting "habits of industry" lacking in most prisoners. The Correctional Systems Study, an extensive study of California prisons, explains that "prisoners are poorly motivated and do not even initially wish to learn how to work."[32] An administrator at West Prison voluntarily elaborated on this statement by noting that ". . . people from ghettos and barrios don't know how to work. It's rewarding for an inmate to learn how to operate a shovel."[33]

Besides instilling good habits there is another aspect of work which is presumed to have rehabilitative consequences. The California system sees work as a means to provide the prisoner with skills that he can use upon release. As such, there is a presumption that work must to some degree be compatible with the interests and abilities of particular prisoners and with the needs of industry and business in the community. To this end, California has developed a Trade Advisory Council composed of businessmen from the private sector. The purpose of the council, as stated, is to:

> (1) Promote better understanding of the industries program and allay suspicions about the impact on the private sector; (2) promote opportunities for employment for inmates after release; (3) provide technical assistance to industrious staff.[34]

The idea that industry should be devoted to developing skills means that prison industries would need to be organized in a nontraditional manner—a manner that can sacrifice productivity and profit in the name of rehabilitation. The goals of profit and genuine training are somewhat incompatible. If a large part of the production day is given over to training and instruction, productivity and profit must diminish accordingly. With a high turnover of workers caused by releases and new admissions, there must be constant training of new workers. The division of labor within the factory furthermore requires that only a finite number of prisoners be trained to perform the same task. It would seem impossible to train the majority of prisoners as skilled machinists when the division of labor calls for only a few.

Because the division of labor in the prison factory conforms to the traditional division of labor in outside industry, many tasks, perhaps most, performed by prisoners do not seem to have much to do with acquiring valuable skills. There are janitors, clean-up men, timekeepers and a variety of assembly line jobs. Thus, prisoners argue that the whole system of prison industry is outdated, irrelevant and counterproductive. At West Prison almost all state-use industries make clothing. Prisoners say that there are very few jobs in clothing manufacturing, even fewer available to those in inner-city barrios and ghettos. Moreover, the prisoners claim that even if jobs were available, prison industry is so technologically backward that most of the skills acquired would not be transferable.

Defining the rehabilitation component of work as dualistic (acquisition of skills and acquisition of habit) provides a means for the administration to meet the criticism of prisoners. According to official doctrine, work does not necessarily need to provide both skills and habits of industry, it may sometimes do the former and other times the latter, although it is hard to tell when it is doing which. But based on this rationale, even the most meaningless jobs can be rescued from criticism by arguing that the vast majority of prisoners are learning habits of industry. If work can provide a means for instilling habits of industry, it has, according to the administration, served a valuable function. A desirable, but not always possible, additional benefit might also be realized, if that work could simultaneously develop skills.

Even habits of industry, though, are assumed by the administration to mean something more than showing up to work. Habits of industry mean productivity, a full day's work at a good pace. Such a work routine is necessary if prison industry is to be profitable. And profit is something the system is acutely concerned with. Since at least 1965, there has been a major emphasis on designing means to improve profit margins. The California system study suggests:

> More markets would be helpful and should be sought for California's prison industrial programs. . . . Recent suggestions for private ownership and management of some prison industries, and the repeal of Federal laws barring prison-made goods from interstate commerce, should be studied carefully.[35]

The system of labor within the institutions provides an important social and economic lever for the administration. Its immunity from attack ended with the beginning of organized labor protest in the early seventies.

Ideology

The final aspect of the institutional system that requires discussion can be termed the system's ideology. "Ideology" is defined as "a pattern of beliefs and concepts which purport to explain complex social phenomena."[36] Marx generally employed the term to describe a "system of ideas" which obfuscated the real content of human activity and institutional behavior. It is in this way that the term ideology is employed.

> The class which has the means of material production at its disposal, has control at the same time over the means of mental production, so that thereby, generally speaking, the ideas of those who lack the means of men-

> tal production are subject to it. The ruling ideas are nothing more than the ideal expression of the dominant material relationship, the dominant material relations grasped as ideas; hence of the relationships which make one class the ruling one, therefore, the ideas of its dominance.[37]

In the prison the ruling class is composed of local and state prison officials. In much the same manner that the ruling class in the political community constitutes a system of "ideal expressions," to hide or rationalize the relations in the systems of production, the ruling class of the prisons fashions an ideology which obfuscates the relations of the system of incarceration.

Being a more unified whole than the ruling class in the outside community, the prison administration is able to construct a durable ideological system, based on wide consensus. In the political community the ideological system must express the variety of material interests that exists among different strata of the ruling class. Because the relative homogeneity of the prison ruling class, the system of ideology emerges as clear and coherent, although by no means impenetrable.

Another factor which strengthens the field of ideological expressions, as well as the ideology itself, is the set of relatively simple activities that the ideology seeks to explain. The prison system has historically been obliged to explain few of its activities publicly. Where a system has been called into question any one of several patent ideologies has usually assuaged critics. These patent ideological expressions are best summarized by the terms "punishment," "retribution," "deterrence," "custody," and "treatment."

Although the pat ideological expressions have been sufficient to justify a prison system in the past, it is at present more difficult to square the ideology of the system with its reality. Many of the present difficulties in employing standardized ideological explanations are the result of political challenges fashioned by prisoners. In California, the official ideology of the system, referred to as "treatment ideology" became an early political target of prisoners and their allies.

A prison ideology speaks not only to the function of the system but equally to the character of the inmates within the system. Particular ideologies, like treatment, usually rest on particular assumptions about the system's clients. For example, theories of deterrence see the client as ready to commit additional transgressions if not incapacitated. The strategy of incapacitation and deterrence are related to this analysis of the offender.[38] The relationship however, is not always linear—a particular assessment of the client's character ending with a correspondent ideology for the system. It is conceivable that the relationship works in the other direction—an analysis about the character of offenders is the product of an ideology that explains the system.

So ideology serves the function of creating a system of ideas which apply equally to the client and the institution. Official policy is supposed to reflect the ideological assumptions of the system. Tasks are also explained by relating them to the system's ideology. The ideological system of the prison becomes a mechanism to explain certain occurrences and disclaim others.

Treatment as an institutional ideology must obviously claim that clients are impaired in some fundamental way. This impairment or deviance is the unifying characteristic of the prison population. The claim that prisoners are all suffering some impairment seems a necessary prerequisite in constructing a treatment ideology. Thus, all forms and strains of criminality are defined as forms of impairment.

The notion that crime is indicative of some organic or psychological disorder has often been used by criminologists in explaining the origin of crime. Theories about the relationship between pathology and criminology seem to rise, gain the favor of the scientific community and then fall from grace, only to reemerge again as a dominant ideology.[39]

> The theories that the criminal is a sick individual in need of treatment—which is promoted today as if it were a recent psychiatric discovery—is false. Indeed it is hardly more than a refurbishing, with new terms of the main ideas and techniques of the inquisitorial process . . . (the deviant) is first discredited as a self-responsible human being, and then subjected to humiliating punishment disguised as treatment.[40]

In the present period certain members of the academic and scientific community continue to argue in favor of pathological theories of criminality. For example, Dr. Karl Menninger, a well-known psychiatrist associated with the school of "liberal" penology writes that unlawful acts are "signals of distress, signals of failure . . . the spasms and struggles and connections of submarginal humans trying to make it in our complex society with inadequate equipment and inadequate preparation."[41]

Treatment is a system of diagnosis, classification and rehabilitation. In California prisoners are admitted to reception centers after sentencing; they are then evaluated and subsequently assigned to particular facilities. From the inception the prisoner is encouraged to cooperate with authorities in the rehabilitation process, a process that must start with an acceptance by the prisoner that he is suffering from a disorder, a disorder that lends itself to expiation through treatment.

Although the treatment ideology claims to be founded on scientific data, there seems to be a general lack of scientific diagnosis or treatment. Some prisoners are diagnosed as paranoids or schizophrenics, but the majority seem to be classified as "malcontents," individuals who have adjusted poorly, troublemakers, those lacking respect for authority. More than a scientific or medical process of diagnosis and labeling, the process seems political, in the sense that most disorders are associated with the inability to comply with the dictates of political society or the inability to utilize freedoms associated with citizenship. Within the institutions there is a high correlation between disciplinary infractions or assertiveness and the official label "disturbed."[42]

Under the treatment ideology, punishment is replaced by treatment. No longer is incarceration a form of retribution, but merely a means to incapacitate an individual to provide the state with time and space to cure the client's malady.

> The underlying rationale of the treatment model is deceptively simple. It rejects inherited concepts of criminal punishment as the payment of a debt owed to society, a debt proportional to the magnitude of the offender's wrong.[43]

The political consequences of employing a treatment ideology are many. Under this ideological banner, the criminal act is completely depoliticized since explanations about the relationship between crime, resources, and environment are not recognized as determinate or decisive. Another political consequence of the treatment ideology occurs in the sentencing process.

> To punish the little man more severely for his little acts, which might appear as open hypocrisy by retributive standards, is no longer a problem if society can be persuaded that "treatment" is not punishment and if the criteria for state intervention are all the social and psychological, but not the moral, deficiencies of the offender.[44]

Sentencing in California follows the logic of the seductive slogan "Let the punishment fit the criminal, not the crime."[45] From this premise it is only a short step to indefinite or indeterminate sentencing.

Indeterminate sentencing, individualization, and discretionary power are the three hallmarks of the treatment ideology. Wide discretionary power is allegedly employed:

> . . . so that the offender's treatment could be matched with his individual needs, and the location of much of this discretionary power is with the agencies responsible for protecting society from criminals.[46]

Three important trends seem to have followed the adoption of the rehabilitation ideology. First, sentences have steadily increased. From 1959 to 1969 the medium time served rose from twenty-four to thirty-six months, the longest in the country. Second, the number of prisoners incarcerated per

100,000 population continued to rise, from 65 in 1944 to 145 in 1965, the highest in the country. Finally, there is evidence that people are not being helped any more by a medium stay of three years in a rehabilitation-oriented prison, than they were by approximately two years in a basically punitive-oriented prison.[47]

When the treatment ideology was first introduced, it was approvingly received by many prisoners. Prisoners were led to believe that they would be able to raise their educational level, to overcome feelings of insecurity and receive help in solving psychological problems. There was a widespread hope that prisoners would be better prepared to deal with the outside world.

Hope that incarceration would increase the prisoner's chance to successfully reenter the society that expelled him has all but evaporated. Treatment is considered a cruel hoax, a ruse known to those grasped by the treatment tentacles, but believed by those far from the body of the monster. Politically, the struggle is to inform unaware prisoners and the outside community about the real nature of treatment, to strip away the illusion fostered in official doctrines, break through appearances and divulge reality. This is the central ideological struggle of many prisoners in California, a struggle that marks a cornerstone of politics.

This chapter has focused on several facets of institutional life, including the institutional rule system, punishment, rewards, prison labor and ideology. The purpose of this review was to acquaint the reader with certain aspects of institutional life necessary to understand much of the material that follows.

Concomitantly, it was necessary to address certain issues in the prison literature that were inconsistent with premises of the analysis that the remainder of the book contains. What is discussed in this chapter forms a foundation of understanding upon which the analysis in the book depends.

The final section of this chapter contains a brief sketch of the two prisons where the study took place.

West Prison

The West Prison was constructed twenty-five years ago in the central part of the state. The main facility was designed as a medium security institution to house a maximum of 2,400 inmates. An adjacent facility is designated as minimum custody and can house 800 prisoners. All the respondents in this study came from the main facility.

The distinctive organizational characteristic of the prison is decentralization. Decentralization of prison facilities was a policy first formulated by the California Correctional Planning Council in 1968. Its report condemned the use of large centralized facilities. The report stated: "Facilities shall be built on the unit concept with a unit capacity of up to 600 inmates.'' Additionally, it was mandated that no facilities should have more than four 600-man units.

> When more than four units are in one institution the benefits derived by the 600-man unit are negated by the lengthening and diffusion of the span of *control* of the administration.[48] (Emphasis mine)

Decentralization was envisaged as a means to increase administration control of the population. The plan is littered with explicit statements showing how decentralizing would increase the administration's ability to monitor and control its captives.

According to the report, the 600-man unit allows correction staff to effectively segregate rebellious inmates from the rest of the population. To call attention to a practical application of the unit's structure, the report notes the ease with which 600 men, as opposed to 3,000, can be controlled when congregating in large groups, for instance, during dining hours.[49] This theme of control should be kept in mind since it tempers much that occurs within institutions.

West Prison was designated the prison structure of the future in California corrections. The recommendations of the 1968 report call for all subsequent prison construction to conform to the standards of West Prison. Not only did the report call for future construction to conform to these standards, but recommended that older prisons seek means to revise their prisons to conform to the unit structure.

The four quadrants at West Prison are designated by letters. Most of my interviews were with inmates in A quad or C quad.[50] Quadrant B contained inmates from other institutions who were spending short periods in West Prison to undergo diagnosis or treatment. Because these were specialized programs that did not always conform to the rhythm and pace of normal institutional life, B quad was eliminated.

Quadrant D contained a large percentage of inmates who received tranquilizers daily. Although some prisoners from all quads were maintained on large doses of tranquilizers, the percentage in D quad was considerably higher than in other quads. Administrators conceded that inmates in D quad were often maintained on such large doses of medication that many were incoherent. The inmates generally referred to D quad as ''space city.'' Because the medical orientation of D quad rendered it somewhat unique within the institution, and the system in general, it was eliminated.

Quadrants A and C were thought to contain the highest percentage of the ''average'' prisoners within the system. C quad is remarkable because it houses the largest percentage of violent prisoners in the institution and presents the greatest management problem.

Although the superintendent of West Prison denied that quadrant placement was selective, abundant evidence shows that much administrative and custodial prerogative was exercised in quadrant assignment. The superintendent said the only consideration in assigning men to particular quadrants is racial and ethnic balance. A subordinate told me "inmates are carefully placed, not to maintain a racial and ethnic balance, but to segregate inmates assigned to particular behavior categories."[51]

This contradiction is more a product of the way information is specialized and secularized through the administration than any conscious effort to deceive the researcher. Selectively composing the membership of a quadrant provides a powerful means for controlling unwanted associations among the inmate body.

Certain matters of policy are decided at the quadrant level. Administering each quadrant is a "program administrator" and a correctional lieutenant. Program administrators are "minisuperintendents" who are instructed to run their quadrants as if they were separate institutions. Each quadrant elects a "Men's Advisory Council," which as the title suggests, acts in an advisory capacity to quadrant administrators. The quadrants are internally segregated into 50-cell units. One representative is chosen from each 50-cell unit. Since no institution-wide prisoner representation organ exists, demands are never recognized as coming from the entire inmate body, but always seen as the desires of prisoners in a particular quadrant. The results of this policy temper the entire mode of government in the institution.

All four quadrants are under the control of the superintendent, four associate superintendents, and a correctional captain. While the program administrators deal with matters particular to their quadrant, the top adminsitrators deal with institution-wide policies. These administrators handle classification, serious disciplinary trials, and act as an appeal body to review decisions reached at the quadrant level. Generally, this stratum of administrators makes a large portion of the decisions that significantly affect the running of the institution.

Aside from being structurally modern, West Prison is also noted for using a wide variety of current programs designated as therapeutic. The most significant of these programs is group counseling, first introduced in the California system in 1944. Although there is no one definition of how the group counseling sessions should be conducted, a set of guiding principles has been articulated by Dr. Norman Fenton, the pioneer of the project.

> Essentially, we are told that a therapeutic technique called group counseling, involving periodic meetings of staff and inmates to talk over matters of concern, has certain consequences for the participants—consequences that are rehabilitative. . . . Operationally, group counseling means that ten or twelve inmates meet one or two hours a week under the guidance of a lay group leader.[52]

Group counseling taking place in a closed institution with regularized motion does not function as a compartmentalized therapeutic routine without political content. One of the lessons of the modern world is that most things are not what they appear to be. Group therapy and control in institutional settings like the prison are not easily separable.

East Prison

The first wing of East Prison was opened in 1901, to be followed by a 350-cell addition begun in 1908. Organizationally and philosophically the prison was envisaged as an intermediate prison, holding offenders whose improprieties could be classified as greater than those in jails, usually held for vagrancy, and lesser than those in the state prison, usually repeat offenders or those convicted of serious crimes.

During the later part of the nineteenth century the ideas of the reformatory took shape. Reformatories were to be the structural counterpart of a penal philosophy which generally held that incarceration should be correctional rather than merely punitive. At the time the discussion of building a reformatory in New Jersey began in the legislature (1890) three reformatories had already been built and were functioning. Planners hoped to incorporate features from the reformatory at Elmira, New York (1870), Concord, Massachusetts (1885), and Huntington, Pennsylvania (1889).[53]

Apparently the architect never fully understood how the reformatory was to correspond to the correctional philosophy. East Prison was an imposing structure of concrete and high walls, a prototype of the maximum security prison. The fact that the structure did not represent the idea was not trivial. Almost immediately after its opening public cries were raised for turning East Prison into a regular state prison and building a new structure which would more fully adhere to the reformatory idea.

Dr. Frank Moore, the superintendent of the institution, led the battle to build a new reformatory. Moore complained that the architecture "was unsuited to the more liberal ideas about discipline and reform that were gaining influence."[54] A Prison Inquiry Commission praised the prison's schooling and progressive ideas, but called it "a prison with reformatory features, . . . too much like its famous prototype, the Elmira reformatory, to be altogether admirable."[55] The commission concluded that its "severity of spirit" resulted in part from the construction "with its inside cells and depressing prison atmosphere."[56]

The prison is one of three maximum security institutions in the state. The types of offenders are similar to those being held in West Prison. The racial composition of the prison is markedly different. At the time of the study the population breakdown at West Prison was: 57.7 percent white,

26 percent black, 13.8 percent Chicano and 2.7 percent classified as other (mostly Chinese and Indian). In contrast, blacks composed about 65 percent of the population at East Prison, whites around 25 percent and Cubans and Puerto Ricans composed the remaining 10 percent.

Notes

1. Richard H. McCleery, "Power, Communication and the Social Order."

2. This view is suggested by John Irwin in *The Felon*. This view is also implicitly held by Sykes and Messinger in their article on the inmate social system, in which they see the structure of the system as a means of preserving and operationalizing a value system measurably different from that of the authorities. See Gresham Sykes and Sheldon Messinger, "The Inmate Social System," in *Theoretical Studies in Social Organization of the Prison*, ed. George Grosser.

3. Erving Goffman, *Asylums*, chapter 1.

4. Joan Smith and William Fried, *The Uses of American Prisons*, (Lexington, Mass.: Lexington Books, D.C. Heath, 1974), p. 57.

5. Sheldon Messinger, "Strategies of Control." [1958, p. 170.]

6. The patterns of communications inherent in the structure of bureaucratic authority in the prison are discussed at length by McCleery in his dissertation and several subsequent articles. The most concise statement of his thoughts can be found in Richard H. McCleery, "The Government Process and Informal Social Control," in *The Prison: Studies in Institutional Organization and Change*, ed. Donald Cressey (New York: Holt, Rinehart, and Winston Inc., 1961), pp. 149-189.

7. Clarence Schrag, "Some Foundations for a Theory of Corrections," in *Correctional Institutions*, eds., Carter, Glaser and Wilkens, p. 158.

8. Sheldon Messinger, Eliot Studt, Thomas Wilson, *C-Unit: A Search for Community In Prison* (New York: Russell Sage Foundation, 1968), p. 39.

9. Richard H. McCleery, "Communications Patterns As a Basis of Systems of Authority and Power," in *Theoretical Studies in Social Organization of the Prison*, ed. George Grosser, p. 61.

10. Messinger, Studt and Wilson, *C-Unit*, p. 65.

11. It is interesting to note that much of the literature on prisons tends to implicitly support the administration's theory of susceptibility. There is a claim, even among many reform groups, that prisons are "colleges of crime," where an inmate is further socialized into the ways of a criminal subculture. Smith and Fried have referred to this as a "germ theory of crime," where criminal ways can be caught through association with a carrier. See Smith and Fried, *The Uses of American Prisons*, p. 57.

12. Gresham Sykes, *The Society of Captives.* See also Schrag, *Some Foundation for a Theory of Corrections.*

13. Sykes, 1958, p. 46.

14. Sykes, 1958, pp. 49-55.

15. Messinger, "Strategies of Control," pp. 28-30.

16. Messinger, "Strategies of Control," p. 234.

17. Daniel Glaser, "Disciplinary Action and Counseling" in *Correctional Institutions*, ed. Carter, Glaser and Wilkins, p. 33.

18. Quoted in Glaser, "Disciplinary Action and Counseling," 1972, p. 33.

19. Messinger, "Strategies of Control," p. 61.

20. Smith and Fried, *The Uses of American Prisons*, p. 80.

21. Messinger argues that no technique "seems to be nearly as effective in organizing the routine activities of the prison community as are the unofficial alliances between staff members and inmates." "Strategies of Control," 1958, p. 253. Sykes argues essentially the same line when he states that ". . . the guard frequently shows evidence of having been "corrupted" by the captive animals over whom he stands in theoretical dominance." *The Society of Captives*, p. 54.

22. Robert B. Reich, "Bargaining in Correctional Institutions," *Yale Law Review*, March, 1972.

23. Elmer Johnson, *Crime, Corrections and Society*, p. 583. For a more detailed analysis of the history of prison labor see Manuel Lopez-Rey, "Some Considerations of the Character and Organization of Prison Labor," *Journal of Criminal Law, Criminology and Police Science*, May-June, 1958, and Manuel Lopez-Rey, *Crime.*

24. Johnson, 1964, p. 583.

25. New Jersey Standards for Work Release, New Jersey Department of Corrections, Trenton, New Jersey, 1974.

26. Elmer Johnson, "Prison Industry," in *Correctional Institutions*, ed. Glaser, Carter and Wilkens.

27. Johnson, *Crime, Corrections and Society*, p. 583.

28. Quoted in Johnson, "Prison Industry," p. 356.

29. Ibid., p. 357.

30. Johnson. *Crime, Corrections and Society*, p. 587.

31. Ibid., p. 586.

32. California Prison Task Force, "Correctional Systems Study," (July, 1971), p. 27.

33. Interview with senior correctional counselor, West Prison, November 1975.

34. California Department of Corrections, *Administrative Manual*, October 9, 1975, section 195-06.

35. California Prison Task Force, "Correctional Systems Study."

36. *Dictionary of the Social Sciences* (New York: Free Press, 1964), p. 316.

37. Marx and Engels, "The German Ideology," in *The Marx-Engels Reader*, ed. Robert C. Tucker (New York: W.W. Norton, 1972), pp. 136-37. Reprinted with permission.

38. Of course there is more to the strategy of deterrence. However, the concept of the offender bears greatly on the way the ideology is formulated.

39. For an excellent historical survey of the scientific explanation of crime, see Richard Quinney, *The Problem of Crime* (New York: Dodd, Mead, 1970), pp. 43-100 and Leon Radzinowicz, *Ideology and Crime.*

40. Thomas Szasz, *Law, Liberty and Psychiatry* (New York: MacMillan, 1963), p. 108.

41. Karl Menninger, *The Crime of Punishment*, p. 19, quoted in Jessica Mitford, *Kind and Usual Punishment*, p. 97.

42. It is also interesting to note that there seems to be a high correlation between the label of institutional "deviant" and feelings about personal efficacy. In a recent study researchers found that 75 percent of the inmates considered particularly deviant by their wardens offered the complaint about their inability to affect their own fate, while among the nondeviant sample fewer than half so complained. For a description of the study, see Smith and Fried, *The Uses of the American Prison*, p. 111.

43. American Friends Service Committee, *Struggle for Justice*, p. 37.

44. Ibid., p. 37.

45. Ibid., p. 27.

46. Ibid., p. 28.

47. Ibid., p. 92.

48. California Department of Corrections, *Master Plan*, August 16, 1968, p. 11.

49. Ibid., p. 17.

50. Certain influential prisoners, those who were widely known as political activists, were also questioned, but not included in the results of the sample reported in a later chapter. The purpose of speaking with the prisoners was to gather information on the historical development of the prisoners' movement.

51. Interview with administrator.

52. Gene Kassenbaum, David N. Ward, and Danile Wilner, *Prison Treatment and Parole Survival*, p. 59.

53. James Leiby, *Charity and Corrections in New Jersey*, p. 135.

54. Ibid., p. 136.

55. Quoted in Leiby, *Charity and Corrections*, p. 136.

56. Ibid., p. 134.

History

The traditional historical accounts of nation-states bear many similarities. History is reported as the sum total of changes in patterns of national leadership and the manner in which leadership reacted to major national events such as wars, famine, or international alignments. History becomes the account of how great people managed great events. The people of a nation-state are the clay, not the sculptors of the national heritage.

The history of a prison can be constructed in much the same way as the history of a nation-state, probably with somewhat more justification because of the relative powerlessness of its subjects. An institutional history can be conceptualized in terms of administrative and policy changes that molded the complexion of the institution, but the actual history of a prison, as well as a nation-state, is considerably richer. The richness is achieved by tracing the patterns of beliefs and activities of the clients—a historical phenomenon usually absent from institutional histories.

There are two broad areas of historical activity in the prison, or two categories of change, which are not always analytically separable. An internal history of a prison can be thought of as a series of events initiated by or confined to a particular institutional setting. Changes in rules which are particular to an institution, such as the time allotted to prisoners to spend in the yard, can be considered as elements of internal history. The administrative and inmate system of governance are additional elements of internal history. Historical change, however, is often influenced by agencies outside a particular institution and has consequences for many institutions. Court-ordered changes in disciplinary procedures are an example of what can be called an external historical stimulus.

The problem is that it is not always clear whether a particular change or event is the product of an external or internal spark. Though court-ordered changes in discipline applied to a variety of institutions, the suit that resulted in the decision was brought by prisoners of a particular institution as a result of the policies practiced in their institution. So whether the court order was an internal or external change for the inmates who brought the suit is problematic.

The purpose of noting this dichotomy or separation between internal and external historical change is to draw attention to the pattern of history prevalent in the institutions in question. Since the reach of the prisoner is short, prisoners are constantly attempting to lengthen their reach by linking up with forces outside the prison. Much of the political history of prisoners is the history of connection, coalition, support groups, and the like—attempts to jostle for position in the wider political and social arena.

This chapter will survey the history of prison politics over the last twenty-five years, giving special attention to the last fifteen, which marked the beginning of the most intense period of political activity among prisoners, and the most serious challenge to the legitimacy of the prison administration. The challenge was aimed at the legitimacy of the political role of the prison administration and correctional staff, who were afforded absolute control over the environment and life of the prisoner. Implicit in this challenge was a protest against the political role that the prisoner was forced to assume as a result of the distribution of power and prerogative.

Early Period

The major political and historical event that marks the path of prison history is the riot. A riot is defined as "the execution of a violent and unlawful purpose by three or more persons acting together, to the terror of the people.[1] Generally, riots have the connotation of being unbridled outbreaks of passion or emotion. It was the riot that brought media and public attention to the prison, often resulting in the appointment of a committee to study the institution and report on causes and possible reforms.

The prison riots of the 1950s were political acts, although not always conscious political acts—ones intended to change the balance of power within the institutions. Major riots occurred with some regularity during the 1950s. In fact, the period is noted as one of the most tumultuous in prison history. There were major riots in both New Jersey men's prisons and riots in San Quentin and Folsom in California.

A period of turmoil began in New Jersey in February 1951 with an uprising of men held in the segregation unit of the prison. In all, fifty-two prisoners were involved, managing to cause considerable damage to the segregation facility.[2] The demands centered on improved conditions for those held in segregation facilities. Because the disturbance took place in the segregation wing, alleged to contain the most troubled offenders, the administration claimed that the riot had "little to do with conditions or practices in the prison as a whole."[3] A similar disturbance occurred at about the same time in the segregation wing at Folsom.

No sooner had the administration dismissed the disturbance as an outburst of a group of troubled and desperate persons, when another major disturbance took place in the New Jersey prisons. In April 1951, sixty-nine prisoners took part in a disturbance that was planned far in advance. This disturbance at Trenton State Prison sent a jolt throughout the New Jersey prison system (as a disturbance in one state prison tends to do) sparking a more widespread riot at the prison farm at Rahway. Sixty-nine prisoners took part in the initial demonstration at Trenton State Prison.

> . . . they captured four guards as hostages and supplied themselves with food and makeshift weapons. They held out for four days. Warden Carty, suspecting trouble, had moved some convict leaders to Rahway. The rumor spread that guards had beaten them severely and a sort of a sympathy riot began at the prison. Two hundred and thirty-one men took nine guards as hostage and barricaded themselves on the second floor. This demonstration lasted more than five days.[4]

The demands of the prisoners centered on improved internal conditions such as food and medical care, as well as new procedures to regulate the interaction between the prisoner and parole board. An independent commission found that "obvious deficiencies in plant, personnel, and programs were basic factors in the riot."[5] However, the commissioner of corrections, Sanford Bates, a noted penologist, disagreed with the report of the investigating committee:

> The riots did not show, he said a need for reform at Trenton State Prison; riots were only possible, in fact, where an enlightened system gives inmates a modicum of freedom and resources.[6]

Bates was asked what the reason was for the riot if not to achieve some reform. Bates pondered the question. "I think it's spring fever. You can quote me on that any time." In addition to the season he pointed to the general unrest in the world.[7]

The character of the so-called riots of the 1950s can be partially understood by the types of demands made by the prisoners. The riot at Jackson State Prison in Michigan was typical. The demands are also considered typical of those compiled during the fifties.[8] The demands included the following:

1. 15-block (the maximum security wing) be remodeled to provide for adequate lighting and treatment facilities.
2. Counselors have free access to the disciplinary cells in the 15-block.
3. Segregation (solitary confinement) policies be revised, and a member of the individual treatment staff be given a position on the segregation board.
4. Only guards who would not be inhumane in their treatment be picked for duty in the 12-block (reserved for epileptic, semi-mentally disturbed, blind, handicapped and senile cases).

5. The carrying of dangerous hand weapons and inhumane restrainment equipment by guards be prohibited.
6. Adequate and competent personnel for handling mental cases, and more adequate screening of such cases.
7. A letter on prison stationery be sent to the Parole Board asking for a revision of procedures to give equal treatment to all parolees.
8. Postoperative care be given under the direction of the medical director (instead of by prisoner technicians).
9. Equal opportunities for dental care for all prisoners, with special regard to the elimination of special buying preferences.
10. Creation of a permanent council elected by prisoners.
11. No reprisals against any leader or participant in the revolt.[9]

James W.L. Park, associate superintendent of San Quentin, and a student of the prison rebellions, discussed the riots of the 1950s in a paper prepared for the Department of Corrections in California. Park defines the traditional prison rebellion this way:

> A typical prison insurrection occurs when enough inmates are sufficiently discontented with their personal situation so that vocal and aggressive leaders are encouraged to agitate action. Usually a list of housekeeping complaints involving food, sanitation, physical handling, housing or privileges is presented as the cause of the rebellion. The grievance list may not be compiled until well after the disturbance starts. . . .[10]

Several characteristics of the early prison riots are repeatedly alluded to by writers concerned with the period. The disturbances generally had a spontaneous character—there seemed to be little or no advance planning of strategy, program, or organization. Leadership thus tended naturally to rise to the top, rather than being selected through consensus. That leadership was in almost all cases entirely white, although many blacks, Puerto Ricans and Chicanos participated in the riots. Finally, the demands put forth by the rioting prisoners primarily dealt with conditions of life within the prison. It is worth taking an expanded look at the context in which the disturbances occurred.

The spontaneous character of the disturbances speaks to a number of issues. Spontaneous political activity will usually occur when no political organizations exist to give direction and clarity to the political will of a group. Often the lack of political organization is attributed to policies of social, economic and intellectual control exercised by those whose position is threatened by the political organization. In some cases the control is subtle, for example the ability to control issues placed on a political agenda.[11] In other cases the control is overt.

During the 1950s, the prison government exerted both overt and covert control over the population. The environment was structured to outlaw communication and political activity among prisoners. Exercising total control over communication, movement, and outside contact, the prison administration was able to effectively block attempts by prisoners to join together for political or even social activity. The administration was the Hobbesian Sovereign that controlled all the axiomatic propositions in the social order and the prison population, the grateful subjects rescued from the anarchy of the state of nature.

Spontaneous political activity can also be, but is not always, a signal of a lack of political knowledge. It may indicate a confusion between the act itself and the causality of the act. In the ghetto riots of the 1960s, the actual insurrection preceded an explanation of the reasons why the riot had occurred. The riot was a means of visibly demonstrating political dissatisfaction.

Most participants in the ghetto riots knew why they were engaging in open insurrection. They assumed that the riot itself would make the conditions that led to the riot clear to the general public. Of course, the riot itself did not express a clear political position. When it became apparent that the conditions that precipitated the riot did not become evident after the riot began, participants in the riot were forced to spell out these conditions. This process of clarification usually led to the publication of a series of demands.

A similar situation occurred in the prison riots. Prisoners felt that rebelling would send a clear signal of their dissatisfaction with conditions of confinement. When the authorities and the general public questioned that signal, the prisoners were forced to spell out the specifics of their dissatisfaction. This is one of the reasons that demands usually appeared after a riot began.

A riot is also the product of the environment in which the riot occurs. It indicates a low level of political efficacy—an inability to change the conditions of life. Riots occur when an environment appears to leave open no paths to effectuate change and when the conditions of life weigh heavily on the individuals within that environment. So, it is among the most helpless, desperate, ravaged, and exploited elements of society that spontaneous political activity occurs. In the American ghettos, in the colonies of Africa and Asia and in the prison, the riot expresses a lack of political alternatives. It is a way of doing something—a way of expressing lingering discontent and neglect. It is a physical and emotional, rather than an intellectual or organizational, critique of alienation.

It is within the category of ideology that an additional explanation of the type of demands put forth in the disturbances of the 1950s can be found. Ideology also helps broaden understanding about leadership and spontaneous political activity. The effectiveness of the ideological system of the prison and the outside community is an important explanatory ingredient in understanding the periods of crisis as well as the periods of tranquillity in the prison in the 1950s.

Marx noted that a strong correspondent relationship exists between the structures and institutions of a society and the dominant ideology.[12] Ideology serves the purpose of providing explanations about the functions of institutions and structures by referencing categories such as personality, human nature, community, democracy. Thus, on the basis of an ideological system, the individual finds a comfortable system to explain the social world and his position within it. In short, structure is intimately related to ideology.

The structure of the prison during the 1950s can be classified as authoritarian or totalitarian. Essentially the prison structure was characterized by several features: First, centralized formal authority and discretion resided in a single administrative officer (warden), who presided over a rigidly organized hierarchy fashioned along military police-state lines. This mode of organization produced rigid status barriers between keepers and wards. Second, prisoners were permitted a bare minimum of formal association. There was no representation of inmate opinion in the formal organization of the system. The inmate publication was rigidly censored—a vehicle of administrative opinion. Contact and communication with the outside was strictly limited. The body of prisoners was classed on the basis of graded privileges with little chance for mobility. Finally, punishment, a central dynamic in the system of prison government, was arbitrary and not restrained by judicial ideals, such as due process rights.[13]

The ideological system that emanated from the system of organization and governance had severe consequences for the prisoner as political and social actor. Structurally, there was no space for prisoners to participate in the system of governance. The proper role of the prisoner, according to the ideological system, was one of subjecthood. The structure legitimated the absolute power of the custodians and the absolute impotency of the captives.

Since the prison is not an isolated institution, but an arm of the state, legitimation has an exernal as well as internal component. The structure of governance within the prison must reflect the community feelings about how offenders should be punished. During the 1950s the two dominant theories of correctional goals were those of retribution and deterrence.

> However harsh an insistence on retribution may appear to be, it cannot be ignored as a social force shaping the nature of the penal institutions; whether in the form of community reactions to accusations of "coddling" prisoners or the construction of budgets by the state legislature.[14]

Theories of deterrence, like theories of retribution, tend to argue for prison conditions that are painful, that inflict misery over and above the loss of liberty. Criminals are not expected to forego crime because of value or attitudinal changes, but rather through a sharpened awareness of the severe costs attached to wrongdoing.[15] Prison conditions must be painful enough to produce this sharpened awareness.

Prison administrators were able to justify the structure of governance on the basis of these two theories. Since custody was the primary goal of incarceration, measures which maximized social control were entirely proper. The prisoner had forfeited his rights to participate in a system of governance—the rights that supposedly secured equal protection under the law. His life became the property of the state to mold and fashion in ways that would accomplish the desired ends of retribution and deterrence.

Rather than questioning the subject-master relationship between the prisoner and the state, the vast majority of prisoners wholly supported the relationship.[16] In denying the prisoner protection and guarantees similar to those of the citizens in the outside community, the state acted in an entirely defensible and legitimate way. As long as prisoners subscribed to this ideology, there was no reason for political action. Prisoners could only question the particular severity of certain sanctions and not the sanctions themselves. It is for this reason that the demands of the 1950s can be properly described as "housekeeping demands." What was at stake in the riots of the 1950s was not the architecture of the house, but the way it was kept.

While the ideology of punishment provided an external form of legitimation, the political climate of the 1950s deepened the effects of that ideology on the client. Devoid of any substantial protest, the quietistic fifties provided neither substantive issues nor strategies for prisoners to emulate. The challenges to public and private government begun by the Civil Rights Movement were to emerge in a later period. Left without any social or political explanations about crime, the prisoner was forced to accept personal inadequacy as the major determinant for incarceration.

So, it was the system of ideology, combined with the apparent widespread social satisfaction of the outside community, that shaped the protest of the 1950s. The demands of the prisoners revolved around equal and humane treatment within the institution, where they accepted the prevailing system of governance. It was, among other things, the weakening of the ideological systems of punishment which would eventually push the prison population into expanded political protest, a path which would move from riot to insurrection.

The Middle Period: The Sixties

The history of the development of the political movements in California and New Jersey shows many similarities. Generally, it appears that the broad movement of political activity proceeded along the same path, although the political movement of prisoners developed much earlier in California. Authorities in California and New Jersey did respond somewhat differently to the developments. Those differences are important and will be examined. However, since the political development of prisoners in both states during the sixties and early seventies are similar, they will be examined and reported as a single history, except when modification is needed to note important differences.

There were three dominant developments that helped build and shape the political arena for the prisoners. The changing political mood of the sixties, including the Civil Rights Movement, the Vietnam War, and the emergence of ethnic and national movements, played a decisive role. Intervention by the courts, especially the federal courts, which had previously steadfastly refused to intervene on the part of inmates, was a decisive element that had ramifications far beyond the amelioration produced by particular judicial decisions. Finally, the development of the Black Muslim movement gave contours to the idea of autonomous prisoner organizations.[17] The development of the Muslim movement was more consequential in California than in New Jersey. Occurring in the early sixties in California, it provided an organizational legacy probably equally as important as the actual activities of Muslims at the height of their success.

Each of these developments will be examined in isolation, then counterposed to see how these currents complemented or clashed with each other, revealing some rather unorthodox political partners. In both California and New Jersey this period of political development in the sixties and early seventies was marked by major insurrections.[18] In California, a general strike took place at San Quentin in 1968 followed by "the longest and the most militant strike in the history of the country at Folsom Prison in November of 1970."[19] These insurrections symbolize the launching of a new political missile.

The Courts

Courts are the agency that first delivered the offender into incarceration. After effecting a ruling that placed the individual in the custody of the state, the courts were almost entirely unwilling to hear cases bearing on the condition of that confinement.

The courts' refusal to act was premised on the acceptance of the doctrine that prisoners forfeited their rights. In 1871 the case of *Ruffin* v. *Commonwealth* defined the prisoner's status as ". . . a slave of the state with no rights."[20] Although the definition was amended in *Coffin* v. *Reichard*, the court persisted in regarding prisoners as having few, if any, political rights.[21]

During the 1960s and 1970s there was a change in the courts' attitude concerning intervention. Courts became more willing to intervene and rule on issues dealing specifically with the conditions of confinement. The change was advanced slowly facing continued skepticism from many members of the judiciary. This shift in judicial policy was hastened by a variety of factors.

In the early sixties there was an expansion of the powers of the federal judicial system. The federal courts produced decisions making the Eighth Amendment binding on states—decisions that held "that petitions claiming infringements of civil rights could be brought to federal courts before state remedies were exhausted—and broadening the use of habeas corpus petitions."[22] Actions brought through the Civil Rights Movement and the tenor of the Warren Court expedited the move toward more active judicial intervention.

But the main impetus for the increasing concern of the courts seemed to be external. The sixties were producing broad challenges to social and economic policies; challenges in the form of vastly increased litigation coupled with protest activism.

> . . . the reasons for the shift lie in the arena much wider than the courts. Changes in the nature of the inmate population and in the legal profession, new ideas about the deviant, about incarceration, and about our society, all influenced the transformation.[23]

A significant change in the prison population began to occur during the middle sixties. A significant number of draft evaders entered federal prisons. Many of these prisoners, of middle-class background, were able to muster the resources to attack policies they found repugnant. Blacks, now in the forefront of the struggle for social change in the community, brought the impulse to struggle into the prison. A disproportionate number of litigations were brought by black prisoners during the sixties. Coupled with this change in the inmate population was a change in the legal community. Civil rights lawyers, knowledgeable from the early struggles, began to broaden their work to incorporate cases brought by the prisoners.

With the attack on American institutions came an increasing interest in the system of ideology which supported the institutional structure. Academics and even policy makers in the field of criminal justice became increasingly critical of retribution as the sole reason for incarceration. The theory of deterrence also met with more frequent criticism. The academic, legal and professional community began to sing the praises of the theory of rehabilitation.[24] Widespread interest and affection for rehabilitating those incarcerated and returning them to the community as regenerated citizens was soon shared by the court. The ideology of punishment for punishment's sake was on the decline. Even prisoners were people and should be treated with some care. The definition of humanity and social justice offered by the Civil Rights Movement in partnership with the growing group of believers in rehabilitation would temper the decisions of the courts in years to come.

The major areas of prison governance that figured in important judicial decisions included discipline, freedom of association, freedom of religion and censorship. My reading of the decisions shows a pattern of cautious interventions, often marked by reversals, rather than a history of bold judicial action. A great many of these decisions reflect the judiciary's adoption of the principle of rehabilitation. A review and discussion of some of what I think are major cases follows.[25]

One of the first questions faced by the judiciary in regard to prison litigation was the question of whether the court had the right to intervene in the administration of the prison. Prison administrators often challenged the court's right to intervene in an administrative regimen, until now immune from judicial intervention. In general, the court turned aside the hands-off doctrine suggested by prison officials. In *Cruz* v. *Beto* the court held that, "Federal courts sit not to supervise prisons but to enforce the constitutional rights of all 'persons' which include prisoners."[26]

The court has generally upheld its right to decide questions concerning the constitutional rights of prisoners. However, the court has provided no systematic interpretation of what constitutional rights prisoners maintain upon being convicted of crime. In referring to this quandary, District Judge Doyle noted, "I discover in the cases scarcely a single beam or joist in a framework of principles within which a particular constitutional challenge to a particular prison regulation can be decided."[27]

There is another legal predicament that clouds the court's role. Specifically, does the same standard for the abridgment of a constitutional right pertain to prisoners and free citizens alike? This predicament remains independent of the determination of what constitutional rights are due prisoners, since a full grant of constitutional rights need not necessarily include the same conditions for the abridgment of those rights.

The question of the range of constitutional protections afforded the prisoner after conviction, and the question of the conditions necessary to abridge those rights are addressed in the case of *Morales* v. *Schmidt*. Although judicial opinions are often obscure and open to a variety of interpretations, the decisions in the Morales case seem to set the parameters for federal judicial action.

In Morales the court is asked to decide whether a prohibition on correspondence by prisoners is unconstitutional. In order to decide the merits of this particular case, the court is forced to render a ruling on the broader area of constitutional rights for prisoners, including the rights to due process under the law. Due process rights include procedural and substantive rights. Substantive rights are those expressly written in the constitution, such as the Eighth Amendment prohibition against cruel and unusual punishment, and due process rights originally found in the Fifth Amendment and later expanded in the Fourteenth. Procedural due process consists of organizational or adjudicative mechanisms for operationalizing these guarantees for citizens in jeopardy.

In the district court decision in the Morales case, the court makes a determination favorable to plaintiff Morales. On the question of the extent of the prisoner's due process (constitutional) protections, the court rules "that those convicted of crime should continue to share with the general population the full, latent protection of the Fourteenth Amendment."[28] This applies to procedural as well as substantive due process.

After ruling that prisoners share Fourteenth Amendment rights with the general population, the court goes on to render a finding concerning the circumstances necessary for the state to abridge those rights. The court holds that the burden of proof to show an interest in differential treatment falls squarely on the state. The decision reads:

> Therefore, if a statute or regulation undertakes to deny to persons convicted of crime one or more of those elements of due process which must be accorded those not convicted of crime, the burden will be upon the state to show a compelling governmental interest in the differential in treatment.[29]

Legally, the term "compelling state interest" has a variety of interpretations. In order to clarify how "compelling state interest" should be interpreted in this ruling, the judge offers the following interpretation:

> . . . if one of these rules of institutional survival affects significantly a liberty which is clearly protected among the general population, and if its only justification is that the prison cannot survive without it, then it may well be that the Constitution requires that the prison be modified. Specifically, if the functions of deterrence and rehabilitation cannot be performed in a prison without the imposition of a restrictive regime not reasonably related to these functions, it may well be that those functions can no longer be performed constitutionally in a prison setting.[30]

This interpretation seems to rule out the "institutional survival" defense often used to justify abridgment of liberties. Prison administrators must at least demonstrate how institutional survival is dependent on usurpation of prisoners' constitutional rights. Even if administrators could prove such a relationship, the decision stipulates that it may well be the prison that requires modification. The Morales decision is a landmark in prison rights litigation. It provides wide latitude for prisoners to press for their inclusion in protections afforded to citizens. Unfortunately, the Morales case was significantly altered in an appeal decision of the Seventh Circuit Court.

The decision of the circuit court sharply diverges from the ruling of the district court. On the question of constitutional protections for prisoners, the court disagreed with the district court ". . . that the equal protection clause mandates the elimination of the distinction between the two classes."[31] Consequently, the state maintains the right to provide differential constitutional protections for prisoners and nonprisoners. While the decision of the district court broadened the constitutional protection available to prisoners by limiting the effectiveness, or totally abolishing, the distinction between the convicted and nonconvicted class, the district court's decision affirms that the distinction exists and should be an operative concept in deciding constitutional questions. The decision does not maintain that the distinction between the "classes" automatically eliminates the potential for prisoners to press for extended constitutional protection. It does, however, limit an important basis for such challenges—the contention that imprisonment should not deprive an individual from fundamental rights enjoyed before imprisonment.

The circuit court's decision also modified the burden on the state to prove that a usurpation of constitutional rights was necessary. The district court held that the state must prove a "compelling state interest" in order to abridge a prisoner's rights. The circuit court introduces the "rational relationship" principle as a sufficient justification for state action. The court defines the rational relationship principle this way:

> The appropriate standard by which to judge the constitutionality of the kind of restriction the defendant wishes to impose in this case is the usual one for analyzing state action, namely, whether the action bears a rational relationship to or is reasonably necessary for the advancement of a justifiable purpose of the state.[32]

The circuit court reverses the district court decision and refuses to make a finding of fact in the Morales case. The decision notes:

> The district court's granting of a preliminary injunction was based upon the "compelling state interest" standard which we hold not to be applicable in the situation before the court. The record is insufficient for a determination of the question of whether the State's proposed restriction is justified under the rational relationship standard, the test which we hold applicable here.[33]

Although it is not absolutely clear what the "rational relationship" principle means, it is apparent that the latitude afforded the state widens. The state can prevail by showing that a constitutional right intereferes with the advancement of a justified purpose of the state. It is assumed that both rehabilitation and deterrence are justified state purposes.

Thus the state is given a technical advantage in deciding how rehabilitation and deterrence should be defined and what interferes with these ends. In the past the court has refused to intervene if the prison administration could make the case that a rehabilitation program is operational.[34] Without such evidence, the administrations found it difficult to convince the court that a restriction interfered with an end of rehabilitation.

For the prisoner, the circuit court's decision removed the possibility that the prisoner could receive a full complement of constitutional rights through the equal protection clause. Collapsing the distinction between "classes" would have in essence provided the prisoner with a constitutional status closely approximating, if not equal to, the nonconvicted citizen. When the circuit court upheld the distinction between classes, the road to democratic protections for prisoners became more winding and considerably bumpier.

The effect of the circuit court's decision in Morales appears in a variety of constitutional decisions concerning prisoners. For example, in the area of freedom of communication, including the right to send and receive mail and certain publications, the court vigorously struck down many prevailing censorship regulations. The administration had failed to prove that the state had a rational interest to justify abridgment of First and Fourteenth Amendment rights. In *Palmigiano* v. *Travisone* the court found:

> In spite of the pronouncement in the cases cited supra that prison officials had broad powers of censorship, I find justification only for fewer restrictions because total censorship serves no rational deterrent, rehabilitative or prison security purposes.[35]

It is clear that rather than affirming that prisoners share in First and Fourteenth Amendment rights bestowed on citizens, the court's decision actually negates the fact. The decision is premised on the administration's inability to show a rational and justifiable relationship between censorship and "the advancement of some justifiable purpose of imprisonment."[36] While prisoners manage to gain access to a First Amendment right on the basis of the decision, they fail to gain the right as a product of a positive affirmation of their democratic rights. Since, if the prison administration is able to successfully demonstrate a rational relationship between censorship and a justifiable purpose of imprisonment, the prisoners would likely be stripped of this right, or more likely, never have received it in the first place.[37]

In 1974 in *Procunier* v. *Martinez*, a California case, the court produced a decision with similar ramifications. The court held that "censorship of prisoners' mail works a consequential restriction on the First and Fourteenth Amendment rights of those who are not prisoners." The court indicated that the case should not be decided by reference to the particular First Amendment rights enjoyed by prisoners, but judged on the basis of First Amendment cases dealing with the "general problem of incidental restrictions on First Amendment liberties."[38]

In Martinez, the court refuses to decide the case based on the important claim of the prisoners that they should enjoy basic First Amendment rights of citizenship. The court provides a decision favorable to the prisoners without including any formal grant of rights. Although the decision in Martinez is somewhat more rigid than in Palmigiano, the end result is similar. The prisoners manage to secure a democratic procedure without securing a democratic right. The failure of the court to grant such rights is politically quite significant. Often the significance of the court's finding and its failure to affirm the unconditional democratic rights of prisoners was lost on the attorneys and the prisoners in the jubilation that followed an apparently favorable decision.[39]

The two remaining areas of judicial decisions that bear directly on political activity are the right to group and religious association and discipline. In the area of religious freedom, the first cases were brought by Black Muslims seeking the right to practice their religion within the prison.[40] In *Sostre* v. *McGinnis*, a case initiated by prison activist Martin Sostre, the court affirmed the right of Muslims to practice their religion while incarcerated. While finding the Moslem faith to be a "religion" qualifying for constitutional protection, the court, as in the previous cases, held that if a subordinate interest exists, the administration is within the law in suppressing the activities of the Muslims.[41]

> No romantic or sentimental view of constitutional rights or of religion should induce a court to interfere with the necessary disciplinary regime established by the prison officials.[42]

In the Muslim cases, the court made reference to the possibility that the doctrine of the Muslims, described by the court as "white-hatred, racial supremacy," would necessitate much administrative latitude in regulating the group. The decision noted that ". . . it is obvious from the evidence in the record that the activities of the group are not exclusively religious."[43] The evidence that the court refers to is accounts of militant activities undertaken by Muslims to secure the right to religious practice. Although the court provided latitude for the administration to regulate the activities of the Muslims in accordance with the "subordinate interest" precedent, it also affirmed the right of the Muslims to exist as a religious group. The decisions opened another consequential chapter in the prisoners' political movement.

Seizing the initiative taken by the Muslims, other groups sought protection under the garb of religious freedom. Many of these groups were not exclusively or even partially religious in nature. Many of the groups that developed and sought recognition were political groups who saw the Muslims' success as a means of gaining official recognition. The court action in recognizing political associations of prisoners had not been nearly as solid as the precedent handed down in Muslim cases. In *Evans* v. *Mosely*, the court affirmed the right of prison administrations to segregate a black prisoner who sought to form a chapter of an organization called the Black United Front.[44] In an opposite decision, a federal district court held that prisoners had the right to form a chapter of the National Prisoners' Reform Association.[45]

Strategically, certain groups of prisoners decided that the fastest and safest route to gaining recognition and the freedom to operate was the claim that the group was religious in nature. In *Theriault* v. *Carlson*, the plaintiff claimed to be founder of a religion called the Eclatarian faith represented by The Church of the New Song.[46] Prison authorities in Georgia denied plaintiff's access to church facilities, refusing to recognize the religion as genuine. The authorities contended that the church appeared to be a front of "a radical political movement."[47] To buttress the authorities' contention, they produced an intelligence report on the activities of the group.

> *The group has members of all races* and has the characteristics of an external group on the far left, completely against the system (whatever it may consist of) and will let nothing stay or stand in its way. (Emphasis mine)[48]

In its decision, the court grudgingly acknowledged the group's religious nature and its right to operate within the prison.

> The court is not unmindful of the very real possibility that petitioners are still engaging in a "game" and attempting to perpetuate a colossal fraud upon both this court and the federal prison system. Nevertheless with all due respect to the respondent, the court cannot declare petitioner's religion illegitimate.
>
> Certainly if respondents could show that a compelling or substantial public interest required the subjugation of petitioner's First Amendment rights, they would prevail. But burden upon respondents is heavy, and a cursory review of the Black Muslim cases reveals how very heavy that burden is.[49]

Finally, in the area of discipline the decisions of the court closely parallel those handed down in cases previously discussed. The decision rendered in *Clutchette* v. *Procunier* allows prisoners expanded due process protections.[50] Citing the Supreme Court ruling in *Goldberg* v. *Kelly*, the court found that,

> . . . the argument that a prisoner is committed to the custody of the Department of Corrections and as such, may be confined in any manner chosen by the Director, subject only to statutory guidelines and the proscription of the "cruel and unusual punishment" clause of the Eighth Amendment is unpersuasive.[51]
>
> Procedural due process must obtain whenever the individual is subject to "grievous loss" at the hands of the state or its instrumentalities.[52]

The decision on disciplinary matters follows the logic of the previous court decisions. In essence, it provides certain safeguards for the prisoner without affirming him as a full member of the political community. In fact, the decisions tend to reaffirm the special place of the prisoner within the political community.

It is fair to conclude that judicial decisions in the area of prisoners' rights had ambiguous results. For example, certain decisions, rendered in the early Muslim cases, acted to expand the avenue for religious and nonreligious groups to gain official recognition and operate publicly. Other decisions produced due process procedures in areas where no such procedures had ever existed. Discipline was probably the most important area of governance affected by these decisions. The term "due process procedure" is used advisedly. It emphasizes the distinction between due process procedures and the actual output of these procedures. Often prison administrators failed to meet the requisites of the court in implementing due process procedures and often even the actual implementation of these procedures did not lead to the realization of anything approaching due process of law.

On the debit side of the balance sheet, judicial decisions stopped considerably short of affirming that prisoners shared many of the constitutional rights of the citizen in the political community. Generally, prisoners were granted certain constitutional rights or procedures by default. Prisoners received some constitutional guarantees because of the administration's inability to prove that a particular sanction was consistent with a justified end of incarceration. On the whole, prisoners received constitutional guarantees as a result of administrative inefficiency rather than as a positive affirmation of their citizenship status.

The Courts and Political Competence

Starting in 1961, the amount of litigation filed by prisoners seeking relief in their own cases or litigating conditions of confinement grew exponentially. Jailhouse lawyers, prisoners with legal expertise, grew up among the ranks of the prison body. The massive increase in litigation secured a special place and need for their talents. Prisoners and administration alike were able to identify the "writ writers."

There were at least two categories of legal activists: One group saw the court and the legal community as a powerful ameliorative weapon able to change the balance of power between the prisoner and the administration. For this group of activists the law was an end in itself rather than a means to some other end. The second group was less hopeful about the results of judicial intervention. They were skeptical of the ability and the desire of the courts to change the status of the prisoner or to produce social justice. This second group saw the legal decision as potentially, rather than immediately, significant. Brian Glick has argued that a particular decision was politically significant in relation to how that decision could be welded into a political strategy. It is on the basis of this understanding of legal action as one method of struggle "by any means necessary" that revolutionaries like Martin Sostre and Rucell Magee have trained themselves to be effective jailhouse lawyers.[53]

Whatever the motive for engaging in legal activity happened to be, those who educated themselves in the law found their talents much sought after. Not only did legal expertise seem to raise the efficacy of the individuals who practiced jailhouse law, but also seemed to provide a vehicle for others to increase their potential power. The use of law in the prison provided a means for the prisoners to independently support one another. In New Jersey, an organization called the Inmate Legal Association, founded to provide legal help and advice to prisoners, had a politicizing effect. Because the association was supposed to deal specifically and exclusively with the legal problems of the prisoners, it gained a certain autonomy, thereby providing an independent base to aid all prisoners.

In the early stages of litigation, most of the prisoners who sought relief from the court were harassed by the prison administration. In three of the major cases of prison litigation, the prisoners who filed the suit were remanded and held in segregation at the time of the court hearing. In *Sostre* v. *Rockefeller*, the court noted,

> It is an undisputed fact that as a result of plaintiff's refusal to cease and desist from "practicing law" in the institution, and his refusal to answer questions about R.N.A. (Republic of New Africa). . . . defendent Follette decided to place plaintiff in the segregation unit.[54]

In one form or another administrative harassment continued throughout the 1960s, and according to several prisoners interviewed, continues into the present. Besides harassing the "writ writers," prison administrations have avoided implementing changes ordered by the courts.[55]

The barrage of litigation also had the effect of opening up some of the reality of incarceration to the general public. Prisoners had for years complained about the inhumane conditions of confinement without stirring the interest of the public or the media. But when a judge comments about the desperate conditions within the prison, the public, and especially the media, seem to take notice. Prisoners' litigation forced the prison authorities and state officials into the open to defend themselves against the charges of prisoners. Of course at the same time, the large amount of litigation and many apparently favorable decisions can convince the public and the prisoners "that an issue has been settled when in fact they have won a very limited victory."[56]

We can conclude at this point that the decisions of the court during this middle period of activity had ambiguous results. Court decisions undeniably opened up important political space for the development and growth of prison organizations. At the same time, the decisions failed to affirm the right of prisoners to carry out overt political activity or uphold other democratic rights.

The Muslims

Through the process of legal activism within the prison and identification with liberation struggles in the community, blacks by 1962-63 had moved to the forefront of struggle within the prison. Traditionally, the prison had been overtly or covertly racially separated, with whites holding most of the dominant positions in the prisoner social system. The development of black activism proved as much of a threat to white hegemony as it did to administrative hegemony, for the acceptance of de facto racial separation promoted a certain quietism among blacks, conditioned to expect nothing more, and whites satisfied to have attained some rank through "white skin privilege."

The first organizational manifestation of the blacks' rise to a position of vocal opposition was the Black Muslim Movement, known officially as the Nation of Islam. The movement founded by the Honorable Elijah Muhammed, was doctrinally the antithesis of the traditional religious teachings of blacks in the Christian establishment. Muslim doctrine asserted the primacy of the black race in shaping the modern world.

> . . . history had been whitened in the white man's history books, . . . the black man had been brainwashed for hundreds of years. Original Man was black, in the continent called Africa where the human race had emerged on the planet earth.[57]

According to the Muslim doctrine, the white race had enslaved the blacks, first physically and then mentally. The white man was the devil. All the institutions of the society were tainted by the white race, especially the black church.

> This religion taught the "Negro" that black was a curse. It taught him that everything white was good, to be admired, respected, and loved. It brainwashed the "Negro" to think he was superior if his complexion showed more of the pollution of the slavemasters.[58]

The doctrines of the Nation of Islam had great appeal to black prisoners in the early sixties, especially in California. The reason the doctrine had such impact among prisoners is class. According to Muhammed, the black prisoner "symbolized white society's crime of keeping black men oppressed and deprived and ignorant."[59]

While the majority of blacks among the ranks of the middle and working class identified heavily with the Civil Rights Movement, blacks within the prison began to unite around the separatist elements of Muslim doctrine. Being from the ranks of the marginal working class gave prisoners little hope of benefiting from the assimilationist approach of the Civil Rights Movement. They saw their hope in the creation of an independent black nation, the stated goal of the Muslims.[60]

The Civil Rights Movement had paid little attention to the plight of prisoners or blacks in the northern ghettos during the early sixties. The Nation of Islam spoke directly to the experience of the black prisoners, who according to Malcolm X, "were the most preconditioned to hear the words,—the white man is the devil."[61] Malcolm X, who was himself converted to the Nation of Islam while a prisoner, testifies to the manner in which the Muslim philosophy became a powerful testament to what is and what could have been.

> You let the caged-up black man start thinking, the same way I did when I just heard Elijah Muhammed's teachings: let him start thinking how, with better breaks when he was young and ambitious, he might have been a lawyer, a doctor, a scientist, anything. You let this caged-up black man start realizing, as I did, how from the first landing of the first slave ship, the millions of black men in America have been like sheep in a den of wolves. That's why black prisoners become Muslims so fast when Elijah Muhammed's teaching filters into their cages by way of other Muslim convicts. *"The white man is the devil" is a perfect echo of that black convict's lifelong experience.*[62] (Emphasis mine)

The success of the Muslims in organizing prisoners went beyond the intimacy that prisoners felt for the doctrine. The organization itself threw its weight behind the drive to organize prisoners. Even in the early days of the movement, Mr. Muhammed personally answered the letters of prisoners

(Malcolm X wrote to Mr. Muhammed from prison). In the first reply sent to the potential convert,

> He told me to have courage. He even enclosed some money for me, a five-dollar bill. Mr. Muhammed sends money all over the country to prison inmates who write him . . ."[63]

Mosques in all major cities initially threw their support behind the prisoners' drive to secure the right to practice the Muslim religion while incarcerated. The support included financial resources, communications between Muslims in the prison and Muslims on the outside, and religious training. They supported the lawsuits and the militant activity of Muslims within the prison to secure a place to worship and practice religious "freedoms".

Along with the support they received from the outside, the Muslim prisoners developed a successful method for recruitment. Contacts with other prisoners were made on a one-to-one basis. The proselytizing inmate spent much time and energy convincing the novices. "During the exercise periods, it was not a rare sight to see several Muslims walking around the yard, each with a potential convert to whom he would be explaining the Message to the Black Man as taught by Elijah Muhammed."[64]

Despite the concerted efforts of prison administrators to suppress the growth of the Muslims, the early sixties produced vast numbers of converts. In California the administration continually transferred or segregated Muslim recruits, forbade the dispensing of literature and prohibited Muslim meetings.[65] The Muslims were a disciplined organization ordered along the hierarchy approved by the ruling order in the Nation of Islam. It was the strength of the organizational discipline, conditioned by religious fervor, that sent shock waves through the correctional bureaucracy. The Muslims showed both a willingness and a capability to produce militant and united action by their membership in order to secure their demands. This show of unity and organizational strength was unparalleled in institutional history. When you add the Muslim doctrine of the "white devil" to their effective organizational power, the administrative reaction was not surprising.

Although the reaction of the administration was predictable, it wasn't entirely rational, a fact the prison administration in California and New Jersey would come to realize. The Muslims shared with the early Christians a dislike, or more specifically, a disinterest in the political community. Muslim prisoners were not interested in changing the power relationships within the prison or in the political community, for their devotion was to a higher authority. Thus, the Muslims shared with the early Christian community a profound sense of other-directedness.

> . . . the Christian political attitude expressed the mentality of a group that regarded itself as being outside of the political order. . . . What is funda-

> mental to an understanding of the entire range of Christian (and Moslem) political attitudes was that they issued from a group that regarded itself as already in a society, one of far greater purity and higher purpose.[66]

The Muslims also shared with the early Christians a willingness to submit to civil authority. Muslim doctrine held that members should abide by the rules of the community in which they resided, whether it be the prison or the larger community. The Muslims were willing to resort to militant activity. But the activity was occasioned by what they saw as the civil authorities' unacceptable entry into the realm of the spirit.

There was even a stronger impulse which drove the Muslim prisoners into a position of unquestioning obedience. Since the prison was seen as a transient community, one which the prisoner would pass through before returning to the outside community, obedience was necessary to ensure that the Muslim prisoner would join the larger community of believers and potential converts. The goal of the Nation of Islam was to recruit disciples who would be active on the streets. Consequently, the primary concern was getting the Muslims out of the prison and onto the streets. Anything that hampered that objective was to be carefully avoided.

To a degree, the Muslim movement was a real asset to the prison administration, since it siphoned off many prisoners who might have otherwise become involved in political activity. Deflecting the prisoner's attention away from his social environment by minimizing the importance of the social arena, the Muslims slowed the process of politization.

By creating a religious paradigm that drew a sharp distinction between the political and spiritual worlds, and a similar distinction between the prisoners of color and whites, the Muslim doctrine also increased racial polarization. Muslim prisoners refused to communicate with or become involved in any activity that included whites. Although racial lines were strictly drawn at the time of the Muslim movement's emergence, the doctrine served not only to justify, but to applaud racial separation. Whatever thin line of recognition existed between white and black prisoners was further erased by the Muslim doctrine. To a considerable degree the Muslims helped further a policy of disunity that the prison administrators had historically fostered.

Administrative opposition was able to slow the Muslim movement but not to stamp it out. By the time the administrators came to realize how effective a religious movement like the Muslims could be in furthering social control, the movement had begun to lose steam, a victim of its own errors. But the lessons of the Muslim movement and its value in promoting disunity and political pacifism were not completely lost on the prison administration. In fact, the Muslim movement helped shape a new policy concerning group affiliation among prisoners—the policy that was previously referred to as "prison pluralism".

Despite the apparent strength and resiliency demonstrated by the Muslim movement in the early sixties, their support began to decline dramatically during the middle sixties. The tactics employed by prison administrators failed to account for the rapid decline. Rather, a combination of internal organizational splits and a growing sense that politics was necessary chewed at the core of the movement. Prisoners were finding it increasingly difficult to accept their conditions of confinement and the structure of power that dominated them. The dichotomy between the spiritual and civil world, so pronounced in Muslim doctrine, became increasingly difficult to accept.

Internally, the Muslim organization seemed to err in promising the prisoners outside support and then failing to deliver. The Nation of Islam's interest in providing resources for prisoners to litigate cases of religious freedom soon evaporated. If the organization was not willing to provide resources for these important class actions, prisoners realized that the organization would never supply resources to help them personally. According to Eldridge Cleaver, an early Muslim convert, the unwillingness of the Muslim organization to struggle on behalf of their membership was sharply illustrated in a well-known case involving a shooting incident at the Los Angeles Mosque No. 27. The four Muslims involved were convicted and sentenced to long prison terms.

> Even though these men were heroes to the Nation of Islam, it became something of a scandal when the officials of the Nation outside failed to come to their heroes' aid with any legal support, so that they were reduced to the common practice of petitioning the courts *propria persona* or appealing to the American Civil Liberties Union.[67]

In 1965 the assassination of Malcolm X, long a hero to black prisoners, alienated many Muslim believers. Malcolm X had represented the possibilities for the transformation of the black prisoner, a possibility that seemed to fade with his assassination. Even before his death, Malcolm had begun to explore new ground—ground not sanctioned by the Nation of Islam.

Malcolm became intensely interested in politics, particularly in the relationship between capitalism and racism. Malcolm's interest in politics undercut the firm separation that the Muslims drew between political and religious activity and signaled the beginning of the period of separation. Of this split between Malcolm X and the Nation of Islam and Malcolm's subsequent assassination, Cleaver writes:

> . . . death made the split final and sealed it for history. These events caused a profound personal crisis in my life and beliefs, as it did for other Muslims. During the bitter time of his suspension and prior to his break with Elijah Muhammed, we had watched Malcolm reorient himself and

> establish a new platform. . . . We watched it all, seeking a cause to condemn Malcolm X and cast him out of our hearts. We read all the charges and countercharges. I found Malcolm X blameless.[68]

It was Malcolm X, according to Cleaver, who was the one-man vanguard of the Black Muslim movement.

> The Black Muslim movement was destroyed the moment Elijah cracked the whip over Malcolm's head, because it was not the Black Muslim movement itself that was so irresistibly appealing to the true believers. It was the awakening into self-consciousness of twenty million negroes which was so compelling. Malcolm X articulated their aspirations better than any other man of our time.[69]

Before the emergence of the Muslims, blacks were fragmented and disorganized. There was a general lack of community spirit and comradery among black prisoners. The fact that blacks tended to associate with other blacks was often more a matter of circumstances than political choice.

The Muslims managed to overcome much of the fragmentation among black prisoners by providing a basis for unity. This unity was founded on spiritual principles, dedication and trust of fellow believers. The failure of the organization to come to the aid of the new community of believers undermined the fragile beginning of the community of black prisoners. If it had not been for the emergence of Malcolm X and his exploration of the political world, the positive aspects of the community experience of black prisoners might have been lost. But Malcolm's stinging critique of the penal system and racism in America supplied sufficient water to keep the ship afloat well after his death. Whatever positive results accrued to black prisoners as a result of the Black Muslim movement can be credited in large part to the work of Malcolm X and his followers.

The organizational legacy of the Muslims had its positive aspects. The Muslims introduced a collective and disciplined form of organization, a form without historical precedent in prison politics. With collective organization came the notion of collective oppression, which tended to blunt the individual pathology model. Collective oppression was defined wholly in racial terms, but, nonetheless, provided a model for prisoners to understand more deeply the society that had incarcerated them and ultimately demonstrated that support of an outside group could make a positive difference in the success of a prison movement. By forming links with outside groups, prisoners were able to extend their power considerably and broaden their political range.

Finally, the Muslims presented the successful struggle of African nations as a testament to the possibility of black independence from white oppression. Blacks could now locate themselves as part of an international struggle against white oppression.

The Growth in Outside Support

Throughout the sixties the prisoners' movement continued to gain momentum through legal and religious activism. It was an intense period, when the practical political gains were not always carefully scrutinized and placed in a political perspective.

By the middle sixties the emerging American Left began to show interest in the prisoners' movement, particularly in California. This started with the entrance of the legal community into the struggle of prisoners, but soon was extended to include a variety of American leftist organizations. Throughout the period of the Left's flirtation with the prisoners' movement, progressive elements of the legal community continued their work within the prisons. Some elements of the legal community began to work more closely with certain Left organizations seeking to broaden the struggle, while others remained aloof, disinterested, or outright hostile.

The division in the legal community was almost identical to the division among the legal activists in prison. One group saw law as a means to enhance a revolutionary struggle which would eventually topple existing legal institutions—institutions that served the interest of the state and ruling class of capitalists. The other group, which was willing to admit that the legal process was slow, expensive, inefficient, and unpredictable, still maintained the courts were the only instrument that would significantly change the status of prisoners.

This group of legal reformers could present concrete court decisions which they claimed had already improved the conditions of confinement. They might not be extraordinarily large gains, but they were gains that demonstrated the real and immediate effect that law could have on the life of the prisoner. The arguments of the legal reformers could have been enhanced during this period if the prison administrations had actually chosen to fully implement some of the decisions of the court. But the administrations in most cases either resisted, stalled, appealed, or implemented the policy of the court in a haphazard fashion. Consequently, the argument of the legal reformers, those who upheld the legitimate role and authority of the prison administrations, were undermined by the very group whose authority they sought to preserve.

Thus the community of prisoners and lawyers, which envisaged law as a means to provide some additional ground for the development of revolutionary organization, gained prominence. From the strategy of litigation developed in the early sixties emerged a strategy of incapacitation. This strategy sought to derive a means whereby prisoners could withdraw their consent from the system and bring it to a halt. The strategy of incapacitation fermenting during the middle sixties closely resembled some of the activities of the Civil Rights Movement, particularly the antiwar strike. Black prisoners formed the vanguard of prisoners, who were then studying ways to broaden and intensify the struggle for prisoner rights. It was quickly discovered that the essential ingredient needed to broaden the struggle was unity. Without racial unity, concerted action against the ruling class was impossible. The emphasis of this group of prison activists therefore turned away from the courts and toward their fellow prisoners. The task was to break down many of the ethnic and racial barriers that separated prisoners.

The interest of the American Left in the prisoners' movement emerged slowly during the sixties. In part the interest in the prisoners grew out of an increasing interest in and awareness of disadvantaged groups in American society. Some organizations of the Left during the early period of interest concerned themselves with publicizing and criticizing the conditions that existed in prison. Other organizations of the Left, who toward the end of the 1960s began to undertake a more sweeping analysis of the society, saw prisoners as victims of capitalist and racial oppression. This oppression seemed to make them natural allies of groups interested in harnessing discontent into a revolutionary spirit.

Groups like Students for a Democratic Society (SDS) gained a romantic attachment to prisoners. They envisioned prisoners as composing the forefront of the revolutionary struggle. As a group, prisoners were severely oppressed and disillusioned, well prepared to lead an armed revolutionary struggle. Growing up in ghettos, experienced in violent struggles, prisoners (according to SDS) were an ideal element to train and lead cadres in armed struggle.

The Left's interest in the prisoners' movement gave impetus to the struggle inside. Outside groups engaged in propaganda and support activities in the form of defense committees for prisoners facing legal action and direct political protest activity at the prison and Department of Correction. The movement inside felt less isolated. Prisoners felt that their political activity had strong links to the struggles of other groups in the community. These perceived links gave politically active prisoners new inspiration to close the division in the inmate body.

The first priority of the inmate political program was racism. With the help of supporters on the outside, the prisoners' movement began to develop some indigenous and powerful leadership. George Jackson, John Cluchette, Eldridge Cleaver, Ruchell McGee, and others became important spokesmen for the prisoners' movement. And when they spoke they constantly emphasized the centrality of racism in the system of institutional control.

Racism and Collective Action

The relative racial peace in the prisons during the 1950s is intimately related to the sociopolitical position of blacks during that time, especially in the

South. Before the advent of the Civil Rights Movement, the notion of racial integration and political equality lived only in the pens of segments of the black intelligentsia. For blacks, the prison was essentially a white institution, and as with other white institutions, blacks behaved in a totally subordinate manner. Nothing was further from the mind of the average black convict than attributing significance to the system of racism in explaining his incarceration.

With the beginning of the Civil Rights Movement, black awareness began to emerge. This initial social awareness would lead to demands for entirely restructuring the system of prison segregation. Once formal segregation was abolished, a void in the prison social structure was created. Black and white prisoners were merged, blacks with a heightened sense of awareness, pride, and political knowledge, and whites with a determination to restore racial segregation and its system of relative benefits. So the problem of racism took on new significance as the sixties progressed.

In addition to anti-integrationist attitudes among white prisoners, white correction officers and administrators also opposed racial integration for practical as well as political reasons.[70] The division of races minimized potential conflict among prisoners by establishing dual social systems, and racial integration, moreover, provided a ready-made means of cleavage among prisoners. If racial segregation was abandoned, the administration seemed to assume, rightly, that a variety of management-political problems would ensue.

In the middle sixties the dimensions of the racial system within the prison began to harden. Although the racial system is constantly in flux, the struggles around the question of racism that occurred during the sixties produced results that endure. Similar to the system of racism in the community, racism within the prison had several elements.

First, racism in the prison was manifested in racial animosity between black and white prisoners. Intensely suspicious of each other from years of isolation, white prisoners challenged the right of black prisoners to hold jobs which were once entirely the province of whites, in addition to questioning the blacks' right to eat and socialize in previously white areas. Simply, white prisoners expressed the attitudes of whites in the community. The attitudes flowed from an overt or covert expression of the doctrine of white supremacy. As a result, the community of black prisoners, if for no other reason than to survive, was knitted more closely together.

Another aspect of racism was institutional. The staff of the prison promulgated differential policies for white and black prisoners. Much of this differentiation was seen as active support by the correction staff to the most vociferous white supremacists. Discipline, job classification, and parole seemed to exhibit extreme favoritism toward white prisoners.[71] Instances of official violence against black prisoners far exceeded that against white prisoners.[72]

All through the middle sixties attempts to unite black and white prisoners were few. Despite the efforts of politically oriented prisoners of both races, but particularly blacks, all the efforts proved futile. In a period where blacks were politically emerging and the whites were, in a sense, on the defensive, unification was impossible. It would take a gradual period of adjustment and education before the racial and political relations could be even partially stabilized.

In California it took a traumatic and tragic event to move the racial struggle away from antagonism and toward partial unity. This tragic event took the form of a mass race riot at San Quentin in 1968, in which about half of the 4,000 prisoners participated.

> The self-defeating nature of such violence was acknowledged by the inmates, and truces were arranged between various black and white groups. An underground newspaper called the *Outlaw* began publication. It attacked the prison system and called for unity among prisoners.[73]

The incident at San Quentin was not an isolated disturbance. Major racial strife developed in other California prisons as well as in other prisons in the United States.[74] The virulence of the racial disturbances in California can be attributed to at least two factors.

One factor was the relative strength of the positions adopted by blacks and whites during the period—blacks had taken a militant position along racial lines years before a similar line was adopted by blacks in other states. Surely, the development of the Black Panther Party in Oakland around 1965, and its subsequent popularity among blacks contributed to the militant posture of blacks in the prison. By 1967 the racial situation was polarized and explosive. Black prisoners were aggressively fighting for racial equality and racial solidarity and white prisoners were fiercely resisting these programs. The new militance of black prisoners was confronted head on by the old conservatism of the white prisoners.

The early arrival of black militance is closely linked to the second factor responsible for the virulence of racial disturbances and the rather abrupt change in the racial situation following the riot. This factor is the speed and intensity of oppositional patterns of political activity in California. This is exemplified by the early appearance of Muslims, their rapid and intense organizing success, and their quick plummet. A number of other oppositional organizations, such as the People's Party, have similar histories.

Because of this speed and intensity, Black Nationalism appeared early, became popular and fostered militance, but never completely took hold. Thus, as community activists, including the Black Panthers, began to question the effectiveness of the nationalist program, prisoners responded to the shifts in community patterns.[75] By 1968 the Panthers and other California community groups began to emphasize class stuggle as well as racial struggle, and prisoners began to follow suit.

The politics of class struggle were also affected by the speed of political change in California. This rapid political development, which often resulted in embracing the form of a political idea rather than its content, made it possible to introduce the concept of class politics (class struggle) without attributing any real significance to the working class.[76]

By 1968 racial relations within the California prison had undergone some major transformations. In February of that year prisoners participated in a work stoppage which completely halted prison operations. In August 1968 during the second Unity Day, demonstrating prisoners remained in their cells during the weekend, voluntarily surrendering their privileges to emphasize the maturity and sincerity of their struggle. Both events were supported and partially organized by outside Left organizations, although the majority of the organization was obviously undertaken by prisoners. The demonstration inside was supported by a demonstration of community supporters outside. James Park, the associate warden of San Quentin, characterized the demonstration in his usual flamboyant manner. But Park's characterization was in large part correct and would soon begin to shape administrative policy.

> These two experiments (San Quentin strikes) were successful from the viewpoint of the instigators because they demonstrated, perhaps for the first time in American penal history, that outsiders could conspire with prisoners to cripple the normal operations of a prison. The age-old dissatisfactions of the convict were translated into a well-planned and sophisticated attack on State laws and policies, the operation of the paroling agency, the limitation on legal rights of parolees, the indeterminate sentence, and other issues far removed from the usual minor food grievances.
>
> The events of 1968 demonstrated that prison operations can be affected, almost at will, given enough publicity, the use of rock bands and other techniques of the New Left, and the participation of dissident outside groups in conjunction with intelligent inmate leadership."[77]

Of course the new expression of racial unity prompted the administration to take decisive action to limit its effectiveness. The strategies included the transferring of inmate leaders to isolate them from their constituencies. Also, according to other authors and prisoners, the correction staff, with the tacit or active support of the administration, began to pass out weapons and promote violence between racial groups. In a matter of months San Quentin was enmeshed in its worst period of racial violence.[78]

Despite the tragic events at San Quentin, the lessons learned from the brief period of racial unity were not lost on many prisoners. The unity demonstration at San Quentin would set important precedents for actions in the near future in California and prisons in other states.

A vast amount of political activity occurred in California and around the United States in 1970. Most of the major prison insurrections were marked by a high degree of solidarity between the races. In fact, part of the fabric of the demonstration and much of its enduring value arose from the degree to which prisoners emphasized class issues. At this point, class issues were still in embryonic forms. But they were class issues to the extent that the identification of prisoners as part of a particular class of people was predominant, while racial and ethnic identification were subordinant. This is not to say that racial issues were not raised or vigorously struggled over, but rather than these issues of race and ethnicity were located at a different level of the political struggle.

During the early 1970s there were several prison insurrections. Major insurrections occurred at Folsom, Rahway, Attica and the Men's House of Detention in New York. In order to examine the political changes the prisoners' movement was experiencing, a careful look at the insurrection at Folsom and a brief examination of the insurrection at Rahway are vital. Although each of the insurrections bears a mark of the particular systems involved, there are many similarities. In this sense, the Folsom demands are fairly representative of the sorts of demands made by the prisoners involved.

Earlier it was argued that the prison disturbances of the 1950s were a political act, but not an act that was directed toward changing the allocation of power between the captives and the administration. The action of the 1950s reflected widespread discontent. But this discontent was trapped within a system of ideology and governance which kept it within manageable lines. The insurrections of the 1970s indicate that the prisoners were successful in extricating themselves from the containers erected through ideological definitions.

The reasons for the success of the new movement in extricating itself from the past have been discussed in some detail. Intervention by judicial authorities both broadened the space inmates had to work within and loosened the system of ideological control which paralyzed the development of prisoners' self and political awareness. The courts' adoption of the principle of rehabilitation undercut the traditional notion of punishment which shaped the severely authoritarian system of governance within the prison. The Black Muslim movement was another factor that prepared the prisoners for their entry onto new political ground. Muslims introduced the notion of collective oppression and disciplined organization into the prison. The Muslims further demonstrated that outside support was vitally important to organizations within the walls. Lastly, the changing political climate of the sixties produced a number of organizations that were willing and eager to link up with organizations within the prison.

The Insurrection: The Culmination of the Sixties

These were the forces that propelled the movement onto new terrain. In a sense, the insurrections of the 1970s showed a dissatisfaction with the antecedents that propelled them. For example, the insurrections were a rejection of the Muslims' notion of strict racial separation and political pacifism. They seemed to demonstrate a disillusionment with both the speed and scope of judicial decisions. The only trend that the insurrections seemed to identify with were forces in the New Left that emerged during the sixties. At Folsom, Attica and other prisons, the insurrections displayed the most powerful show of collective activity and consciousness in prison history. Although the struggle toward ethnic and racial unity during the sixties had many disappointing periods, it seemed, in the main, to have produced the basis for a truly phenomenal show of unity.

The Folsom rebellion of 1970 was the longest in American history. Nearly all 2,400 inmates held out for nineteen days, refusing to leave their cells or contribute to the running of the prison.[79] The prisoners published a list of thirty-one demands labeling prison as the "Fascist Concentration Camp of Modern America." The demands can be divided into three categories: First, there were a set of "housekeeping" demands that resembled those of the 1950s, but were actually much broader in scope. Second, there were a set of political demands, totally absent in the 1950s. Third, there were a set of demands that dealt directly with conditions of labor within the institution. These demands reveal the new political character of the prisoners' movement shaped by the forces of the 1960s. Some of the new areas where the prisoners sought redress had been the subject of earlier court action. For example, prisoners sought procedures that incorporated elements of due process and equal protection into discipline, sentencing, and visitation policies. In part, these demands reflected dissatisfaction with the speed and scope of the administration's policy of implementing court-ordered changes.

These expanded housekeeping demands had another interesting current. The demands sought to get the administration to apply what prisoners saw as the spirit of many federal court decisions to areas of internal governance. In a sense, many of the housekeeping demands were aimed at pushing the administration to broaden the spirit of court decisions into areas where formal decisions had not yet been reached. Having made some initial gains through the courts, but being dissatisfied with the manner and speed that the gains were incorporated into the system, the prisoners sought to shift a greater responsibility onto the shoulders of the administration. An example of this tendency can be seen in Demand No. 4, from the Folsom manifesto:

> We demand that each man presently held in the Adjustment Center be given a written notice with the Warden of Custody signature on it explaining the exact reason for his placement in the severely restrictive confines of the Adjustment Center.[80]

The purpose of this demand is to push the administration into implementing due process procedures in the area of punitive segregation. Courts had previously indicated a willingness to provide certain due process protections to prisoners. Although the courts had not ruled on due process protections for prisoners in punitive segregation, the decisions of the court seemed to be moving in this direction. Thus, this demand, in an attempt to push the administration, was extending the spirit of court decisions dealing with due process. The demand reflects an interest in obtaining individual rights begun by the Civil Rights Movement.

The numerous political demands seemed to have no antecendent in the riots of the 1950s. These demands both reflected a new degree of political consciousness on the part of prisoners and new concrete conditions within the institution that found roots in the development of the sixties. Some of these political demands were:

> **Demand No. 7.** We demand an end to political persecution, racial persecution, and the denial of prisoners to subscribe to political papers, books or other educational and current media periodicals that are forwarded through the United States mail.
>
> **Demand No. 6.** We demand an end to the segregation of prisoners from the mainline population because of their political beliefs. Some of the men in the Adjustment Center are confined there solely for political reasons and their segregation from other inmates is indefinite.
>
> **Demand No. 24.** We demand annual accounting of Inmate Welfare Fund and formulation of inmate committee to give inmates a voice as to how such funds are used.
>
> **Demand No. 28.** We demand an immediate end to the agitation of race relations by the prison administrations of this state.
>
> **Demand No. 29.** We demand that the California Prison System furnish Folsom Prison with the services of Ethnic Counselors for the needed special services of Brown and Black population of this prison.[81]

Three themes seem to run through this group of "political demands": First, there is a series of demands that fundamentally, seeks the right of prisoners to engage in political organizing and political activity within the prison. Second, there is a realization of the administration's position in the system of racism. And finally, there are demands for increased power in the system of governance and increased opportunities to interact with the outside community.

The expanded rights sought by prisoners were of two types—individual and collective. Individual rights included the right to receive desired publications; the right to be free from official harassment; certain constitutional rights like due process and equal protection; the right to hold certain political views. Collective rights included the right for prisoners to meet together to further some legitimate (legal) end. In certain cases this required an extension of an individual right, like the right of the individual to organize an association of prisoners.[82] In fact, the right to organize was a particularly important demand.

During the period of organizing activity in the sixties, it became clear to many of the prisoners involved in the activity that some degree of safety was needed in order to organize more effectively. If the administration was able to freely segregate organizers from their immediate or potential constituencies, the already difficult task of organizing would become nearly impossible.

This set of demands seeking to secure some formal guarantees for potential organizers was similar to the demands made by the early labor movement. In 1932 the Norris-LaGuardia Act gave labor the full freedom of association, self-organization, and designation of representatives for the purposes of collective bargaining.[83] These were the types of protection that prison organizers sought to obtain.

Demanding democratic protections for organizers reveals the important emphasis that prisoners, especially the leadership elements of the movement, put on the task of organizing. The demands demonstrate the knowledge that organization was the key element in building and solidifying a prisoners' movement. In this sense, the demands of the movement in the 1970s show a qualitative leap forward from the 1950s. Yet, the movement in the 1970s was still somewhat unclear about the implications of the demand or its potential for neutralization. It was clear that the prisoners were demanding the right to organize, but unclear exactly whom or what they wanted to organize. Without an organization similar to the organizations of the trade unions in the 1930s, the demand for organizing rights was vulnerable to overt and covert subversion.

The second theme in the political demands concerned racism. The demand that the administration desist from provoking racial conflict between prisoners was the first collective statement of prisoners that formally identifies administration policy as pivotal in the prison system of racism.

Although this realization was of great importance in furthering the political knowledge of prisoners and the public alike, the demands contained no mention of amelioration policies beyond hiring ethnic and racial counselors. The effect of this demand was to subjectivize or internalize an objective or collective political process. Without a formal program to place the racial practices of the administration within a political context, the potential for the issue receding into the background—out of the field of vision of the prisoners as a whole—greatly increased. This left open to the administration the enviable option of discussing relief without admitting to the problem.

The final theme that runs through the "political demands" and is also very prominent in the set of "economic demands" is power. Here, the prisoners attempt to attain formal guarantees that their power in the system of governance be increased. The word "formal" is key in this set of demands. The formal or informal power that prisoners might exercise in the governance system of the prison is entirely contingent upon the ability to create some organization that could independently and autonomously reflect the political position of prisoners as a whole. It is the power contained in a collective organization that would seem to be instrumental in a prisoner's gaining a position within the prison's system of governance. Labor unions achieved whatever power they have in the labor-capital arena by drawing on their collective direction—collective interest.[84] Formal guarantees of participatory rights are important, but seem highly dependent upon the ongoing ability of the organization to promote collective action. Thus the type of guarantee most desirable is one that secures the right to autonomous rather than collaborative power sources. This position was not embedded in the demand for increased participation.

The final category of demands issued by the Folsom prisoners is "economic demands." Although they are called economic, this set of demands, like the political demands, sought to change the balance of power within the prison's governance system. They are referred to as economic demands because they specifically deal with the economic structures of the prison—the system of prison industries.

There was no equivalent of the economic demands contained in the demands that emanated from the riots of the 1950s. The presence of this set of economic demands reflects the changes in the political base of the movement. Once the notion of class politics was introduced into the prison, the stage was set for an attack on the prison labor system. Without question, the labor system of the prison epitomized the notion of the exploitation of labor at the core of Marxist theory.

The economic demands include:

Demand No. 11. We demand that industries be allowed to enter the institutions and employ inmates to work eight hours a day and fit into the category of workers for scale wages. . . . Those industries outside who desire to enter prisons should be allowed to enter for the purpose of employment placement.

Demand No. 12. We demand that inmates be allowed to form or join Labor Unions.

Demand No. 15. We demand that all institutions who use inmate labor be made to conform with the state and federal minimum wage laws.

Demand No. 21. We demand updating of industry working conditions to standards as provided for under California law.

Demand No. 22. We demand establishment of inmate workers insurance plan to provide compensation for work related accidents.

Demand No. 23. We demand establishment of a unionized vocational training program comparable to that of the Federal Prison System which provides for union instructors, union pay scale, and union membership upon completion of the vocational training course.

Demand No. 8. . . . Prisoners at Folsom and San Quentin Prisons, according to the California State Penal Code, cannot be compelled to work as these two prisons were built for the purpose of housing prisoners and there is no mention as to the prisoners being required to work on prison jobs in order to remain on the Mainline and/or be considered for release. Many prisoners believe their labor power is being exploited in order for the State to increase its economic power and continue to expand its correctional industries which are million dollar complexes, yet do not develop working skills acceptable for employment in the outside society, and which do not pay the prisoner more than the maximum sixteen cents per hour wage. Most prisoners never make more than six or eight cents per hour. Prisoners who refuse to work for the two to sixteen cent pay rate, or who strike, are punished and segregated without the access to the privileges shared by those who work. *This is class legislation, class division, and creates class hostilities within the prison*. (Emphasis mine)[85]

As with the political demands, three themes seem to run through the economic demands. First, there are demands that serve the function of describing the place of the economic system within the prison. Demand No. 8

is such a demand. While it asks that something specific be rectified, it also presents a picture of the economic system—the relationship of the prisoner to the state. Second, there are demands which parallel the sorts of demands made by the trade union movement in its incipience. Demands 21 and 22 are examples of what will be referred to as "union demands." Finally, there is one demand, No. 11, which in effect seeks to narrow the public sphere of control within the prison by introducing private industry.

The first set of economic demands, those that describe the economic system of the prison, mark the beginning of a period of dissension over labor-power that prevails right up to the present period.[86] What the demand (No. 8) represents is a challenge to the contention of the state, long embedded in penal policy, that the labor of the prisoner is at the disposal of the state during a period of incarceration. The demand portrays a system of divisiveness and punishment concentrated within the prison labor system—a system that creates a class of workers with relatively privileged access to certain goods and services, and a class of unemployed who are systematically excluded from the privileges.

Separating a producing from a nonproducing class serves a twofold purpose. First, it creates a sizable obstruction to class unity by making the cost of unity variable among the prison population. Second, it provides a system of incentives that is necessary, although not always adequate for recruiting a labor force. The prisoners' recognition of the divisive effects of the labor system has not led to its abolition, but has severely hampered the administration's ability to maintain an effective ongoing labor force.

The second theme or cluster of demands within the economic demands can be called "union demands." Once again, this type of demand reflects a qualitative leap in the political understanding of prisoners. It was the union demands that the administration seemed to fear above most others. Concessions in this area were quickly ruled out. Union organization would provide a base for collective action with the potential to strike a powerful blow at the economic system of the prison. Demand No. 12, asking that prisoners be allowed to join labor unions, could conceivably give prison labor unions protections available to workers in the community, including the right to strike and collectively bargain with the administration. If this demand were met it would likely have a transformative effect far beyond that of the other demands. Despite administrative resistance the idea of unionization is still alive within the California prisons.

Finally, there is demand No. 11 which asks that private industry be allowed to operate within the prison. This is a particularly difficult demand to analyze since the rationale and ramifications of the demand are not entirely clear. The demand could be aimed at increasing the collective power of the prisoners by centralizing their role in the system of profits. This assumes that the structure of profits developed through the scheme would in some way pay a part of the costs of incarceration, thus becoming a crucial source of funding for the system. No doubt this would occur in one form or another since the state would have little incentive to participate otherwise.

There is an additional consequence probably unforeseen by everyone except the state. If prisoners were employed by private industry, it would likely bolster their claim that they should be represented by labor unions. Since workers in the private sector have formal democratic rights that allow them to organize collectively, the prisoners would be in a position to strongly argue through the courts that they should also be included under these protections. In fact, there are precedents which support the prisoner's right to unionize. In *Goodwin* v. *Oswald*, Judge Oakes wrote:

> There is nothing in federal or state constitutional law or statutory law of which I am aware that forbids prison inmates from seeking to form, or correctional officials from electing to deal with, an organization or agency or representative group of inmates concerned with prison conditions and inmates' grievances.
>
> The formation of a prisoners ''union'' even in its nonrhetorical sense, does not strike me as a proposal totally unacceptable to society.[87]

It is also conceivable that the rationale behind the demand for admission of private industry into the prison is much less complex. Wages in the private sector are considerably higher than in prison. It is entirely possible that prisoners thought that the introduction of private industry would provide a means to increase the wage scale.

East Prison

Two years after the uprising at Folsom, in the wake of Attica, prisoners at East Prison staged a similar rebellion. They held a number of hostages for several days and presented a series of demands.

The demands of the prisoners at East Prison contain many elements of the demands at Folsom and Attica, but appear to be somewhat less politically integrated. For example, there are no union demands—demands about the conditions of work. There is a demand concerning wages and forced labor, but the demand seems isolated—not attached to a larger context, program, or analysis. There is a heavy emphasis on cultural and religious identity, especially freedom for Muslims to practice their religion within the prison. The demand concerned with the right of the Muslims to practice their religion reflects their central position among the prisoners in New Jersey in 1972, long after the time that their influence in California had subsided.

Although the positions surrounding particular types of demands are not well articulated in the statements of the New Jersey prisoners, most elements of the Folsom demands are there. There are demands concerning racism, participatory rights, freedom of association, educational and vocational training and a demand that private industry be allowed to enter the prison.

The demands of the New Jersey prisoners suggest that the movement had developed at a slower rate than the movement in California or even New York. The demands of the New Jersey prisoners reflect an interest in cultural and ethnic identification. Yet, the rebellion itself had been preceded by intense efforts to unite ethnic and racial groups within the prison. There was recognition in the demands of the East prisoners, as there was in the demands of Folsom prisoners, that racism was key to the policy of social control. The demand concerning racism reads in part:

> . . . The favoritism of white inmates over Black and Puerto Ricans is overt. This is a method that is used to keep inmates disunited so that they do not come together to discuss dissatisfaction with prison policies.[88]

Conclusions

With the view that the present state of a movement can be explained by its history, this chapter has sought to examine the history of the movement of prisoners toward forms of political organization. Although the history of the movement does not effectively explain every nuance of development, it does provide a framework upon which an understanding of the present political situation can be built.

All historical examinations tend to locate a theme or a number of themes believed to have important explanative value. This examination was no exception. Political processes within the prison were shaped by three major currents: legal activism among prisoners, the Black Muslim movement, and the politics of the Civil Rights Movement and the New Left.

Throughout this chapter there was an attempt to interweave the three central areas of interest discussed in chapter 1 into the history. In a sense, the history presented is formed in a way intended to put into sharper relief question of changes in the ideological system, the system of governance and the labor system within the prison. A few final remarks about these three key aspects of institutional life should help recapitulate the manner in which they were affected or themselves affected the history of the prisoners' movement.

In the area of ideology there were at least three marked changes in the 25-year historical period outlined. First, the introduction of the treatment model provided the court with an ideological device to justify many decisions rendered during the period of judical activism. In addition, the ideological shift to the treatment model legitimized the indeterminate sentence and provided a different definition of the offender—a definition couched largely in terms of organic-functional disorders.

Another change in ideology arrived via the Black Muslim Movement. The Muslim's philosophy implicitly rejected the assumption of individual pathological disorder contained in the treatment ideology in favor of the ideology of collective oppression—the oppression of blacks by whites. This challenge to the prevailing ideology not only burst the ideological container that encircled black prisoners, but also lessened the hold that the ideology had on white prisoners.

Finally, the impulses brought into the prison by way of political activity on the outside also affected the prisoners' ideological structure. Of the impulses funnelled through the walls by outside groups, the politics of individual rights and class analysis were most important.

The "individual rights" movement grew out of the Civil Rights Movement of the early sixties. In essence, the movement argued that certain groups previously excluded from the umbrella of democratic rights (blacks, welfare recipients, youth) ought to receive the same protections as other citizens. The movement claimed that these groups were excluded for a variety of reasons. But whatever the reason, the result was that these groups had the status of second-class citizens. The notion of "citizenship" contained in the ideology of the movement was adopted by many prisoners, who held that race, poverty, prison, had relegated them to the status of second-class citizens. These prisoners would hold that the problem was not pathological but political. Thus, the solution to the problem was not rehabilitation but restoration.

Class analysis was first introduced into the prison well after the "citizenship analysis" was made available by the Civil Rights Movement. It quickly gained a good number of articulate and committed adherents. Class analysis viewed crime as essentially an economic phenomenon. Thus, the solution to the crime problem and the prison problem was revolution, rather then rehabilitation.

The system of labor within the prison received almost no critical attention by the prisoners until the early seventies, when rebellious Folsom prisoners stamped it as a central area of discontent. Of the thirty demands made in the Folsom Manifesto, ten deal specifically with the economic-labor system of the prison. The prisoners' movement was for the first time in history challenging the state's hegemony over the labor of prisoners. In place of a system of total domination, the prisoners were demanding the rights that capitalism offered the worker—the right to sell his labor.

The final area that the discussion on history sought to emphasize was the prison system of governance. Here, the prisoners sought a greater role in decision making and procedural guarantees to limit the tyranny of the rule system. Many of the court cases cited in the chapter, along with some of the political demands of the Folsom prisoners are aimed in this direction. Court decisions and political activity did bring about alterations in the governance system. Some analysis of these alterations has already been discussed; more will follow.

Notes

1. The American College Dictionary, New York: Random House, p. 1047.
2. James Leiby, *Charity and Corrections in New Jersey*, p. 316.
3. New Jersey Committee to Examine and Investigate the Prison and Parole System of New Jersey, *Report*, November 21, 1952, p. 3.
4.Leiby, *Charity and Corrections*, p. 316. It is interesting to note that the demands of the rioting prisoners are not even mentioned in the book, which is thought to be the definitive study of the New Jersey institutional complex. This is some indication of the status of the demands in relation to the event (riot) itself.
5. Ibid., p. 316.
6. Ibid., p. 317. My intent is to show that the opposite relationship actually pertains—that riots as a political act occur because of deficient resources and freedom.
7. Ibid., p. 317.
8. John Pallas and Robert Barber, "From Riot to Revolution," in *Politics and Punishment*, ed. Erik Olin Wright, p. 239.
9. Ibid., p. 240.
10. James W.L. Park, "Power To the People": Social Revolution and the Prison. Although the paper is undated, it was probably written between 1969 and 1971. The purpose of the document is to alert California Prison authorities to changes in political patterns among the prisoners. I received the paper from an unofficial source who could not verify the date of publication, but thought the paper to be a "working document" for the California prison administration. (See appendix G.)
11. See Peter Bachrach and Morton Baratz, *Power and Poverty* (New York: Oxford University Press, 1970), chapter 3, "Decisions and Non-Decisions," p. 39.
12. In the context of this discussion, "structure" is meant to denote organizational patterns. Structure connotes the internal governmental or bureaucratic relations within a particular institution. Structures within an institution could run the gamut between totalitarian and democratic. Structure also refers to the manner in which certain institutions combine to form a system, or structure, larger than any of the individual institutions. An example of a structure of this type would be the criminal justice system.

13. These categories are used by McCleery in describing the early prison regimes of OHAU Prison in Hawaii, but they also describe the broad systems of governance in most American prisons during the 1940s and 1950s. See "Power, Communication and The Social Order," p. 25. One should be careful to note that the characteristics of the authoritarian prison that are used fall into at least two distinct types: There are characteristics which essentially describe the way things are done (decisions) and those that describe the way things are organized. Some categories refer to procedure, while others refer to form. Although the relationship between structure and decision might seem evident, it is not so; democratic mechanisms may not always result in democratic decisions. However, in this particular case the process and form do correspond, which makes the criteria used both correspondent and applicable.

14. Sykes, *Society of Captives*, p. 10.

15. The theory of retribution and deterrence are considerably more complicated than what appears here. There is a vast literature on the subject in political and legal philosophy. It is a subject that will receive more attention in subsequent sections. For a concise explanation of the theories of retribution and deterrence see H.L.A. Hart, *Punishment and Responsibility* (New York: Oxford University Press, 1968).

16. The acceptance of this relationship can be assumed from the lack of protest against the power-relations within the prison, even in the demands that preceded riots. Evidence of the political attitudes of prisoners during the 1940s can be found in Donald Clemmer, *The Prison Community*, (Boston: Christopher Pub., 1940). Some evidence of political attitudes in the fifties can be found in John Irwin, *The Felon*.

17. These major aspects of political activity among prisoners reflect some of the basic problematics of social and revolutionary change. For example, the use of the courts to seek amelioration raises the problem of the advisability and effect of seeking broad change through organs of the state. The Black Muslim movement provides some insights into the question of the political potential of national, ethnic or religious groups. Tracing out some of the implications of these sorts of political activity within the prison should provide some insights applicable to other groups involved in seeking social or revolutionary change.

18. I use the term "insurrection" rather than "riot" because of the compositional, structural and political changes in the disturbances of the 1960s. These changes will be closely analyzed at the end of this section. For now, it is sufficient to say that an insurrection differs from a riot on the basis of degrees of planning and the political nature of the goals.

19. Pallas and Barber, "From Riot to Revolution," p. 253.

20. *Ruffin* v. *Commonwealth*, (1871). Unless otherwise indicated, full citations appear in the court cases section of the bibliography.

21. In theory, *Coffin* v. *Reichard* (1944) would seem to be an extremely pivotal decision although in practice it seemingly had few ripples. The decision stated that a "prisoner retains all the rights of an ordinary citizen, except those expressly, or by necessary implication, taken from him by law."

22. David J. Rothman, "Decarcerating Prisoners and Patients," *Civil Liberties Review* (Fall 1973) p. 12.

23. Ibid., p. 12.

24. This was especially the case in California, where the rehabilitation ethic had massive support in the early sixties. For a discussion of rehabilitation in California see American Friends Service Committee, *Struggle for Justice*; Kassenbaum, Ward, and Wilner, *Prison Treatment and Parole Survival*; and David Rothman, "Decarcerating Prisoners and Patients."

25. Most of these cases are taken from Sheldon Krantz, *The Law of Corrections and Prisoners Rights* (Minnesota: West Publishing, 1973), and Michele G. Heiman and Marilyn G. Hart, *Prisoners Rights Source Book*, (New York: Clark Boardman Co., 1973).

26. *Cruz* v. *Beto*, (1972).

27. *Morales* v. *Schmidt* (1972). Krantz, p. 325.

28. Ibid., p. 328.

29. Ibid., p. 329.

30. Ibid., p. 332.

31. *Morales* v. *Schmidt*, F 2nd. (7th Circuit 1973). Krantz, p. 336.

32. Ibid., p. 337.

33. Ibid., p. 338.

34. One of the earliest cases in which the administration's claim of successful rehabilitation was upheld concerned the Patuxent facility in Maryland. See *Tippett* v. *State of Maryland* (1971). Patuxent is an institution devoted to the use of behavioral modification to treat criminal offenders. The prison authorities argued that behavioral modification was a new and surprisingly effective rehabilitative technique and the court agreed. The court ruled that behavior modification was a justified end of incarceration and that certain constitutional guarantees could be amended to meet this end. As the use of behavioral modification techniques, such as chemotherapy, aversion therapy, shock therapy, etc., spread, more administrative officials repeated the claims of Patuxent officials that constitutional abridgments were in the interests of the new rehabilitation. For a short review of the "new rehabilitation" programs and the legal ramifications, see David Rothman, "Decarcerating Prisoners and Patients," p. 25.

35. *Palmigiano* v. *Travisone* (1970). Krantz, p. 341.

36. Ibid., p. 343.

37. I know of at least three cases where the court made precisely this finding of fact, ruling that censorship furthered a justifiable purpose. *Abernathy* v. *Cunningham* (1968) bans Muhammed's *Message to Blackman in*

America and issues of "Muhammed Speaks." See also *Rowland* v. *Jones* (1971), *Walker* v. *Blackwell* (1969).

38. *Procunier* v. *Martinez* (1974) in Krantz, p. 315.

39. The phrase "unconditional democratic right" is meant to take into account the restrictions placed on rights in the outside community. The condition that it precludes is exclusion based on the particular status of the recipient. For an excellent review of some conditions attached to the exercise of democratic rights, most specifically First Amendment Rights, see Thomas Emerson, *The System of Freedom of Expression*.

40. The first important cases in this area are *Cooper* v. *Pate* S.Ct. and *Pierce* v. *Lavalee* (1961).

41. *Sostre* v. *McGinnis* (1964) Cert. Denied 379 U.S. 892, 85 S.Ct. 163, Bl. ed. 2d. 96 (1964), Krantz, p. 417.

42. *Sostre* v. *McGinnis*, Krantz, p. 418.

43. Ibid., p. 417.

44. *Evans* v. *Mosley* (1972). Krantz, p. 390.

45. *National Prisoners Reform Association* v. *Sharkey* (1972). Krantz, p. 391.

46. *Theriault* v. *Carlson* (1972).

47. Ibid., p. 426.

48. Ibid. The fact that the group had members from all races was extremely significant to the administration, which attempts to avoid collective activity across race lines at all costs. In the court decision in *National Prisoners Reform Association* v. *Sharkey* (1972), the court noted the peculiarity in the authorities permitting various prisoner groups to function and prohibiting the group in question. The decision reads: "The only thing which seems to be unique to the plaintiff organization out of all these groups is its interracial character." Krantz, p. 393.

49. *Theriault* v. *Carlson*, Krantz, p. 341.

50. *Clutchette* v. *Procunier*, 328 F.Supp. 767 (N.D. Calif. 1971). Krantz, p. 640.

51. *Goldberg* v. *Kelly* (1969) held that process benefits "are a matter of statutory entitlement for persons qualified to receive them. Their termination involves state action that adjudicates important rights. The constitutional challenge cannot be answered by an argument that public assistance benefits are a privilege and not a right. Krantz, p. 64.

52. *Clutchette* v. *Procunier*, Krantz, p. 647. The Clutchette decision is an important one to remember, for it will provide an excellent opportunity to evaluate how a judicial decision was handled at the prison.

53. Brian Glick, "Change through the Courts," in Erik Olin Wright, ed. *Politics of Punishment*, p. 308.

54. *Sostre* v. *Rockefeller*, 312 F.Supp. 863 (SPNY 1970). Krantz, p. 310. The other prisoners held in segregation at the time of the hearing were the plaintiff in *Theriault* v. *Carlson* and plaintiff John Clutchette in *Clutchette* v. *Procunier*.

55. An example of a case of administrative resistance to court-ordered change can be found in *Theriault* v. *Carlson* (1973), where the defendants were held in contempt for failure to comply. Other examples can be found in Glick, "Change through the Courts" in Wright, *Politics of Punishment*.

56. Glick, "Change through the Courts," Wright, *Politics of Punishment,* p. 309.

57. Malcolm X, *The Autobiography of Malcolm X*, p. 162. For a more complete examination of Muslim history and doctrine, see E.U. Essien-Udom, *Black Nationalism*, or Eric C. Lincoln, *The Black Muslims in America*.

58. Malcolm X, *Autobiography,* p. 163.

59. Ibid., p. 169.

60. John Pallas and Robert Barber, "From Riot to Revolution," in Wright, *Politics of Punishment*, p. 244.

61. Malcolm X, *Autobiography*, p. 183.

62. Ibid., p. 183.

63. Ibid., p. 129.

64. Eldridge Cleaver, "The Muslims Decline," in *Prison Life*, Frank Browning and Ramparts Magazine, p. 101.

65. This policy of suppression was elucidated to me in a personal interview with the director of research of the California Department of Corrections, Dr. Lawrence Bennet, in a meeting in his Sacramento office in September 1975.

66. Sheldon Wolin, *Politics and Vision*, p. 99.

67. Cleaver, "The Muslims Decline," in Browning, *Prison Life,* p. 103.

68. Eldridge Cleaver, *Soul on Ice*, p. 60.

69. Ibid., p. 65.

70. For a discussion of the racial attitudes of corrections officers and administrators in the California prison system during the period in question, see, Min S. Yee, *The Melancholy History of Soledad Prison*, Robert Minton and Stephen Rice, "Using Racism at San Quentin," in *Prison Life*, ed. Browning and George Jackson, *Soledad Brother*.

71. "We found few blacks in the more desirable trade training areas, namely, the maintenance shop, print shop, hospital, dentistry." California Senate, Black Caucus Report on California Prisons, July 15, 1970., p. 14.

72. Ibid., p. 12.

73. Pallas and Barber, "From Riot to Revolution," in Wright, *Politics and Punishment*, p. 250.

74. In California a similar racial disturbance occurred at Folsom and Duell Vocational Institute. For a brief discussion of the events at Duell, see Sheldon Messinger, Eliot Studt and Thomas Wilson, *C Unit: A Search for Community in Prison* (New York: Russell Sage Foundation, 1968).

75. For a good account of the activities of the Panthers during this period, see Bobby Seale, *Seize The Time.*

76. It is precisely this politics of form that accounts for the ambiguity and the popularity of Governor Brown. Brown, a master of the politics of form, seems to provide progressive form with conservative content. The activities of the Symbionese Liberation Army also present an illustrative example.

77. James Park, "Power to the People": Social Revolution and the Prison. Appendix G.

78. For a complete description of the racial situation at San Quentin, see Robert Mirton and Stephen Rice, "Rice War at San Quentin," *Ramparts*, January 1970.

79. I was able to learn much about the strike at Folsom by interviewing prisoners who were incarcerated there during the time of the rebellion and were subsequently transferred to West Prison.

80. The Folsom Manifesto of Demands, 1970. The complete text of the manifesto is reproduced as appendix F.

81. Ibid.

82. For the purposes of this discussion individual rights associated with collective organization should be thought of as "collective rights." This distinction is important since the general political aim of the individual right to organize and the individual right to wear the clothes one desires are usually distinct. In the one case the individual right is aimed at enhancing the collective power of a group, while in the latter case the individual right is aimed at ameliorating a personally repugnant prohibition, or broadening rights associated with the "quality of life." In terms of political power, individual and collective rights are not always at cross-purposes. However, in the case of the prison, different groups of prisoners prioritized rights differently—often in direct opposition to each other. The opposition usually results from different political ends.

83. For a further explanation and critical discussion of the Norris-LaGuardia Act, see William Z. Foster, *American Trade Unionism* (New York: International Publishers, 1947).

84. For a discussion of the importance of collectivist activity in labor unions, see J. Matles and J. Higgins, *Them and Us.*

85. Folsom Manifesto.

86. For some background on the prison labor system, see chapter 1.

87. *Goodwin* v. *Oswald*, 462 F.2d 1237, 1245-1246 (2nd Cir. 1972) in Krantz, p. 397. This particular case does not refer to prisoners forming or joining labor unions, and, in fact, does go on to elaborate a number of restrictions that would need to be placed on any form of "unionization" within the prison. I cite the case to demonstrate that there was potentially favorable sentiment within the federal court system toward the idea of unionization, especially during the early 1970s. I trust that along with other prison matters the court's opinion in this area has probably hardened somewhat now.

88. Report of the Governor's Committee on Negotiations, June 1972, p. 26.

A New Era in Prison Labor

The demands raised by the Folsom prisoners in 1970 had become a model program for the prisoners' movement. Rebellious prisoners in New Jersey, New York, and Massachusetts used the Folsom Manifesto to construct the broad outline of a political program.[1] The fact that the Folsom demands were interchangeable reflects the degree to which prison politics around the United States were closely aligned. Although modifications in the demands were made to accommodate to specific institutional features, the Folsom demands can be said to represent the political aspiration of a majority of the prisoners engaged in political activity.

The California administration, at both the state and local levels, recognized that the general political aspirations of prisoners were contained in the Folsom Manifesto. Realizing this, the administration would attempt to devise policies to deal with these aspirations, not only at the specific institutions where insurrections had occurred, but also, and perhaps more importantly, at institutions where insurrections had not yet occurred. The policies of the administration would have to contend with the growing ethnic, racial, and class identification of the prisoners, the solidarity exhibited during the rebellions, discontent with the system of labor, and the demands for increased political power.

Of course the first task of the local administration was to bring a halt to the insurrection and punish those thought responsible for leading the demonstrations. At some institutions like Rahway there was a negotiated settlement which brought the rebellion to an end. At other institutions like Attica, and to some degree at Folsom, force and coercion were used. In all cases large numbers of prisoners were immediately transferred to other institutions while the state prepared indictments charging them with a variety of offenses ranging from disorderly conduct to first-degree murder. The transfers and indictments were a powerful first step in counteracting the new spirit of solidarity and unity tenuously achieved by the prisoners. But the state recognized that a policy of repression would have to be accompanied by other programs to remake the foundation of social and political control within the institutions.

The degree of demoralization among the prisoners varied from one institution to another. There were few immediate results that could be pointed to as victories achieved through insurrection. Many prisoners seemed to feel that the spirit begun in the insurrections was a real concrete achievement, one worth sacrificing for.

> The strike may have fallen short of our goal, but was not a failure. We accomplished something that has never been accomplished before. Not just the record length, but more important is that the spirit of awareness has grown, and our people begin to look around and see what's happening. The seed has been planted and grows. If we have accomplished nothing else, we have accomplished this.[2]

But in fact the insurrection had done more. The administration (seeing the prisoners armed with outside support and internal solidarity as a serious force), took the demands of the rebelling prisoners as a serious challenge to the system of governance. In this respect, the demands made a greater impact on the prison administration than the prisoners suspected. While the prisoners temporarily abandoned the demands articulated during the demonstration, the administration was devising a strategy to contend with them. The prisoners underestimated the administration's reaction to the demands, assuming that no new policies would be devised to meet criteria set out in the Folsom Manifesto. This left the administration free to fashion policies aimed at reinforcing the system of social control in the institutions. Of course the program of state repression and transfer severely weakened the leadership structure in the institutions and deflected attention away from the demands. But the administration's ability to deflect attention by transferring known leaders showed the centrality of the leadership elements and the relative lack of political sophistication among many participants. This lack of sophistication, nonetheless, was no accident—it was the product of the objective circumstances that preceded and followed the insurrections.[3]

The demands of the prisoners at Folsom and East Prison were divided into three categories: housekeeping, political, and economic demands. Our concerns lie with the political and economic demands and those aspects of the housekeeping demands that dealt with the expansion of individual rights. Those elements of the housekeeping demands that dealt with individual rights are discussed with the political demands.

The first part of the prisoners' movement program contained demands for a transformation of the system of prison labor. The remainder of this chapter is concerned with the system of labor.

Economic Demands

The set of economic demands put forth by the Folsom prisoners expressed the sentiment of the vast majority of prisoners throughout the state.[4] The system of prison industry is seen by the prisoners as exploitative and by the administration and state bureaucracy as essential.

Recall that the economic demands of the prisoners had several aspects.

There were demands that challenged the state's contentions that it had total control over the prisoners' labor-power, and that labor itself had rehabilitative consequences. Other demands asked for the right to form labor unions, upgrading of wages and working conditions, and the introduction of private industry into the prison.

In any one California prison there are at least two potential employers of prisoners. One is the administration which allocates jobs within the prison facility itself—janitors, kitchen help, maintenance men. The second is the State-Use Industry Corporation, a semipublic corporation under the umbrella, but not the absolute control, of the Department of Corrections. The corporation has a great deal of autonomy in all areas.

The Correctional Industries Commission (CIC) which guides state-use industries

> was created in 1947 and was given certain powers and duties relating to the work programs of the Department of Corrections. The purpose of the act was to create in the department an agency to aid in the development of the work programs for persons in the custody of the Director of Corrections which would contribute to their rehabilitation, training and support with minimum competition with private industry and free labor.[5]

Within every California penal institution that houses a state-use factory, there is a separate plant administrator, whose direct superior is not the institutional superintendent, but the CIC. The budget of state-use industries is separate from the institutional budget, a factor that leads to considerable dissension between the prison and CIC administrators.

According to the Folsom Manifesto, the stated purposes under which the CIC was created in 1947 have not been realized. Instead of providing "rehabilitation, training and support," the industries system, according to prisoners, is solely a means of extracting labor for profit. Actually, the official statement of the department concerning state-use industries tends to support this contention. Correctional industries, according to the department, "operates as a business venture on a profit and loss basis."[6]

The 1970 demands asking for a complete restructuring of the system of labor rest on the assumption that the state does not have unbridled liberty to extract surplus value from those incarcerated. Once this premise was internalized by the prison labor force, a new period of labor history was destined to begin.

After the rebellion of 1970, the state commissioned a study of prison labor. The study alludes to some of the demands made by the rebellious prisoners at Folsom. For example, on the question of private ownership the report reads:

> More markets would be helpful and should be sought for California prison industrial programs. Recent suggestions for private ownership and

> management of some prison industries, and the repeal of Federal laws barring prison goods from interstate commerce should be studied carefully.[7]

While some of the demands of the prisoners are mentioned in the study, none of the demands were conceded. The prisoners' rejection of the conditions of labor within the prison, however, which first emerged at the time of the Folsom rebellion, continues throughout the prison system.

Since at least 1970, the correctional industries system and the entire system of prison labor have been beset by crises, centering on the inability of state-use industries and the prison administration to recruit labor and meet productivity standards. The authorities' refusal to meet the demands for collective organization of the work force has neither thwarted the prisoners' desire to form unions nor stopped the mass of individual protests against the labor system.

The crises themselves have been propelled by several factors. The search for increased profit requires that a means be found to require prisoners, most of whom find little personal or material incentives in prison labor, not only to work, but to work faster. The most important step in that direction was creating a dual wage system, whereby prisoners who worked for correctional industries would receive substantially higher wages than those working directly for the institution.

Coupled with this wage differential, Correctional Industries (CI) in 1973 and 1974 began to provide additional incentives for its labor force. These additional incentives reflect the inability of the wage differential to promote "just and efficient" work by the labor force.

The new set of incentives contained provisions for more pay based on increases in productivity, paid holidays, vacations and bonuses. The administration maintained that the incentive system was not inconsistent with the principle that work was rehabilitative, the same principle which prisoners challenged in 1970 and continued to challenge. Productivity itself, according to the California Systems Study, is rehabilitative. *"Work done at a slow pace can undermine its rehabilitative potential."* (Emphasis mine)[8]

In relation to the conditions of labor that had pertained since the inception of state-use industries in 1947, the incentive plan seemed a tempting package. In the area of pay increases based on growth in productivity, the plan stated that:

> any incentive increase in hourly pay will be based on a percentage of production in excess of predetermined reasonable quotas. Such increases will not exceed $0.02 per hour for each full 5 percent over the established quota.[9]

Additionally, the incentive plan provided one week paid vacation on the condition that the worker had a "satisfactory work performance rating for that year, a clean disciplinary record . . . and no unauthorized absences." There were also provisions for shift differential and some bonuses.[10]

In less than a year, CI modified this plan to provide for even more incentives and benefits. Obviously, after twenty-five years of rigidity in the wage and working structure of CI, these two major modifications, one coming on the heels of the other, pointed to the ever deepening crisis within CI. In October 1975 the Department of Corrections published the following directive:

> It is the policy of the Correctional Industries Commission and Director that wide use be made of various incentive programs to encourage and reward inmate productivity and to create a working environment within correctional industries as much like private industry as possible. Such programs may include, but need not be limited to, group bonus pay plans, inmate suggestion cash awards, vacations with pay, supplemental rations for industries inmates who eat the noon meal separately, and separation bonuses at time of parole or discharge.
>
> Use of correctional industries funds to supply athletic equipment for use at breaks, to establish branch canteens, to establish family visiting facilities for exclusive use of correctional industries inmates, and other similar facilities as outlined upon approval of the general manager.
>
> Correctional Industries institutional management is encouraged to establish some formal communication channels with the inmate employees, such as inmate advisory groups, to keep inmates informed about incentive programs and to ascertain possible additional ones of value to inmates at that particular institution, as well as other items of mutual interest. Such incentives should be clearly identified as directly related to productivity so they do not become regarded as vested interests.[11]

The revisions suggested in this directive went far beyond those published just the year before. The department was mandating the establishment of a separate prison environment for CI workers. This policy was not warmly received by local prison officials. In an attempt to meet the crisis caused by diminished productivity, the local administration accused correctional industries of fanning the flames of the smoldering crises in prison labor.

Correctional Industries versus the Prison Administration

Creating a dual wage system within the prison had the effect of dividing up and forcing the two branches of the labor administration into conflict and contradiction with each other. It also created some stratification among prisoners, although this was not nearly as serious as the contradictions in the sphere of the ruling strata.

The dual wage system provided industry workers, employed in exactly the same capacity as institutional workers, with wage premiums. For example, a janitor who worked within the prison complex might receive $13 a month or no wage at all. Whether the prisoner employed by the institution would receive a wage depended on a set of highly arbitrary criteria, including the availability of funds. A prisoner employed by CI as a janitor could be paid as much as $32. His wage was determined by a set of precise wage standards.

In effect, the dual wage system put CI and the prison administration in the position of competing with each other to recruit the number of workers they needed.[12] But the competition did not proceed on an equal footing. CI possessed more resources, which ultimately enhanced its competitive position. The state-use budget for 1975-1976 was $174,000, while the support budget for the entire West Prison complex was only $135,910.[13]

The ability of state-use industries to outbid the prison administration for available labor means that state-use industries eventually capture all those who want or need to work. Consequently, the prison itself suffers from a constant labor shortage. West Prison administrators also see the structure of the two-tier labor system as creating an economically powerful class within the prison, that would soon beget the wrath of the excluded prisoners. On balance, though, the administration is more concerned about the former condition—the labor shortage—than the latter.

Rather than simply representing a myopic policy formulation on the part of correctional industries, the labor policy is designed to attempt to diminish the crises in the labor system of the institutions. Starting in the late sixties and coming to fruition in the early seventies, the prisoners' movement had severely shaken the material basis and the ideological tenets of the prisoner labor system. An incentive system was desperately needed to revive productivity and boost the shrinking labor supply. Although the incentive system was bound to create control problems for the prison administrator, profit was apparently seen as a more important priority at this juncture.[14] The state must have been aware that the relative economic strength of CI would put them in a superior bidding position for labor. Capital invested in CI, however, yields a greater return, since CI produces commodities sold on a restricted market while capital allocated to the prison administration goes entirely for services. And, of course, the services are directed at areas where the prisoners themselves will be primary recipients. So, the policy promulgated by the state earmarked increases for the productive sector and cutbacks for the welfare sector (unemployable and partially employed prisoners).

Many of the modifications suggested in the new departmental memoranda have been implemented, some remain on the drawing board, while others are sharply contested by prison officials. The stratified labor system feared by prison officials has for all intents and purposes become a reality. Yet, the results of the policy that created a system of privileges for those employed in state-use industries seem to be falling far short of the expectations of those who championed it.

Not only does the administration suffer from an inability to recruit the necessary labor, but CI, whose economic position is considerably stronger, suffer a similar malady. The quarterly management report of West Prison indicates that 579 jobs are available in state-use industries within the West Prison complex. In 1975, only 467 of these jobs were filled.[15] In economic terms, this would mean a labor shortage of approximately 20 percent of the needed work force. It means that CI at West Prison is probably around 15 to 20 percent below capacity, or more precisely, below desired levels of output. To date, the incentive system has not produced the desired results for CI, but has adversely affected the prison administration's ability to meet its labor needs. The administration has responded to the crisis—a response that will be examined after taking a closer look at where and in what form the prisoners' resistance has developed.

Prisoners and Labor

In reviewing the uprisings that occurred in the 1950s and the demands that emerged from those uprisings, work-related demands were virtually absent. The first significant demonstration of discontent with the system of labor in the prison appeared in the rebellions of the 1970s. The appearance of these sorts of demands was a distinguishing characteristic of the insurrections of the seventies. These demands emerged out of the politics being imported into the prison during the late sixties in California, and somewhat later in New York and New Jersey. Included in this importation of political ideology was the Marxian concept of "class analysis".

Although the theory surrounding much of the Marxism that entered the prison was weak and often contradictory, it was sufficiently powerful to lead the prisoners' movement onto the unturned political ground of the labor system. In California the industrial system within the prison was sizable and important. Prisoners who had begun to study Marxism quickly realized that the labor system was a primary point of exploitation. Prisoners also began to theorize about the vulnerability of a system that depended for much of its support on profits produced from CI.

Sparked by the demands made at Folsom, prisoners employed in CI at West Prison began a campaign to increase their power in the workplace. In a meeting on November 11, 1972, the Men's Advisory Council (MAC) of D Quad at West Prison advanced a proposal submitted to it by industry workers.[16]

> Proposal: That a MAC representative be elected by the majority of workers in the Industries Area (Maintenance) shoe factory, tag plant, knitting mill, laundry) to represent workers in their grievances to their supervisor and plant managers.[17]

On January 2, 1973, the superintendent of the institution responded thus:

> The MAC was developed to produce dialogue between the entire general population and administrative staff. A concentrated MAC within Correctional Industries would be inappropriate.[18]

The workers' demand was aimed at building some collective organization in the work place, was apparently recognized as such, and was subsequently rejected by the administration. Within a month, the workers again submitted a proposal which sought to merge the Trade Advisory Council (seen by prisoners as a completely ineffective organ of workers' viewpoints) with the MAC, which at the time had a larger constituency and somewhat more power. This merger between the prison workplace and the representative organ at the quadrant level (MAC) was drafted and accepted by both groups. On December 12, 1972, the MAC D quad made a slightly watered-down proposal, which was envisioned as a possible first step toward a merger.[19]

> Proposal: That the Men's Advisory Council be made a part of the meeting of the Trade Advisory Council.[20]

On January 2, 1973, the superintendent responded:

> The TAC (Trade Advisory Council) works closely with people in vocational training and with instructors. Both MAC and TAC are adequately represented by inmates from each quad. They have two different purposes, with adequate mechanism of feedback from each group to the main populations. I fail to see any significant input from MAC to the meeting.[21]

In the next few years MAC continued to make proposals linked to the interests of prisoners working in CI. From what can be garnered from reading the minutes of MAC meetings, the administration continued to resist any attempt to alter the political base of industry workers, while conceding certain minor proposals having no organizational consequences.

In late 1973, prisoners began to prepare plans for an institutional work stoppage. The plan was to declare a general strike of industry and prison workers to press the demands for total revision of wages, working conditions, and organizational structure. Administrators at West Prison maintained that the strike was being coordinated by the Lawyers Guild, which was printing literature for the prisoners and smuggling it into the prison.

Administrators, on the basis of information supplied by informers (prisoners) who had infiltrated the prisoners' organization, learned of the strike a week ahead of time. The administration acted quickly and decisively. Prisoners who were identified as being in the leadership of the group planning the strike were immediately transferred to other institutions, and Lawyer's Guild attorneys were banned from the institution. The proposed work stoppage never occurred.

Refusing to accede to any demands that would lead to collective organization of prison workers, the administration was able to keep the work force from engaging in any collective activity. However, administration policy did not change prisoners' attitudes concerning the need for collective organization. The mass of prisoners strongly supported the economic demands made in the Folsom Manifesto. One was the right of prisoners to form unions.

In order to ascertain attitudes toward unionization, I asked prisoners at West Prison, "Do you think that prisoners should have the right to form unions?"[22] Of those asked, 92 percent felt that prisoners had the right to be represented by a union. Another question asked whether one union should represent all inmates.[23] Almost all prisoners thought that one union could and should represent all prisoners, indicating that many prisoners felt that a union was needed to represent working and nonworking prisoners alike. It is certain that many prisoners had in mind the California Prisoners' Union (an organization attempting to become the bargaining agent for prisoners).

Many prisoners held the view that although a union was necessary to represent all prisoners, it was needed most in Correctional Industries. A 37-year-old white prisoner, serving a term for manslaughter, argued that "it was very important for the inmates in the industries to get a union; that's where some of the greatest exploitation takes place." He felt, as did the prisoners who devised the Folsom demands, that "all inmates should be given at least a minimum wage."[24] A 39-year-old prisoner answered the question by saying, "I wish we had a union to represent us here. The industries here are making a hell of a profit by paying peanuts!"[25]

The strong preferences shown by West prisoners for a union suggest the degree to which the economic demands of the Folsom Manifesto reflected the feelings of the vast majority of the prisoners. When we examine the administration response to other issues raised by the prisoners' movement, the resistance shown by the administration in refusing to yield any ground in the workplace will be seen in sharper relief. The administration's choosing to stand firm in opposition to collective organization of the work force reveals the central importance that labor has in the California penal system. Not only does labor provide the basis for the accumulation of profits, but it is essential for the maintenance of certain crucial institutional functions. It is the one contribution of the prisoners that, if withdrawn, could severely affect the entire system. The authorities find themselves in the position of needing the prisoners' labor more than the prisoner needs the fruits of his labor (wages).

Recognizing their vulnerability, the administrators have sought to limit their dependency on prison labor. Messinger, who studied Duell Vocational Institution in 1965, noted at the time that the authorities consciously attempted to curb their dependence on inmate labor:

> Although many inmates had important jobs, the institution made sure that it wasn't dependent on any worker or group of workers. There was always free, custodial and staff people available to man crucial posts in case of emergency.[26]

While this particular strategy could be effective in limiting the leverage of workers employed directly by the institution, it could not be used in industry. Present conditions limit the effectiveness of the strategy even for labor used to accomplish institutional tasks.

Labor Protest and Administration Strategy

The prison administration presently finds it difficult, if not impossible, to reduce its dependence on prison labor. Cutbacks in staff, resulting from state-wide budget cuts, have increased the number of important positions held by prisoners. Thus, the administration seeks a new policy to enforce work discipline.

It has already been noted that a twofold crisis exists in the labor system. There is a division in the ruling strata of the prison and widespread dissatisfaction on the part of the prisoners, resulting in an inability to recruit the needed labor force. The incentive system has failed to promote the desired number of inmate workers. Thus, the administration has been forced to adopt other mechanisms to ameliorate the problem. At present, the administration relies heavily on two methods.

First, the administration has fallen back to a policy of active repression. Although the policy is not publicly articulated, evidence shows that it is operative. For example, in the quarter ending June 1975, the administration's statistics reveal that 59 prisoners were given work-related disciplinary charges, which include a variety of offenses associated with work performance. These charges were the second highest category of charges, only exceeded by the category of "disrespect." This figure indicates that 5 to 7 percent of the full-time work force received a disciplinary charge. By the end of the next quarter, the situation had either deteriorated further or the policy was being applied with more vigor. In October 1975, the quarterly report shows that 116 prisoners were charged with work infractions, double the number of the month before, representing 10 to 20 percent of the entire work force.

There are several types of behavior which are the subject of these disciplinary charges—charges which can adversely affect the prisoner's chance for release. For example, in October 1975, a charge was filed against a prisoner for failing to report to an administrative (as opposed to industry) work assignment. The report written by the correction officer assigned to the dining room reads:

> At approximately 7:50 A.M. on Oct. 19, 1975, I telephoned Building 7 and asked that Inmate X be sent to the Quad Dining Room as a server for the breakfast meal. I was informed that Inmate X refused to report to his work assignment.[27]

The inmate was called before the disciplinary committee where, according to the report, he refused to go to work, was found guilty and sentenced to be locked up in his cell for five days. After serving his sentence, the prisoner would again be given a work assignment. If he refused to comply, he would once again be sent before the disciplinary committee.

Another sort of disciplinary charge concerns work performance. An example of this sort follows:

> At approximately 8:20 A.M. on Monday, October 13, Inmate X . . . , was assigned to serve oleomargarine on the Building 7 side of the D Dining Room. This writer instructed Inmate X on several occasions to serve a level scoop of oleomargarine. The subject refused, and continued to serve an unauthorized portion . . .[28]

At his hearing, the prisoner contended that he thought he was being asked to serve less than the ration and didn't feel that was right. The prisoner was found guilty.

The disciplinary reports cited above were written by corrections officers against prisoners who were employed in jobs under the administration budget. In CI, work supervisors are given the authority to write disciplinary charges against the prisoners. The total number of disciplinary charges are divided fairly equally between industry jobs and prison jobs. A typical charge written against a prisoner working in CI is cited below:

> Inmate Z is assigned to the shoe factory on a full day basis. Z failed to report to his job assignment on Tuesday, Oct. __; Upon calling D Quad at approximately 1:00 P.M., Z finally reported to work. Again this date Oct. __, Z failed to report. It should be noted that he missed a half-day on Sept. __, all day on Sept. __ and four hours on Oct. __. Z has been counseled extensively to no avail. His attendance, attitude, and work habits have deteriorated to the point that he is considered unsuitable . . .[29]

Issuing disciplinary charges to curb the decline of inmate participation in the labor system is one of the only available gambits in the face of the breakdown of the "work ethic." Disciplinary charges have become one of the two main strategies for coercing the work force.

The second mechanism that the administration employs to overcome the labor crisis could be called "selective stratification." Primary to the system of social control is a system of stratification. Stratification creates a division in the prison body, with the effect, in economic terms, of varying the costs of certain actions. Simply, it creates pockets of prisoners who have more to lose or gain, as the case may be, than other pockets of prisoners. Policies like classification, job assignments, and honor units exemplify what can be referred to as policies of selective stratification. Historically, this process has proved successful in counteracting the unification of the prison body.

Within West Prison there are several specialized programs, the most important of which is titled "the Stress-Assessment Program." The stated purpose of the program is to assess the way prisoners with a history of violent behavior are able to stand up to extreme stress. (See appendix C.) Prisoners who participate in the program are very close to a parole date. Their participation is not voluntary, but a condition for release established by the paroling authority. Therefore, successful completion of six months in the stress-assessment unit is required before these prisoners can be paroled.

Being very close to a parole date and participating in a program mandated by the paroling authority, the prisoners in the stress-assessment unit are particularly vulnerable. Failure to complete the program is taken by the paroling authority as an indication of the prisoner's inability to deal with the pressures of the free world—sufficient evidence to require the prisoner to serve more time before again being cycled through stress-assessment. Part of the requirement of the stress-assessment unit is work.

Two prisoners who had been through the stress-assessment unit described the work requirement. One said, ". . . they work you as hard as they can. You worked in the kitchen, and outside on the grounds."[30]

Another prisoner who had gone through the stress-assessment unit described the experience:

> The Adult Authority (paroling agency) sent me to the stress-assessment unit—you have no choice, you must go. The unit is a means of supplying inmates to perform the most menial jobs in the institution. Everyone in the stress unit is required to work in the kitchen for at least eight hours a day without pay. It's the job that no one in the institution is willing to do for money. When you get done working like a dog all day, you're forced to go to group in the evening. In group they don't do anything but drag you down—drag you through the mud. The stress unit has done nothing but make me more bitter—expose me to more degradation.[31]

The stress-assessment unit can provide 50 prisoners to do the most menial jobs in the institution at no cost. Although 50 working prisoners can not totally ameliorate labor shortage in the range of 200 workers, they can make it somewhat less acute. It is a short-term strategy that provides needed time to construct a more viable long-term policy.

Conclusions

The system of prisoner labor in California and other states provides ripe investigative territory for understanding how ideology functions in the service of the system of control. As the previous discussion has attempted to demonstrate, the labor system in California was in part disabled as a result of the prisoners' recognition of the differences between ideological declarations and material conditions. That chasm between appearance and reality has historically existed. But the knowledge was largely unobtainable until a prisoners' movement began to translate the logic of labor into political terms.

California's contention that labor was primarily a means of rehabilitation was not a unique or even particularly modern ideological gambit. In studying prisons in North Carolina, McCleery concluded that labor policy:

> . . . served the interest of the ruling authority to the maximum extent, although they were supported by the classic argument of penal government that the results would be to teach prisoners the meaning of discipline and the importance of work.[32]

Labor within the prison has the primary objective of providing a monetary savings for the state, since, "performance of (these) critical services would otherwise require employment of additional civil service personnel."[33] Whether one examines a particular labor function like vocational shops, which primarily serve as maintenance shops for the institution rather than training facilities, or the entire web of labor departments, one conclusion is inescapable: "Efforts to maximize economic return from industries require emphasis on output, rather than on corrections of faulty attitudes of the prisoner-worker."[34]

Political information that became available as a result of the insurrection of 1970 led to a weakening of the ideological system that explained the relations in the prison labor system. Ideology tends to erect a set of laws or propositions that not only explain a particular interaction like labor, but hold up the explanation as a natural law or timeless phenomenon. Without some internal or external disturbance, the ideological explanation draws strength from its apparent ability to capture a system's logic.

Ideology can become weakened when a crisis penetrates the formal character of the laws on which it rests, or there is some change in the system it seeks to explain. In the case of the ideology of prison labor it was the former.

> On closer examination, the structure of a crisis is seen to be no more than a heightening of the degree and intensity of the daily life. In its unthinking, mundane reality that life seems held together by 'natural laws'; yet it can experience a sudden dislocation because the bonds uniting its various elements and partial systems are a chance affair even at their most normal.[35]

This statement by Lukac in part explains why the ideological systems that rationalized prison labor for so long were damaged by the uprisings of the 1970s. But it is not only the dislocation caused by the crisis itself that accounts for the damage, but the process set in motion by the crisis. While a crisis produces a weakening of an ideological system, it can never assure that another like system will not be erected after the most severe shocks have passed. The process of change can be initiated in a period of crises, but only a sustained organizational effort is sufficient to prevent inertia from setting in after the storm has passed.

A crisis, like the one caused by the 1970 insurrection, provides the opportunity or space for the introduction of new explanations. In the case of the prison labor system, the explanations produced by the prisoners' movement more accurately expressed the reality of the labor system than those contained in the previous ideological framework erected by the administration. It was for this reason that the ideology of labor and the labor system itself have undergone what may be irreparable damage.

In this situation the administration has two possible options to increase its control over prison labor. It can either entirely restructure the system to diminish the most grossly exploitative elements or attempt to reassert control through the suppression of dissent.[36] The administration tried both alternatives, although each could have been, and may still be, pursued with more vigor. Both options have failed. An incentive system has not been sufficient to legitimize the labor system. Repression can under certain circumstances produce acquiescence, but can almost never produce the kind of active participation needed to legitimize a system that has fallen into disrepute.

The division in the ruling strata creates an additional obstacle to the formulation of coherent policy. This obstacle was not created by a myopic bureaucracy, nor is it a policy that can be attributed entirely to the manner in which the bureaucracy is organized. Rather, the division in the ruling class concretely expresses the different interests held by the local bureaucracy and those in CI.

This cleavage in the ruling strata is particularly interesting because it can be extended to capture a similar, although less apparent, cleavage between the state (legislature, executive, judiciary) and capitalist enterprises. In the case of the prison, the administration is concerned with the objectives of control and legitimacy, which at certain times can reinforce each other. The state is also concerned with maintaining control and legitimacy. In both areas, ideological warfare and repression are often used to accomplish this end.[37]

While the state is primarily interested in control and legitimacy, the capitalist sector is interested in maximizing profit.[38] The same situation obtains between CI and local administrations; that is, CI is interested in securing and maximizing profit. At times the requirement of legitimacy, control and profit maximization can and do reinforce each other. At other times, profit maximization and control can become contradictory. This is exactly what has occurred in California and is seemingly occurring on a wider scale in the United States.[39]

Correctional Industries is mainly concerned with producing commodities for sale in an efficient and inexpensive way. It sees this as its function—a function that is part of a total system of institutionalization. The labor system is a variable that the administration has to contend with, whether it likes it or not. Since CI produces profit that helps cut the costs of institutionalization for the state, it performs an invaluable and irreplaceable function in the institutional scheme. CI does not see its own functions as antagonistic to those of the local administration; therefore, it refuses to take responsibility for the crises that exist.

If CI does not see its function as antagonistic, the local administration surely does. Although the local administration does not deny the importance or even the value of having a factory system within the walls, it does dispute the way the system is organized—the goals that it pursues. Ideally, the administration would opt for industries either paying a competitive wage or some direct form of control over the policies and objectives of CI.

The administration would like to live in a world where all prisoners are paid a decent wage, whether they are working or training. The superintendent of West Prison, with no apparent sense of implicit contradiction, argued that relative economic deprivation within the prison leads to criminal activity within the walls. For purposes of control, nothing would suit the superintendent more than a system of relative equality among prison workers. This would overcome the local administration's inability to secure necessary labor, while at the same time limit illicit activity that, according to the superintendent, necessarily occurs when there is a class without economic power.

The other option that the local administration would choose would entail placing CI under the control of the local administration.[40] While this would probably not maximize profit, it would likely maximize administrative control.

At present, and at least in the near future, the contradictions between state and local correctional officials will not be solved. In fact, the problem is not soluble unless the state invests substantially more money in the institutional system. Barring some massive shift in the health of the economy and a correspondingly massive shift in the priority given to prison expenditures, this prospect does not seem likely.[41]

The situation in the labor area is presently a classic stand-off. The administration has failed to promote desired levels of participation and output through incentives, repression, or the use of special programs. No means has been devised to solve the basic contradictions that plague the system. Out of desperation, the California correctional administration recently agreed to start a test program at Soledad Prison, allowing the California Prisoners' Union to represent inmates at the institution. To date, the program has not begun because of difficulties in reaching agreement about the areas and conditions under which the Prisoners' Union would function.

For the most part, the prisoners are in the same sort of malaise as the administration. While prisoners continue to rebel individually, no collective protest has occurred, partly because of the great risks involved. Prisoners are looking to groups like the Prisoners' Union to carry on the fight for unionization. In the meantime, the individual protests have affected the system to the point where the state administration is looking toward new solutions.

Notes

1. For example, at Folsom, Rahway and Attica there appeared demands that sought to: increase the wages and benefits paid to inmate labor; combat racism in the institution; protect prisoners involved in political activity from suppression. Since these sorts of demands appeared in prisons on the West Coast as well as on the East, it can be assumed that administration policies were similar.

2. A letter written by a prisoner at Folsom, cited in Pallas and Barber, "From Riot to Revolution," p. 254.

3. It should be remembered that the demands themselves did not in most cases set down some criteria or program to satisfactorily accomplish the goal of the demand. This lack of specificity, which we will allude to later, also strengthened the administration's position.

4. Although I know of no studies that surveyed prisoners in the California prison system to test their attitudes toward the labor system of the prison or the modifications suggested in the Folsom Manifesto, I believe that prisoners strongly line up behind the program suggested in the manifesto. First, my own questionnaire results, and the conversations I had with prisoners in California support that conclusion. Second, the vast popularity of the California Prisoners' Union, an organization built on many of the demands in the Folsom Manifesto, is evident within the prison.

Finally, it is clear that the economic demands contained in the Folsom Manifesto are clearly in the best interests of prison workers. Based on my experience I believe that the prisoners recognize these demands as being in their interest.

5. California Department of Corrections, *Administrative Manual* (1974), Section 195.02

6. Ibid., Section 195.0341.

7. "California Prison Task Force Correctional Systems Study," p. 21.

8. Ibid., p. 36.

9. California Department of Corrections, *Administrative Manual* (1974). Sec. BA 37-11.

10. California Department of Corrections, *Administrative Manual* (October 9, 1975), Section 195.07.

11. California Department of Corrections, *Administrative Manual* (October 5, 1975), Section 195-07.

12. This is in some ways not dissimilar to the historical contradictions that have often appeared between the state sector and monopoly sector, especially during periods of labor shortage. For example, see James O'Connor, *Fiscal Crisis of the State,* St. Martins Press, 1973.

13. Figures supplied by superintendent of West Prison, November 1975.

14. This particular example, although it occurs within a very specific context, seems to run counter to the argument of some economic theorists who argue that management, in creating policy and technology, is primarily concerned with systems that will maximize control over the workplace and labor force. This argument's most eloquent statement can be found in Steve Marglin, "What Do Bosses Do?", *Journal of Radical Political Economics,* December 1972.

15. California Department of Corrections, *Management Quarterly Reports,* quarter ending Oct. 1975, p. 38.

16. The Men's Advisory Council is a group of prisoners elected by other prisoners in their cellblock (50 prisoners per block) to represent them in meetings with administrators.

17. Minutes of the meeting of the Men's Advisory Council of D quad (November 11, 1972).

18. Superintendent's response in minutes of the meeting of the Men's Advisory Council of D quad (January 2, 1973).

19. This account was received from two prisoners who participated in these negotiations.

20. Minutes of the meeting of the Men's Advisory Council of D quad (December 12, 1972).

21. Superintendent's response in minutes of the meeting of the Men's Advisory Council of D quad (January 2, 1973).

22. Question 1 in Unions section, questionnaire. See appendix B.

23. Question 2 in Unions section, appendix B.

24. Interview with inmate.

25. Interview with inmate.

26. Sheldon Messinger, "Strategies of Control," p. 121. Reprinted with permission.

27. California Department of Corrections, "Rules Violation Report," Violated Rule DR 1301; DR 1302.

28. Ibid., Rule Violation DR 1301 and DR 1302.

29. Ibid., Rule Violation DR 1301 and DR 1302.

30. Interview with inmate, 30-year-old black.

31. Interview with inmate, 50-year-old white male.

32. Richard H. McCleery, "Power, Communication and the Social Order," p. 161.

33. California Department of Corrections, *Master Plan* (1968), p. 27.

34. Elmer H. Johnson, *Crime, Correction, and Society,* p. 588. Other evidence could be collected to support this statement. What vocational programs are available at West Prison are small and selective. Some programs, such as electronics, have a two-year wait for admission. Other programs cannot be filled at all.

35. George Lukac, *History and Class Consciousness,* p. 101.

36. Because the prison labor system is modeled on the capitalist labor system, exploitation cannot be eradicated. Exploitation is embedded in the very relations betwen capital and labor, and therefore, cannot be abolished without the abolition of the nexus or axiomatic relations of the system. The option that is conceivably open to the administration is to restructure the system to a point where improved conditions might lead to cooperation or passive participation by the work force. This is what the admininistration had in mind when it created an expanded incentive system.

37. A particularly good practical examination of how the state constructs and utilizes policies of control, while at the same time reinforcing certain ideological premises of the system can be found in Frances Fox Piven and Richard A. Cloward, *Regulating the Poor.* In the sense that welfare agencies of the state rely on ideology and arbitrary sanctions to regulate their clients, they differ in degree, rather than kind, from prisons.

38. I owe this idea in part to James O'Connor's *Fiscal Crisis of the State.* O'Connor labels these state outputs used for central purposes "social expenses." They are "projects and services required to maintain social harmony—to fulfill the state's 'legitimization functions,' " p. 7.

39. With social critics paying increasing attention to the state, many of the contradictions between the state and monopoly capital are receiving more careful attention. This emphasis undercuts the presumptuous, and rather undialectical approach of Marxist scholars in treating the state as an essential captured and static institution. Some of the more important work

in this area include: Ralph Miliband, *The State in Capitalist Society*; Nicos Paulantzas, "The Problem of the Capitalistic State," in R. Blackburn, ed., *Ideology in the Social Sciences*; Ernest Mandel, *The Marxist Theory of The State*; and J. O'Connor, *Fiscal Crisis of the State,* especially chapters 5, 7, 8, 9.

40. The superintendent of West Prison also felt that the paroling authority should work more closely with, if not be totally controlled by the local administration. Because the paroling authority does not solicit recommendations from the local administration, it reduces a potentially powerful weapon of administrative control. Messinger discussed this very point in "Strategies of Control." My findings seem to support the fact that the local administration is dissatisfied with the separation between the Adult Authority and local administration. What distinguishes the problem, however, from the problem in CI is the motive for the mode of organization. In the case of the Adult Authority the motive is political. In the case of CI the motive is economic. This is a distinction with a difference.

41. I should note that the New Jersey system has avoided many of the labor problems of the California system because it has more effectively limited its dependence on prison labor. The prisoners' movement in New Jersey did not give the emphasis to the problem of labor that the California movement did. Therefore, the crisis in the system of labor was less traumatic, limiting the amount of political education (alternative explorations) that could be effectively introduced. So far, the ideological system that supports prison labor in New Jersey may have a few bruises but is essentially in good health.

Origins of Political Development

The political demands adopted by the prisoners' movement, particularly the expansion of individual and collective rights, are inextricably bound up with the various strains of political thought. Unlike the economic demands, which first emerged around 1970, the political demands had been fermenting for a long time. Behind the set of political demands were several embryonic organizations, each devoted to a particular ideology. Consequently, the demands were related to certain activities and practices that these structures were carrying out or were desirous of carrying out. Also, the administration's response was grounded in its assessment of the organizations behind the demands and their particular political beliefs.

Because of the interconnection between the political demands and the political organizations, reflecting the civil rights, class analysis and Muslim doctrines, it is impossible to discuss the administration's response without flushing out these interconnections. This chapter is devoted to a discussion of political alignment and political ideology, as well as an analysis of the administration's policy formulation based on its assessment of political development.

Political Demands: The Background

Many of the political demands had their roots in the early struggle over racism. Since blacks had been in the forefront of these early struggles, they had been targeted by the administration as political agitators. Once blacks emerged as a visible political force, they became the victims of widespread harassment usually occasioned by arbitrary and capricious segregation and punishment. A majority of the litigation in the sixties dealt with treatment black prisoners received.

Blacks entered into the leadership of the movement for several reasons. There was a very sizable portion of black prisoners, far exceeding their actual proportion of the total population. In New Jersey, approximately 65 percent of the prison population is black. In California, the black proportion of the prison population is smaller but still three or four times greater than their proportion in the total population. Moreover, many of the outside political currents were either directly aimed at blacks or bore a greater relevance to the life experience of blacks. The doctrine of the Black Muslims was, of course, aimed directly at black prisoners who imported it into the prison. The Civil Rights Movement, while having a somewhat wider base, was still generally geared to black prisoners. Class analysis (Marxism) while not exclusively aimed at a black constituency, rang truer to black prisoners than it did to white prisoners.

Aside from providing a system of ideas that blacks strongly identified with, the various outside movements also provided organizational impetus. The Muslim movement was the first to attempt to erect a strong organizational structure to support its doctrine. On the heels of the Muslim overtures came similar attempts by the civil rights and Marxist forces.

Although blacks were more intimately affected by the ideas introduced during the sixties and emerged as the central political actors, the activity and ideas also deeply affected white prisoners. Both the organizational and political forces of the movement jarred the white prisoners into an increased political awareness of their own situation. When black prisoners raised the issue of the rights afforded to blacks in general and black prisoners in particular, white prisoners quickly extended the "rights model" to their status as prisoners. Soon whites joined blacks in active litigation and political struggle to secure citizenship rights. By 1970 whites and blacks together rebelled against the tyranny of the prison system and the society out of which it grew.

By the time of the Folsom insurrection, the various political forces within the prison had begun to harden. This process continued until after the end of the insurrection. As these positions hardened, blacks and whites formed into various political camps.[1] These alignments would eventually become the basis for the administration's response to the political demands of the prisoners. Therefore, it is imperative to look closely at the issues and programs of the surviving political alignments as a prelude to discussing the administration's reaction to the political demands.

The first victim of these new political formations was the Muslim movement. Prisoners rejected the separation the Muslims drew between civil and religious society, black separatism, black superiority, and the "white devil" theory. But while black prisoners dispensed with most aspects of Muslim doctrine, they did not reject the more positive moments of the Muslim movement. These included the powerful organizational form adopted by the Muslims, along with its rejection of pathological explanations of criminality. Black prisoners retained elements of the Muslims' use of racism as an analytic and explanatory tool.

While the fortunes of the Muslims declined, the numbers of Civil Rights Movement adherents grew.

The central demand of the Civil Rights Movement was the demand to extend constitutional rights to afford blacks the same constitutional status afforded whites. Certainly the charismatic leadership of the movement and the abundance of media attention that it drew enhanced its appeal. The

Civil Rights Movement tended to draw a close correlation among rights, freedom, and justice. Freedom and justice were seen as almost mechanical outputs of a system of citizenship rights. This tendency to see the accumulation and protection of democratic rights as springboards to freedom and justice had profound effects on black consciousness.

Blacks attracted by the Civil Rights Movement adopted its programs and began to investigate means to press for the protection and extension of the rights of black prisoners. Groups of black prisoners attempted to form chapters of the NAACP and other black civil rights organizations. They demanded that the prison administration protect the rights of blacks and increase the opportunities for black prisoners to gain upward mobility. Mobility meant providing opportunities for blacks to hold positions formerly held by white prisoners. Protection of rights in the prison would most often mean curbing the racism of correction officers, white prisoners and the administration itself. The movement to obtain and protect personal rights would become the predominant model for politics within the institution.

While Muslim doctrine had clearly identified an "oppressor" or race of oppressors, the Civil Rights Movement was either unwilling or unable to assign responsibility for the plight of blacks. The Civil Rights Movement did attack a number of American institutions—the courts, Congress, local government, the executive—but at no time did a coherent and identifiable picture of the locus of oppression emerge. This eclectic approach to political activity, attacking here, retreating there, was adopted by elements in the prisoners' movement.

Without a methodology that could identify a responsible person or agency linked to the system of racism, or a concrete political strategy, blacks who identified with the movement exhibited considerable political vacillation. Before and after the uprising, this group worked for change through the courts, state legislatures, prison bureaucracy and a variety of other agencies. Although the Civil Rights Movement did not discount interracial political activity, it also did not encourage it. Thus, while prisoners attached to the ideas of the Civil Rights Movement were more willing to participate with whites than Black Muslim prisoners were, they lacked the sort of analysis that could have produced sustained political coalitions around broad issues. Lacking a substantive political analysis and strategy, the issue of race was presented as an issue unrelated to most other issues on the political terrain of the prison.

The insurrections of 1970 represented a point of disillusionment with the Civil Rights Movement. Predominantly, the disillusionment centered on the tactics of the movement. Prisoners were dissatisfied with the speed in which reforms mandated by the courts, legislatures or prison authorities were being implemented. Prisoners felt that hopes for amelioration through established institutional channels were less likely than they had once anticipated.

Participating in an insurrection like the ones that occurred in Attica, Folsom or Rahway indicated a willingness on the part of black prisoners to raise the level of struggle.

Besides the growing impatience with the tactics of the Civil Rights Movement, there was also dissension over the program laid down by the movement. Doubt emerged about the ability to carry through any comprehensive program. Even if such a program could be realized, many black prisoners were uncertain what the effects of those reforms would be on their lives. The notion that the enforcement and allocation of full citizenship rights would constitute a means to alleviate the effects of a repressive system became more problematic. Although criticism about the program's ends appeared less frequently and with less voracity than the criticism concerning means, it nevertheless existed.

Both the adherents of the civil rights model and the Muslim model were shaken by the introduction of class analysis into the prison. Indeed, the class analysis model caused some profound changes in the way the questions of race were being posed in the institutions. Many allies of the Muslim and Civil Rights Movements changed their posture as the model of class analysis became more widely accessible to black prisoners.

At the time of the insurrections of 1970 in California, it seems that the class model had the attention of a sizable number of black and white prisoners. I have argued that the demands of Folsom prisoners in 1970 represented the first time that prisoners raised class issues. In terms of the struggle against racism, it meant that the category of race and ethnicity became located at a different level of the political struggle.

Concretely, this signaled the beginning of a disillusionment with a major premise of the Civil Rights Movement—that equality for blacks could be achieved through legal reforms. This disillusionment would not have occurred at the brisk pace that it did without the presence of another analysis that could loosen the foundations that the Civil Rights Movement's strategy of reform rested upon. The initial power of the prisoners allied with the class analysis model lay precisely in their ability to provide such an analysis. Added to the power of the analysis was the assertion on the part of those forces that beside a correct analysis they also had a strategy to correspond to the analysis. Coming on the heels of the failure of the Muslim and Civil Rights Movements to provide a cogent analysis and strategy for both the long- and short-term struggles, it seemed that class analysis had fertile soil in which to take root.

Class analysis maintained that racism was a phenomenon historically rooted in capitalism. Fundamentally, racism was portrayed as an economic strategy, a means to keep a reserve army of labor and prevent labor costs from rising. Racism served as a tool to keep the labor force divided. Consequently no real change was possible as long as capitalism determined the economic and political agenda of the society.

But racism was only one strategy employed by the ruling class to secure its hegemony; there were various others. The fundamental strategy to maintain its economic dominance involved its control over the means of production. Controlling the means of production, the wealth of the society, the capitalist class was able to extract labor power on its terms—terms that secured its control and the workers' exclusion and exploitation. One needed to look no further than the labor supply system of the prison for a concrete example of how capitalist industry functioned. George Jackson, a heroic figure in the prisoners' movement, and the most articulate spokesman of the anticapitalist movement, analyzed the effect that capitalism had on the black population:

> The new slavery, the modern variety of chattel slavery updated to disguise itself, places the victim in a factory, or in the case of most blacks, in support roles in and around the factory system (service trades) working for a wage. However, if work cannot be found in or around the factory complex, today's neoslavery does not allow for a modicum of food and shelter. The sense and meaning of slavery comes through as a result of our ties to the wage.[2]

Capitalists, by control exercised through the state and in the workplace, could effectively pit one group of exploited people against another, similar to the way the prison administration could pit blacks against whites as a means of maintaining control. Racism functioned as a medium for these divisions. Blacks were portrayed as a grossly exploited class, but a class whose exploitation served a particular master.

Of paramount importance was the fact that within this analysis blacks found a class of potential allies. The capitalist system had created other oppressed groups—Puerto Ricans, Chicanos, Native Americans, women and many white workers. What was necessary in light of this analysis was the unification of oppressed peoples who could collectively struggle against oppression. The analysis opened the door to class action between blacks and whites:

> We need allies, we have a powerful enemy who cannot be defeated without an allied effort. The enemy at present is the capitalist system and its supporters. Our prime interest is to destroy them. Anyone else with the same interest must be embraced, we must work with, beside, through, over, under anyone, regardless of their external physical features whose aim is the same as ours in this. Capitalism must be destroyed, and after it is destroyed, if we find that we still have problems, we'll work them out.[3]

The analysis also provided hope that the ranks of the opponents of capitalism, and by definition, allies of blacks, would naturally grow. The growth would occur because the economic system would by necessity squeeze people out when it no longer needed their labor. Thus, allies would multiply with each new member of the working class who rose to recognize the implicit exploitation embedded in the system.

These were the essential elements contained in the class analysis brought into the prison.[4] Within the analysis, prisoners themselves formed a stratum of the working class, systematically excluded from participation. While the vast majority of the prisoner class fitted this definition, blacks were still viewed as a class who suffered from a special form of exploitation.

Although the analysis tended to relocate the black struggle at a different level in the overall political struggle, it by no means liquidated the question of racism. Even though blacks were a part of a larger class of oppressed peoples, they still faced different problems than whites in the class. Because racism was particular to blacks, the praxis flowing from Marxist doctrine would encourage blacks to form organizations to deal with the problems faced by blacks and assure that these problems were recognized by class allies.

In 1970 the class analysis of racism had emerged to contend strongly with the civil rights analysis. The Muslim doctrines had by this time fallen into disrepute. The collective protest at Folsom and other California institutions evidenced the fact that collective action among the races had gone beyond theory. Although class analysis had penetrated the movement, advocates of the civil rights model, which did not share the view that the destruction of capitalism was a precondition for black freedom, maintained considerable influence in the circles of blacks and other prisoners of color.

Almost the same pattern of political activity occurred in East Prison, albeit two years after California. What distinguished the political situation in East Prison from that at West Prison was the relative strength of the Black Muslim force at the time of the 1972 uprising.

The position of the forces allied with class analysis at the time of the insurrection at East Prison was not as strong as at Folsom. However, they did have significant influence on the demands and negotiations. It was shortly after the actual insurrection that the Marxist analysis began to reach a significant number of prisoners. In sum, the class forces at East Prison by early 1972 were a small but significant force in the political arena. Unlike those in California, the New Jersey prisoners who declared themselves Marxist and argued for a race program constructed along Marxist premises faced opposition not only from prisoners aligned with the Civil Rights Movement, but also from a fairly strong and well-disciplined group of Muslims. This naturally slowed their development.

In California the various alignments of prisoners around political doctrines were recognized by administration forces. James Park, associate warden at San Quentin, saw the civil rights or reformist faction as predominant;

> First, and characteristic of the majority, are those who are working within the existing socioeconomic system to make that system share some of the power and affluence. There is no revolutionary intent although strong rhetoric and even violence are applied to put pressure on the system.[5]

The more class-oriented group within the prison is described by Park this way:

> On the second level, a smaller but more attention-getting segment has adopted the revolutionary ethic and actively advocate destruction of the existing social order through a Maoist or Castroite social revolution. They are encouraged by elements of the largely white New Left who capitalize on the impatience of minorities with the slowness of the establishment in meeting their needs.[6]

Park describes the way these forces play themselves out in the organizational struggle in the institution.

> Two inmate self-improvement organizations at San Questin, SATE for black inmates and EMPLEO for Mexican-Americans, have had continuing leadership struggles between those who seek identity and increased opportunity and those who would demand, confront and destroy, thus reflecting similar division in the outside community.[7]

These prisoner organizations referred to by Park formed the backbone of the prisoners' movement. Most of these organizations had operated surreptitiously within the prison and were dominated by black and minority prisoners. There were, however, several white revolutionary organizations that also functioned, sometimes in coalitions with black organizations. These group formations, in which there existed varying degrees of political heterogeneity, were to become a focus of administrative policy. It is now important to examine these prisoner groups in some depth.

Collectivism, Pluralism and Political Policy

Informal groups of prisoners have existed for some time within the prison.[8] A relatively recent phenomenon is the appearance of a large number of formal, or recognized, inmate groups. Almost nothing has been written about these new inmate organizations although they are a significant force within the modern prison.

It is somewhat difficult to trace the historical development of groups, since some have at times operated clandestinely, and at other times in the open. Other groups have always operated surreptitiously.[9] Because the composition of these groups has changed, both in terms of membership and organizational banners, there is in most cases no cumulative history. Therefore the history to be discussed and the groups included in this history are those that were accessible—those I was able to locate and communicate with through one means or another.[10] Although I am certain that I was not able to make a connection with every underground tendency within West Prison, I believe that I reached most of them.

Within particular prisons in California and New Jersey the policy toward groups varies somewhat. Therefore, while the policies of East and West Prisons generally represent the main tenets of state prison policy toward inmate groups, particular prisons will show variations. These variations reflect the position or function of the particular institution within the state system or the degree of volatility the group movement seems to present at any particular point.[11]

At West Prison, the superintendent attested to the fact that only two groups, Alcoholics Anonymous and the Men's Advisory Council, existed when he began his tenure in 1966. All the groups that exist or have recently existed came into being after that year. Most of these groups actually began to function between 1971 and 1974, the period that marks a change in the state and local administrations' policies toward groups. This change was occasioned by the events of 1970.

In East Prison a few groups were functioning before the 1971 uprising; the most visible and important was the Inmate Committee, which dates back to the early 1950s.[12] Most of the groups, however, began after the 1971 insurrection. As in California, the incident at East Prison in 1971 prompted a reexamination and subsequent revision of policy concerning prisoner organizations.

The reason for the change in policy in California was certainly the character of the insurrections at Folsom and San Quentin in 1968 and 1970 respectively. Although making the case that New Jersey changed policy direction for the same reason is a little more difficult, I remain convinced that the changing political attitudes of the prison body were the most significant in generating new policy.

The character of the uprisings in California and New Jersey have been previously described. The two most important elements were the massive shows of collective unity among prisoners of color and whites, and the new demands that emanated from the insurrections. The policies that followed these events were aimed at undermining the unity of the prison body and counteracting the new political forces that had developed. I hope to prove that the new policy, originated in the early 1970s, was explicitly aimed at accomplishing these ends.

Although certain embryonic and even more advanced group structures existed prior to the events of the 1970s, these groups were largely out of the administration's sight. That is, the administration had no means, other than developing informers, to find out about the groups' activities, ideology, and membership. Although these groups were out of sight, they were not out of the administration's mind.

Almost all these groups consisted of ethnic and black prisoners, although in California there were at least three white groups of some significance. James Park alluded to the existence of SATE, a black organization, and EMPLEO, a Chicano group. Other groups included the Black Muslims, the Black Guerrilla Army (BGA) whose cadre were later to become members of the Symbionese Liberation Army, the Polar Bear Party and Venceremos, (both essentially white organizations), and the multiracial Prisoners Union. When the administration was able to identify members of a group, it did all it could to crush it. Lew Fudge, a high-ranking Corrections Department official expressed the rationale behind this policy, "The administration fears organizations. That is why they tried to suppress the Black Muslims, out of fear of their very tight organization."[13] But what the administration feared more than tight organization was interracial organization.[14]

When I first began to research the development of prison organizations, I was uncertain how the policy actually evolved. At first it seemed the administration, had almost by accident, come upon a policy that accomplished, or seemed to accomplish, the desired end of interrupting collective organization. But after accumulating more evidence, it became apparent that the policy was not entirely an accident. Although the policy in New Jersey developed out of the same impetus as the policy in California, I am not prepared to prove empirically that it developed in exactly the same way. I am going to trace the way the policy actually developed in California. In the case of New Jersey, I have less documented evidence to substantiate the claim that it developed in the same way. Whether the New Jersey administration happened on the approach or designed it, it functioned to accomplish the same end.

The Demand for Collective Organization

Implicitly and explicitly the demands of the Folsom prisoners and the movement that developed subsequently sought the rights of prisoners to join collectively and organize other prisoners within the institution. This meant that organizations representing black, Chicano, and white prisoners should be allowed to function openly and receive certain protections. Essentially, the groups wanted their status transformed from illegitimate to legitimate. This demand was met with immediate and stiff resistance from a majority of correctional officials who saw every inmate group as destructive. The policy of continuing repression might have carried the day, except for the dissent of some keenly intuitive and (relatively) politically aware administrators. In California, James Park stands out as one of those.

Park is a veteran of the California prison system. He started his career in the early fifties as a clinical psychologist at the Chino facility. After working in Department of Corrections headquarters at Sacramento, followed by some years at Soledad, he became associate warden of San Quentin.[15]

The policy on group activity and outside community groups first outlined in Park's memorandum[16] formed the backbone of the policies that would be adopted by the Department of Corrections. It is, therefore, important to examine Park's suggestions in some detail.[17]

Park is a political realist, at least in comparison to some of his colleagues. In his memo, Park first stressed the idea that administrators should keep abreast of "current trends, tactics, and goals of major social movements." According to Park, this sort of information was vital if the local administrators were to understand the influence of inmate leaders. It is also a means for making sound judgments about the implications of certain types of demands;

> The positions of various black and Mexican-American groups in the community should be studied and understood. What appears to be unacceptable militancy by minority group inmates may reflect no more than the opinions of responsible community leaders. Staff must develop capacity to work calmly with inmates who express views in a militant manner and must recognize that militancy is not necessarily insurrection, although the distinction is sometimes difficult to make.[18]

Although the intent of this statement is not entirely clear, it seems aimed at administrators' taking a hard line on the existence of minority political groups. The intent becomes clearer as Park lays out his position on ethnic organizations;

> Ethnic identity is here to stay whether or not ethnic organizations like SATE and EMPLEO are allowed to operate. The needs and feelings expressed by these groups will not go away and must be given consideration. The prospect of keeping such groups in a noninsurrectionist mode of operation is open to question but there is no doubt that equivalent communication channels have to be open. The prospect of keeping inmates in constructive, evolutionary, modes of operation improves with the speed and flexibility shown by the administration in making reasonable changes while recognizing that the revolutionaries can never be placated.[19]

This paragraph is the crux of the policy that Park is recommending. First, it notes that the concerns of the ethnic organization have now become firmly rooted among ethnic constituencies. The likelihood of isolating a fraction, a leadership grouping or singular leader is no longer a possibility. A vast majority of the ethnic population of the prisoners recognizes ethnic-racial identity as a political issue—an entitlement.

Once the issue is perceived as legitimate by the largest part of the ethnic constituency, Park asserts that the administration must establish channels of communication to deal with the issues raised by the group. If not EMPLEO or SATE there must be "equivalent communication channels." This opens the way for the formation of prisoner groups composed along ethnic and racial lines.

In essence, Park was suggesting that the California prison system accede to the demand that prisoners be afforded extended rights of collective organization. Park saw a legalized group structure as producing positive results for the administration. If properly designed, Park further indicates that the group structure could aid in promoting moderation by providing incentives in the form of resources and increased privileges. This conception is not very different from the use of incentives in state-use industries.

Park's plan gained the favor of the state prison bureaucracy. After 1972, the number of inmate groups began to increase quickly throughout California. Groups were seen by the administration as a mechanism to promote moderate ideas, while at the same time isolating radical ideas from the political arena. As one correctional administrator noted, "The department should maximize the number of popular viewpoints . . . so that inmates have a more balanced perspective."[20]

Most of the prisoners welcomed the endorsement of group activity. Organizing clandestinely was a massive endeavor requiring much energy and great risk. Many prisoners saw the acceptance of group activity as a means to increase organizational efficiency, enlarge constituencies, and decrease risk. Some prisoners recognized that the group policy was being structured to increase the administration's control over inmate political activity. But even most of these prisoners were forced to accept the policy out of a sense of hope and because so many other prisoners accepted them.

In many ways the acceptance of group politics is analogous to the shift from the authoritarian to the liberal state. It inaugurated the beginning of the period of "prison pluralism."

Notes

1. Before embarking on this discussion, I should note that the analysis does not pertain to all inmates—black or white. Essentially, the political tendencies existed within the prisoners' movement—among prisoners active in the movement. However, the politics were not confined to movement activists; they affected a large number of prisoners. That number has varied

from time to time. During the mobilization leading up to the insurrection and for a period of two to four years thereafter, many prisoners were affected by these ideologies. Many still are.

2. George Jackson, *Soledad Brother*, p. 190.

3. Ibid., p. 202. Of course Jackson was not the only prisoner to embrace class analysis. The beginning point for the introduction of the analysis into the prison can be located in the later thoughts of Malcolm X. Malcolm argued that capitalism could not produce liberty for the black man. For a discussion of Malcolm's thought in this area see Breitman, *The Last Year of Malcolm X*, especially chapter 2.

4. The level of theoretical comprehension of Marxism and its American application varied from prison to prison. What I have presented is something like an "ideal" analysis. For example, Marxism was often presented as a system which could liberate blacks, without reference to the centrality of the working class within the theory.

5. James Park, "Power To The People": Social Revolution and the Prison, (see appendix F).

6. Ibid.

7. Ibid.

8. For example, Donald Clemmer's 1940 classic, *The Prison Community*, devotes a full chapter to informal groups. The modern literature on prison is permeated with writings concerning informal inmate groups. For example, see Lawrence Hazelrigg, ed., *Prison within Society*, or Leon Radinowicz and Marvin Wolfgang, eds. *The Criminal in Confinement* (New York: Basic Books, 1971).

9. I specifically exclude organized gangs (in California, probably the largest underground force) from the discussion. I define a group as being composed of prisoners who have a common (noncriminal) interest and who act to further that interest. The interest may be shared by prisoners who are not, strictly speaking, part of the group.

10. Many of the groups that I eventually reached in West Prison, were groups that the administration had never mentioned. Almost all of these groups had been, or were currently, banned from carrying out any organized activity. In most cases it was a prisoner who informed me of the existence of the group and made arrangements for me to speak with a prisoner from the group.

11. Sheldon Messinger was one of the first to emphasize the function that a particular prison plays within a state penal system. Messinger has noted that the particular functions assigned to a prison by the state severely limit the possibilities for the development of certain policy alternatives. He illustrates the point by showing how Duell Vocational Institute, used as a dumping ground for unmanageable juveniles, was robbed of the important policy alternative of transfer. See Messinger, "Strategies of Control".

12. The historical records concerning the Inmate Committee at East Prison start in the late forties. Although the committee was officially sanctioned in the fifties, apparently periods of three or four years went by between meetings. Before the 1972 uprising, evidence indicates, the committee was, in effect, dormant.

13. California Department of Corrections, "Working Papers of the Task Force to Study Violence," (minutes). I received the document from an unofficial source. The date of the meeting was March 22, 1974. Of course, as I previously noted, the policy of suppressing the Muslims was widely known.

14. In the judicial opinion in *National Prisoners Reform Association* v. *Sharkey*, the court inferred that the administration seemed particularly interested in preventing formation of this group because the group was composed of black and white prisoners. The decision noted that, "The only thing which seems to be unique to the plaintiff organization out of all these groups is the interracial character". Krantz, p. 393. This is an example of the administration's abhorrence of interracial collective organizations.

15. Jessica Mitford, *Kind and Usual Punishment*, p. 236.

16. James. W.L. Park, "Power to the People: Social Revolution and the Prison."

17. Not every prison adopted the same group policy. However, Park's analysis is representative of the general strands that run through all institution policies in this area.

18. Park, "Power to the People."

19. Ibid.

20. California Department of Corrections, "Task Force to Study Violence."

Prisons and Pluralism

Pluralist Theory

The similarities between pluralism in and out of the prison are striking. Both schools of pluralist practice depend on a concept of "interest" as a key political determinate. The concept of interest employed to structure the political domain tends to be narrow and particularistic. It tends to reinforce one mode of conceptualizing interest at the expense of others. This narrow definition of the concept of interest limits the degree to which interest can be seen as interchangeable or relational, thus limiting the possible forms of political behavior. The bias in the way groups are sliced up on the basis of this notion of interest contributes to a "pattern of one-dimensional thought and behavior in which ideas, aspirations and objectives that, by their content, transcend the established universe of discourse and actions are either repelled or reduced to terms of this universe."[1]

Another characteristic common to pluralism is competition. Pluralist theory is based on the competition between various groups and various interests, each attempting to assert the priorities of its constituency into policy consideration. The actual patterns of competition are regulated by the way resources happen to be distributed between the competing parties. In the prison, unlike the outside communities, the groups within the pluralist structure would appear to have access to similar resources. But in reality, there is much inequality in group resources. On the outside the market is the primary tool for the unequal distribution of resources, but in the prison the governing body of officials holds great sway over where resources happen to fall.[2]

The role of the state and the prison administration goes beyond influencing or directly participating in the distribution of resources like information, accessibility, and money. The governing power can use other means to prevent certain interests from getting into the political arena. Bachrach and Baratz coined the phrase "non-decision-making" to describe the phenomenon. A non-decision, as they define it, is "a decision that results in suppression or thwarting of a latent or manifest challenge to the values or interest of the decision maker."[3] According to the authors, non-decision-making is simply "a means by which demands for change in the existing allocation of benefits and privileges in the community can be suffocated before they are even voiced."[4]

A non-decision can take any one of several forms. It would be helpful to keep these in mind, since at one time or another the prison administration has employed all of them.

The first involves suppression by force. Within the prison this is the means that has been historically used, although it may be giving way to more scientific-managerial forms of control.[5]

A second, related, form of non-decision is one in which an actor uses a quotient of his power in applying or threatening to apply certain sanctions. "The threat of sanctions against the initiator of a potentially threatening demand may be positive or negative, ranging from intimidation (potential deprivation of valued things or events) to cooptation (potential rewards)."[6] In regard to cooptation, Phillip Selznick has accurately observed that "participatory democracy" may serve as a powerful coopting vehicle. Participatory democracy can, according to Selznick, give "the opposition the illusion of a voice without the voice itself, and so stifles opposition without having to alter policy in the least."[7]

The third form of non-decision-making is indirect. Bachrach and Baratz say it is one that "invokes an existing bias of the political system—a norm, precedent, rule, or procedure—to squelch a threatening demand or incipient issue."[8] An example of this form of non-decision might be a demand for a change being "denied legitimacy by being branded socialistic, unpatriotic, unmoral, or in violation of an established rule or procedure."[9]

The fourth and final form of non-decision-making is the most indirect. "It involves reshaping or strengthening the mobilization of bias in order to block challenges to the prevailing allocation of values."[10] This may involve invoking additional rules and procedures for processing demands for change or altering the boundaries of jurisdiction.

With some understanding of the way political challenges can be muted within the pluralist system, it is now possible to turn to a more direct discussion of the manner in which pluralist policy took shape in West Prison.

Prison Groups and the Grand Definer

An associate superintendent at West Prison acknowledged that the growth of inmate groups is a result of policies devised in the central office of the Department of Corrections. According to the official, the "central office has encouraged all administrations to deal with groups. Enomoto [director of the Department of Corrections] will not tolerate suppression of groups."

In November 1975 when I began work at West Prison, there were approximately eighteen recognized groups. The number of recognized groups varied, new groups being recognized or old groups voluntarily or involuntarily disbanding. The number of prisoners involved in group activities also varied. In October 1975, the administration estimated that 502 prisoners, or fully one-fifth of the inmate population, actively participated in group activities.[11]

The pluralist landscape is populated by groups formed on the basis of particular interests. In the outside community, these interests often represent recognized constituencies in the community. The division of interests within the pluralist arena thus reflects traditional patterns of interest aggregation, within which are contained the major islands of power in the society. The American Medical Association, the National Association of Manufacturers, and the labor bureaucrats of the AFL-CIO are all examples of pluralist groups who reflect the current balance of power in society. The state employs a variety of mechanisms, discussed by Bachrach, Baratz and others, to buttress attempts by those outside the power pockets to gain equal footing. Part of the state's power to limit access by certain constituencies resides in its capacity as a "power definer."

This power to control the mode and content of communication reinforces a system of control. In the authoritarian prison the agency that controls the power of definition is able to set the priorities within the institution. "The institutional pressures and requirements that dominated the office where communications centered (captain's office) dictated its content and its use, namely for the constant reassertion of custodial values in all aspects of institutional life."[12] In the traditional prison the custody forces controlled the environment by controlling the dialogue.

Although the custody forces still hold considerable sway in the communications process, their influence within California began to diminish between 1968 and 1970. The policy begun by Park, which legitimized group activities, ran counter to the desires and interest of the custodial force. The subsequent acceptance of the policy had the effect of transferring a significant portion of the "power of definition" from the custodial forces to the administration.[13] The power to define what group conduct is to be taken as legitimate now resides in the hands of the state and local prison bureaucracies. Locating this power to control the axiomatic propositions of the communications system with the administration has changed its orientation, but not diluted its effectiveness.

The actual definitions of acceptable and legitimate group activity are formally elaborated in the Department of Corrections *Administrative Manual.*[14] These guidelines define parameters within which group activity must reside:

> Inmate activity groups are groups of inmates who are authorized to meet on a voluntary basis to pursue specific interests and activities during their leisure time. These interests may range from discussion groups for improving self-understanding, to making and flying model aircraft.

> Inmate activity groups stress wholesome, constructive activities, but are not substitutes for other institutional programming such as academic or vocational education and work assignments.[15]

The guidelines explain what sorts of interests are viewed as acceptable; they can range from improving self-understanding to flying model airplanes. Similar guidelines in the outside community result in groups like the NAACP's being recognized as a legitimate voice for a particular constituency, while groups like the Black Panther Party, SNCC and CORE have, at various times, been relegated to the status of illegitimacy.

The administrations at West Prison and other California institutions interpret the state guidelines as excluding groups involved in political activity. The associate superintendent in charge of inmate groups has constructed a definition of "political" that he feels is consistent with state guidelines. According to this official,

> Nonpolitical groups are involved in the betterment of individuals in the group, in cultural education, and in projects related to integration, such as job placement. Anything that goes beyond this is political.[16]

Besides the guidelines which establish a range of acceptable interests, various other guidelines regulate the actual activity of the groups. The administrator responsible for group activity must devise a master plan to be transmitted to the Director of Corrections:

> This plan will include the institution controls on the size and frequency of group meetings, the amount of employee supervision required for various kinds of meetings, guidelines for participation of outside guests including methods of screening guests, and number permitted to attend group meetings and the plan for handling the financial affairs of the activity groups. It is additionally required that each institution maintain a training program, so that inmates, group sponsors, outside guests and supporters, understand the *limits on group activity and rhetoric*, the necessity to stay within stated aims of the group, and that no incitement to violence or disruption can be allowed.[17]

There are myriad guidelines regulating almost all aspects of group activity. But one especially important regulation dealing with group sponsorship is worth attention. According to the guidelines, each inmate group must have a sponsor and one or more cosponsors. The sponsors must attend every meeting to ensure "that the group's activities are confined to the written purposes authorized for that group and neither violence nor disruptive behavior is advocated."[18] Another provision states, "sponsors of groups structured *along ethnic or social issues lines* must be permanent full-time employees, co-sponsors may be probationary employees."[19] (Emphasis mine.) These regulations and guidelines provide the formal structure for group activity.

Administration Policy

In the workplace the administration steadfastly refused to accept any collective organization of prisoners. It chose a policy that sought to promote effectiveness through individual monetary incentives. This policy precluded recognizing the right of prisoners to form organizations based on common interests in the workplace. Outside the workplace the administration was more receptive to the pluralist groups as long as it felt that these groups were being kept within desired bounds.

The task of keeping group activity within a "wholesome" framework has several facets. Group policy must be administered with a degree of equilibrium. The group structure must be afforded a degree of legitimacy and credence to encourage prisoners to participate—demonstrating that participation in this type of activity can produce some results.

If the administration pulls the reins of a group too tightly, the constituency sees the whole group as a puppet. The result is that the administration loses touch with, or alienates, the faction it is trying to promote.

On the other hand, if the administration allows the group too much latitude, it feels the group will move toward insurrection and hence be taken over by a militant faction. Group activity was designed to avoid this very occurrence. Consequently, the administration must fashion a policy that will give groups a degree of legitimacy and prevent them from engaging in any form of radical politics.

This balance can be accomplished by several methods. One method favored by several top administrators involves manipulation of behavior through the use of what one administrator calls "scientific management skills," or "Prison Taylorism." As Harry Braverman pointed out, ". . . control had been the essential feature of management throughout its history, but with Taylor it assumed unprecedented proportions."[20]

The associate superintendent for classification and treatment, one of the exponents of the scientific position, equated the task of controlling group activity to structuring a business. In relation to groups the scientific approach has several layers.

First, according to this official, a group sponsor must act as a conduit for information about group activities. Since the superintendent "can really see little about the group activities, the sponsor is his eyes and ears."[21] A sponsor's primary allegiance must be to the administration rather than to the group he or she sponsors.

Second, the functions of the group must be clearly and exactly formulated; they must be specific and limited. Overlapping interests must be avoided. Each group must find a foundation of interests and activities not explicitly or implicitly linked to another group. Such ties could result in groups engaging in collective action to further common interests. If there should be activity, despite the manner in which interests have been formally fenced off from one another, the administration can officially intervene by claiming that the group or groups involved are acting outside the provisions of their charter. Simply, this policy of narrowly focusing the interests of the groups works in the interest of containment. The official who outlined the policy, along with other administrators, believed that all "political movements can be contained as long as no coalitions are formed."[22]

Third, leadership elements are encouraged to get into as many organizations as possible, under the premise that it is easier to coopt two or three leaders than it is to coopt fifteen or twenty.

The associate superintendent asserted that if you create interlocking leadership patterns and you could influence that officer, you could create continuity in all organizations. This policy was eloquently stated by a member of the Department of Corrections task force:

> The British made good use of the native chiefs in governing their empire, educating them and getting them involved in the problem-solving process. You should make maximum use of paraprofessionals and inmate leaders. Tell them if they keep the peace, you will help them obtain their objectives.[23]

The adherents of this scientific management approach tend to see groups as an administrative asset rather than a liability. If the policy were successful, it would lead to groups structured along narrow lines of interest, effectively preventing any coordinated activity. At the same time the administration could be more effective by working with, or more accurately, working through certain leadership elements. Although the scientific school has not yet gained complete hegemony over administrative policy, its influence has grown to a point where it can exercise great power in policy formulation.

The other school of administrative thought concerning group activity views the group structure and its participants with considerable suspicion, if not outright cynicism. Adherents of this school tend to come from the custody side of the administration. They favor contacts with prisoners on an individual rather than collective basis. Although this cluster of administrators tends to be supportive of some groups (those that have been around for awhile and have proven helpful) it would generally prefer to see groups kept to a minimum.

According to these administrators, groups would not be necessary if the staff and administration were properly carrying out their assigned duties.[24] Groups are seen as a device to make maintaining security more troublesome. Almost every group is seen as a harbinger of some revolutionary doctrine. A quadrant administrator echoed the suspicions of many of the staff who share this perspective:

> I've seen evidence of the development of underground groups in the prison. During cell searches writings of Communist China are found. Bylaws for the development of political organizations have been found. I generally have an idea of who the people are within my quadrant who are involved in these activities. I suspect a good deal of men. And they usually show their true colors.[25]

A corrections lieutenant noted the manner in which the custody staff handles certain inmate groups:

> We watch the Black Muslims very carefully. Whenever they get too strong we rip off the leadership and send them to another institution. After a leader is shipped the group usually stabilizes until another strong leader emerges, then we have to rip them off again.[26]

Although these two groups of administrators have different ways of conceptualizing and approaching prisoner groups, they have on occasion joined forces in a unified effort to destroy certain groups. In the early period of group activity in West Prison (1970-1971) the administrators of the "scientific school" were relatively inexperienced at handling the groups: they found it difficult to maintain the proper equilibrium. Therefore, a number of ideologically advanced and organizationally efficient groups formed. During this period the administrators in the scientific school were forced to join forces with the custody-oriented group in order to curb these groups' activities.

One of the groups that formed during this period and was eventually disbanded by the administration was a black group, an offshoot of a Black History class that the education department was offering. Prisoners at West Prison who had participated in the group estimated that at its peak the Black History group had 150 active members. These persons claim that the group had never engaged in any illegal activities, but that administrators disbanded the group because of the large number of black prisoners who actively participated.

The associate superintendent of custody said, "The group had been taken over by Maoists who had threatened to use violence to meet their objectives. Approximately forty inmates were transferred to other institutions and the organization was broken."[27] The superintendent of West Prison elaborated on the tactics employed at the time. "The way we had to deal with this, is we isolate the hierarchy and ship them off to other places. *This group was actively recruiting other inmates and there was no other choice.*"[28] (Emphasis mine)

Although a chasm exists in the administration ranks over group activity, the relative strength of the scientific school has resulted in a clear picture of how the pluralist arena of groups should be put together.

If the administrative policy yielded the desirable results the group structure would bear several distinguishing marks. Groups should be kept small to avoid any group from establishing a powerful constituency within the institution.[29] The charter, required before a group is granted permission to function, should clearly spell out the ends and activities of the group. A group's "interests" must be drawn along narrow and contained boundaries to prevent the group from interfacing with others. Associations along religious, racial, and ethnic lines are tolerated, while interracial associations are actively discouraged.

The results that the administration expects this policy to yield are aimed at maximizing control and depolitizing the prison environment.[30] Depolitization should be achieved through the administration's ability to give legitimacy to certain groups' interests and deny it to others. By controlling the objectives of associations, the administration expects to control the way interests are formulated and acted upon.

Depolitization is also the expected result of other policy outputs. Participating in group activities should require prisoners to depolitize not only interests and objectives but language as well. Since the administration controls the distribution of resources, groups can be obliged to function in a quasi-bureaucratic, as opposed to an antagonistic or insurrectionist, mode if they want to receive certain disbursements such as money, privileges, or outside contact.

The process of acquiring resources also breeds a considerable amount of hostility among the groups. Since resources within the prison are very scarce, the competition for acquiring resources should be keen. It should be expected that when scarce resources are being sought by many competing groups, divisiveness rather than unity will emerge as the dominant political characteristic. Divisiveness can also be expected when the group structure is only large enough to incorporate a portion of the entire prison population.[31]

Finally, the administration suspects that the group structure will result in increased control of leadership elements. This strategy is a more visible variation of the process of bargaining between prison leaders and correction officers.[32]

Although we have seen that formal and informal barriers exist to prevent certain groups from forming, the administration expects that the group structure will be viewed by prisoners as a means for all interests and opinions to be represented. Within this view the administration itself would like to be viewed as a neutral force in relation to group policy.

Attitudes of the Prisoners

Most of the questions in the questionnaire dealt with the attitudes of the administrators and prisoners concerning group activity.[33] Similar questions were asked of group members (usually its leadership) and prisoners who did not participate, or only participated marginally, then or in the past.

The sample of prisoners was drawn from two quadrants in the prison. A representative from the Men's Advisory Council (MAC) of each of these quadrants was included in the group sample.

At the time I began the study, there were approximately seventeen groups which were known to the administration and functioned aboveground. Four of these were the MACs from each quadrant. During the seven weeks of interviews, the status of several groups was in flux. That is, there was some disagreement between the administration and the membership as to whether the group was permitted to meet and function.

In total, I interviewed members of twelve inmate groups, although the administration officially recognized only ten of these. One group was banned by the administration (the administrator and members both agreed on this point) and one was in a state of flux. The group responses that follow constitute only the responses of the ten groups officially recognized.

The responses of the other two groups were not included because it was impossible to determine whether they actually had a membership or following at that point or were groups in name only. Also, my primary concern was with groups that functioned aboveground as opposed to those that functioned clandestinely.

Of these ten groups, three claimed that they were permitted to function because of court-mandated policy. The other groups claimed that their beginning came as a response to prisoners' interest in the organization's ideas. The ethnic groups, including a Chicano, Indian and Black Muslim group, formed to increase ethnic awareness, according to the leadership.

Most of the groups, except the MACs, saw their roles as educational. One or two groups maintained that their major activities were social rather than educational. An officer in the Chicano group said the educational activities in the group included "everyday problems like cell shakedowns, a prerelease program, writing, theatre, poetry."[34]

All except two of the ten groups interviewed said that organizational leadership was chosen through democratic elections. In the Chicano group there were elections every six months. The member interviewed said that "each candidate develops a platform, like a tortilla on everybody's plate." In a somewhat more serious vein, he noted that "most people running for leadership promise to take the bus ride if it is necessary." Many of the groups required that members be active for specified periods before running for leadership positions. Although only two groups said they chose leaders on the basis of interest and motivation, rather than by elections, the administrators all said that none of the groups, except the MACs, chose leadership through elections. Administrators contended that leadership was chosen in popularity contests or on the basis of a prisoner's strength or ability to articulate.[35]

Structurally, the groups at West Prison conformed fairly well to the design embedded in the administration's policy. Except for a Peer Counseling Program which was quite distinct from all the other groups, membership of most groups ranged from twenty to fifty members.

Membership is generally limited through the use of covert rather than overt initiatives. The administration accomplishes this by manipulating the mobilization of bias in favor of some groups and away from others. This manipulation of bias is accomplished by increasing the quantity of uncertainty involved in the prisoner's choice to participate in a group. Administrators could let it be known that the Adult Authority might look unfavorably on a prisoner's participation in certain group activities. The success of this method was demonstrated when many prisoners mentioned that participation in certain groups would mean increased difficulty with the Adult Authority. This method of limiting a group's membership, by mobilizing either a real or imaginary bias, as suggested by Bachrach and Baratz, is similar to the use of biases to block decision making.

Besides keeping the membership of groups limited, the administration has also been somewhat successful in limiting and containing the interests of groups. Specifically the administration forced groups to put a formal limit on their range of interests as a condition for becoming chartered. So at least on paper, most groups are limited to very specific activities primarily associated with the real or perceived interests of the membership. Almost all of the groups (except the MAC) are organized along racial, ethnic, or religious lines. No interracial group of any consequence exists within the formal group structure. Dividing groups along these lines is a natural way to limit the interests and purposes of organization.

In their relations with the administration the groups appeared to have adopted a quasi-bureaucratic mode, which the administration expected would depolitize dialogue between the administration and prisoners.[36] Groups are required to fill out reams of forms covering every aspect of group activity (meetings, speakers, publications, outside guests).

A continued bureaucratic relationship with the administration was a necessity for almost every group. As Bachrach and Baratz observed, the invocation of rules, precedents, and procedures can act as an impediment in bringing forward a political challenge. The bureaucratic relationship between the administration and the groups acts as this sort of impediment by involving the organization in a series of operational rather than political procedures. In the realm of bureaucratic relations, the administration controls the expertise that shapes the modes of its interaction with prison groups.

The Unity Question

To evaluate the degree to which group participation affected the attitudes of prisoners who participated, it was instructive to compare the responses of participants and nonparticipants. A chasm between the responses of the two groups appeared on questions concerning group cooperation.

The actual question where the divergence occurred read, "Do most inmate groups cooperate and work with each other?" Of the ten group leaders who answered the question, only two felt that cooperation among the groups was good. Most explained this lack of cooperation by pointing the finger at the administration. A chairman of the MAC said, "The administration keeps us separate, won't allow us to come together. There's a divide and conquer strategy."[37] Another MAC chairman pointed out another dimension of the strategy. "[The] institution has and is thwarting all efforts at interinstitution communication among groups. Quad setup makes inmates from different quads unable to communicate with each other; the architectural setup keeps groups from cooperating and working together."[38]

Among twenty-eight non-group members, the responses to this question were almost evenly split: 34.4 percent—Yes, groups do cooperate; 43.3 percent—No, groups do not cooperate; 23.3 percent—Sometimes groups cooperate. Those who responded that groups do not cooperate offered reasons very different from those given by group members who also answered that groups do not cooperate. While the group respondents singled out the administration as the agent of disunity, the nongroup members tended to blame the groups themselves for the low level of cooperation. There was a general feeling that the groups were competing with one another for resources and administrative access. One of the prisoners who saw the disunity problem as a problem of competition described it in this way:

> They are really fighting against each other. It doesn't matter whether they are white, black, or Chicano groups, they are all trying to look good to the staff. Looking good to the staff, most of the time, involves making other groups look bad.[39]

What do these findings mean in terms of the expectation that competition between groups would occur? Prisoners who participated in a group were aware that cooperation between groups was problematic. Unlike the nongroup respondents, however, group members always pointed the finger of responsibility away from the groups themselves. Group membership produced a reluctance to criticize the policies of the group in the area of cooperation. On the other hand, nonparticipants placed the blame solely on the groups.

The truth lies somewhere in the middle. Administrative policy strives to create an environment where coalitions among groups becomes impossible. Undeniably, the administration does play an active role in sowing disunity among groups, a gambit group members correctly spotted. Yet, the policies followed by many groups also contribute to the levels of disunity. It is this dimension that group members failed to mention.[40] This is one area, but not the only area, where the perceptions of members and nonmembers collide.

The group structure has produced competition among groups. The varying perceptions about where the root of the competition lies should not obscure the fact that competition does exist, and many prisoners realize it. As expected, the results of many parties contending for finite and relatively scarce resources has resulted in intense competition.

This particular divergence of prisoner opinion also demonstrates that the group structure does result in the creation of certain barriers between group and nongroup prisoners. In this case, the barrier is perceptual. However, perceptual barriers are often destined to lead to divergence over actions and goals.

One of the aspects of this particular perceptual cleavage that is provocative is the positions held by the different sides. Considering the prospect that group activity was expected to produce a moderation of the views of the participants it might be expected that the group members would have a more moderate view of the administration's role. Of course, the opposite actually occurred. Members tended to be more critical than nonmembers about the role of the administration in contributing to disunity. Whether this shift away from expected attitudes is confined to this particular area, or will be evident throughout is a question to keep in mind when evaluating the responses that follow.

Another question, concerning unity, solicited opinions on the administration's attitude toward group activity. The question asked the prisoner to describe how he saw the administration's attitude toward groups. The respondents could choose between hostile, neutral, or helpful/supportive as an answer. The respondent was asked to elaborate and explain his answer.[41]

Four of the groups thought that the administration's attitude was generally hostile.[42] This would seem to be a logical extension of the position held by most groups in relation to the question involving cooperation. A respondent from the group aiding prisoners with legal problems thought that the administration's attitude was often concealed.

> While some of the groups think that the administration is helpful, they don't realize that the administration is using them as a barometer to measure what's going on in here.[43]

Three groups chose to answer "neutral" to describe the administration's position. Upon exploring the answer, two prisoners explained "neutral" as meaning that administration policy towards groups was flexible but usually nonaligned. Finally, three groups described the administration's attitude as helpful. "Helpful" usually indicated a belief that the administration would help a group to develop and meet certain goals.

When the same question was asked of nongroup members, the

responses were different. The most important difference occurred with those who chose "hostile" to characterize the administration's attitude. While 40 percent of the group members described the administration as hostile, only 18 percent of the twenty-eight nongroup members chose that answer. The remaining nongroup prisoners split their answers between neutral (39 percent) and helpful (43 percent). Once again, the expectations about attitude configuration are turned upside-down. The nongroup members are kinder in their evaluations of the administration than the group members.[44]

Although the respondent was asked to choose a word which best described the administration's general attitude, each prisoner was asked to elaborate on his choice.[45] When the answer was probed, many prisoners suggested that the administration's attitude could best be described as selective—favoring some groups and not others. Of a total of thirty-eight respondents, thirteen mentioned the policy of selectivity when they elaborated on their answers.

Representation

The next set of questions sought to probe the broad area of representation. Specifically, did the prisoners believe that the group-pluralist structure represented the major viewpoints or interests of the prisoners? Questions were designed to see if prisoners thought the pluralist structure acted as a springboard for the representation of major interests, and if the administration was viewed as a neutral force in allocating space for all opinions.

Was there a consensus concerning whether prisoners thought all viewpoints should be represented? Except for a few respondents who thought that the opinions of child molesters and medicated prisoners should not be represented, there was a general consensus that all viewpoints should be represented. Of the six administrators who were asked the question, all agreed that all inmates' opinions should be represented.[46]

After determining that a degree of consensus about representation existed, a question that sought to probe the degree of representation achieved in the present structure was poised. "Do you think that groups within the prison are generally representative of the major viewpoints held by prisoners?"

Among the group respondents the answers were split right down the middle—five groups said that all major viewpoints were represented and five groups said that they were not. Significantly, all the minority groups (the Chicanos, Black Muslims, Indians, Gays, and the legal group) thought that the groups in the present structure did not represent the viewpoint or interests of many prisoners. The two representatives of the MAC, the newspaper group and the Peer Council Group (Newspaper Group and Peer Counseling Group have the same leadership) all believed that all interests and viewpoints were represented by groups. Of those groups who believed that all interests were not represented, most mentioned legal, minority, and certain political interests as among those excluded.

Among the nongroup respondents, there was a more prevalent feeling that all viewpoints were not represented in the present pluralist configuration. Sixty-one percent of the prisoners thought that the major viewpoints of the prisoners were not represented within the group structure. There was a strong feeling that certain political and ethnic group interests were systematically excluded from participation. One prisoner characterized the workings of the group as a sort of game:

> . . . groups are allowed to pretend they're part of society. As soon as they stop pretending and begin to address themselves directly to the problems within the institution, the administration loses patience.[47]

There are at least two possible explanations of why certain interests are not represented in the pluralist arena. Conceivably, there could be interests, perhaps latent, that have not yet jelled. These interests could become part of the pluralist arena once structured and a supportive constituency organized. Another possibility is that the forces that shape the parameters of the pluralist arena, the administration, have constructed the landscape in a way that prohibits certain interests from congealing and becoming articulated.

In order to find out what the prisoners felt was the cause, or causes, of major viewpoints not being represented, they were asked: "Do you think the administration is in favor of all opinions being represented?" Among group members, the answers were once again split right down the middle—half thought the administration was in favor of all opinions being represented and half thought not. As might have been expected, the groups that answered the previous question positively (about groups representing the major viewpoints of prisoners) tended to answer this question positively. The groups who answered the previous question with a negative answered this question with a negative. However, there was some variance. Two groups switched sides on this question. One group which previously answered the question about "represented viewpoints" in the negative (major viewpoints are not represented) thought that the administration was in favor of all opinions being represented.[48] And one group moved in the opposite direction, thinking that major viewpoints were represented, although the administration was not in favor of all opinions being represented.[49]

When the nongroup participants were asked this question about the administration, their opinions varied sharply. Only 10 percent of the thirty nonparticipant respondents thought that the administration was in favor of all opinions being represented.[50] This seems to indicate a shift away from the previous two questions, where the group members tended to be more critical of the administration than nonparticipants were.

In responding to a follow-up question about which opinions the administration did not want represented there was a general consensus that political opinions, or opinions that did not support administration policy, were not favored by the administration. The responses to the follow-up question also revealed that certain prisoners do believe that the administration has been forced to accept certain inmate opinions. The case of Muslims, whose right to function within the institution was supported by the court, was mentioned by many of these prisoners.[51]

Structure versus Attitude

Although the structure and even the composition of the groups closely conform to expectations, the political attitudes that the administration assumed would have resulted from this structural configuration did not totally appear. This raises questions about the relationship between political structures and political attitudes.

The group structure was ideally supposed to be seen as an open arena for the articulation of prisoners' interests with the administration playing the role of referee. All legitimate (nonviolent) interests could be articulated and furthered through participation in the group structure.

Contrary to this, there was a strong feeling among the prisoners interviewed that groups did not represent the major viewpoints of the prison body. Sixty-one percent of the nonparticipants and fifty percent of the participants held this view. Coupled with this was an especially strong feeling among nonparticipants that the administration was not in favor of all views being represented.

Ninety percent of the nonparticipants believed that the administration was not in favor of all inmate opinions being represented. Fifty percent of the group members interviewed also believed this. Although group members had a more moderate view than nonmembers concerning the administration's willingness to see all interests represented, there was a powerful feeling that the administration was not in favor of wide representation of inmate opinion.

The responses from these two questions indicate that the prisoners did not perceive the pluralist structure in the way the administration thought they would. The administration was seen by approximately 70 percent of all prisoners interviewed as a partisan rather than a neutral force. In this area, it is fairly clear that prisoners were able to see through the form and into the substance of the group structure.

As to the objective of coopting prisoner leadership, the results were ambiguous. If the group leadership had been successfully coopted, it could be expected to hold significantly more temperate views toward the administration than counterparts in the general population. However, on the questions of group cooperation and the administration's attitude toward groups, the group members exhibited a more hostile view of the administration than nongroup members did. On the question of representativeness and the administration's role in group politics, the respondents from groups were moderate. To try to explain these switches it is necessary to examine each of the responses separately.

Being close to the actual transactions that occur between the administration and the groups, the group members would apparently be better equipped to judge the administration's attitude toward them. Historically, recruiting members of a community to interact in some formal way with a bureaucratic organization has often resulted in increased antagonism on the part of the participants rather than the expected cooptation. The local control project in school districts in New York City provides some evidence of the potential for increased hostility. One participant in a school board project related a sort of transformative experience:

> Governing board experience has changed my views on what can be accomplished . . . I had no idea that the time and effort to accomplish a needed response would be so long. I was not fully aware of the underhanded methods which could be used by the power structure to hinder self-determination.[52]

In terms of ends, the experiment in group organization and community control of education are both concerned with moving leadership elements onto a peaceful cooperation terrain. One scholar of the community control movement described what the bureaucracy could expect from community control experiments:

> [Community control should] in addition to eliminating numerous issues that have proven insoluable [*e.g.*, large scale busing to achieve racial integration], create a substantial class of black politicians with jobs to do other than agitating. Their jobs . . . would tend to place them among the moderate activists in the black community. It has been noted, moreover, that representatives of the poor who have regular dealings with the institutions of the larger society are susceptible to being coopted.[53]

These expectations were not wholly achieved during the first years of community control in education. Marilyn Gittell, who closely followed the beginnings of the project, reported that:

> The political ideology of the governing board members did change in Ocean Hill-Brownsville. Militants were not necessarily moderated, while at the same time many moderates became increasingly more militant. In P.S. 204, for example, the militants have not moderated their tone, but have become more sophisticated in their operation.[54]

Although the group leadership in the prison did not become more radical as a result of participation in group activity, neither were they completely captured and coopted by the administration. Segments of the group leadership structure were significantly moderated by participating. The administration succeeded in developing a cooperative relationship with some leaders, mainly from the ranks of the groups dominated by whites and those groups in existence for extended periods. But even most of these leaders were not concretely situated in the camp of the administration. Rather, they performed a precarious balancing act between the identification as a "convict" and their role as group leader.

Among the leaders of minority groups there seemed to be strong antiadministration sentiment. This cluster represented 50 percent of the group leadership.[55] Besides the sort of formal collusion necessary to maintain a legitimate status, there was almost no evidence of collusion between this segment of group leadership and the administration. In almost all instances this cluster of leaders' answers conformed closely.

The fact that only 18 percent of the nonparticipating prisoners, as opposed to 50 percent of the group members, were willing to describe the administration's attitude toward groups as hostile is indicative of several factors. First, as the administration expected, group activity does produce a chasm between the perceptions of participants and nonparticipants. Second, the prison body as a whole tends to view the relationship between the present groups and the administration as more collusionary than it actually is. The group of nonparticipants who responded with an answer of neutral or helpful/supportive seemed to be indicating a belief that the groups and administration are closely aligned. This perception was fueled by past events. Since it was known that a number of groups were officially disbanded and prohibited by the administration, it was assumed that those that remained must be compatible with the administration's desires. If these remaining groups survived in the pluralist arena, it seemed clear that the administration could not be hostile, for if the administration were hostile, the group couldn't exist.

Although this analysis is logically coherent, it does not reflect much more than its own tautological premises. In fact, the administration viewed several of the functioning groups with considerable hostility.[56] There were, however, several factors which prohibited the administration from putting an end to the groups' existence.

Administrative Limitations

Some groups that the administration viewed with hostility could not be easily disbanded because of their connections with the courts. At least three groups in the prison came into being as a result of favorable court decisions.

While the administration could conceivably have ended the tenure of these groups, given court permission, the task would have been arduous. If the administration had sought to outlaw these groups, they would almost certainly have challenged such a decision in court. In court, the burden of proof would have fallen squarely on the administration. It would have had to prove that the existence of the group interfered with a justified end of incarceration. While the administration could possibly have won such a case, the costs of mounting such a campaign would have been high, in terms of both public and departmental publicity. A local administrator is not anxious to involve Sacramento in legal battles that originate at the local level, nor would such action be helpful to his career.

Another factor that prevented the administration from disbanding some groups was the problem of balance. Since the administration felt that the group movement served some positive function, it could not delegitimate the group structure to the point where prisoners would refuse to participate at all. If the administration had prohibited all the groups that it felt hostile toward, only about half the present structure would have remained. In such an arena it would have been tremendously difficult for prisoners to continue to participate in the remaining groups.

This problem of balance is crucial. During the time I was at West Prison, an incident involving the Chicano group illustrated the difficulties. These difficulties unfolded soon after the administration had been forced to severely curb the functions of the Humanist group. In fact, the Humanist group itself claimed that the administration had forbade the group to meet. Earlier the administration had disbanded several other groups.

The incident began when the Chicano group used the word "Gringos" in its newsletter. The administration proceeded to ban the group from further printing and distribution of the newsletter. However, the associate superintendent of Inmate Affairs later confessed to certain doubts about the policy. He didn't want his decision to cause the Chicano group to cease operations, nor did he want custody people, or the state administration, to think that the group was out of hand. After some lengthy discussions with the group's leaders, a compromise was reached. The administration would allow the Chicano newsletter to be distributed to all prisoners if the group would agree to delete the word "Gringos".

From the administration's point of view the compromise was the perfect solution. Disbanding the Chicano group, known as a militant and principled organization, on the heels of disbanding the Humanist group would have assuredly diminished whatever credibility the group structure had. The interests of the administration were best served by a compromise solution, which explains why the administration was willing to compromise.[57]

Contrary to the nonparticipant majority view, the administration exhibited considerable hostility toward a number of groups. It was not ready to remove these groups from the arena because of pressures from the courts and state administration, and because of its own desire to have the pluralist structure appear legitimate. Yet, the fact that the nonparticipants envisaged the administration stance as "nonhostile" was itself a victory for the administration's policy. It had the effect of creating a severe division in political perceptions and knowledge among the prisoners.

Two more dimensions contained in this set of responses need analysis. Recall that 50 percent of the group members felt that the administration favored all opinions being represented and an equal percentage thought that the current structure did represent all viewpoints.

There is considerable reason to believe that the responses of group members in relation to representativeness, and the administration's view about interests are the product of a process of cooptation. But the cooptation has an element over and above the normal or expected administration cooptation. Participating in the group structure itself tends to have a coopting, or at least neutralizing, effect apart from any administrative stimulus. It must also be honestly noted that white participants showed more signs of being liable to one or another form of capture.

The cooptation that occurs as a result of group participation has a number of causes. The actual structure of the pluralist arena, tailored by administration policy decisions, is probably the most significant causal factor.

With group membership, as well as the number of groups, being held to minimum size, participating in group activity becomes a possibility for only a small number of prisoners. The effect of clustering a small number of prisoners in a relatively unknown structure and activity is increased suspicion among prisoners. Simply, many nonparticipating prisoners are highly suspicious of the relationship between group members and the administration, as well as the groups themselves. As a reaction to the widespread suspicion, group members tend to take on a sort of fortress mentality, which at times seems to blur political attitudes and produce seemingly contradictory responses to questions. As a group their answers tended to place a great deal more legitimacy in group politics and the administration's position in the scheme than the responses of their fellow prisoners did.[58]

An important cause of the cooptation, or ideological capture of group members, is related to the group structures. Combined with the relatively small size of the groups, the groups are well contained—sealed off from the rest of the population. Barriers on movement and communication make it very difficult for the groups to reach out to the entire population. Even if they could reach out to nonparticipants there is very little that they could offer in the way of participation, since a large membership is actively discouraged by the administration. The actual bureaucratic and formal regulatory relationship between a group and the administration is privileged—not open to public scrutiny. This serves to contain the various groups even further.

In a very real way, the centripetal force pulling group members into this defensive posture is a product of their own isolation. Without any public means to legitimate their activities to the rest of the prisoners, group members seem to make their actions and goals even more private; they defend their activities and structure to a point where the positions must be seen as unrepresentative of the factual evidence, and out of step with the vast majority of their fellow prisoners.

However, this cooptation was not universal. On the whole a pattern appeared which seemed to separate minority group members from white group members. Those representing groups of minority prisoners did not perceive the group structure as representative, nor the administration as anxious to achieve full representation. Because of their more militant stance toward the administration, and their frankness about group politics, some of these groups seemed to be held in high esteem by their constituencies as well as by many white prisoners.

Militant Groups

Many of the nonparticipants see things differently than group members. Their actual opinions about group activity may be suspicious, but cannot be characterized as completely hostile. The attitudes of the prison body have not become completely hostile because of the existence of groups that are seen as fighters. The actual number of these groups is decreasing, as the administration slowly and carefully weeds them out.

A reading of the cumulative attitudes of prisoners in relation to group activity comes from the responses to two questions. Prisoners were asked whether they thought that "groups have acted to increase or decrease the political awareness of prisoners". They were then asked to explain how that happened. Two-thirds of the thirty nonparticipating prisoners thought that group activity as a whole did raise political consciousness. Prisoners mentioned a variety of ways they thought awareness was increased, ranking from learning to work collectively with others to learning how to begin to capture state power. One prisoner saw the groups as an "educational conduit":

> There are different types of convicts now, more of the convicts are highly educated, guys who come in here from the outside know more about political ideology. The groups act as a vehicle for other convicts to get that political knowledge.[59]

Among group members, there was, not unexpectedly, a greater feeling that groups acted to increase political awareness. Seventy-eight percent of the nine group respondents held this view. A chairman of MAC thought that groups increased political awareness, but could do a more effective job:

> There are no people-power groups. Groups shouldn't be divided racially. Racial divisions among groups keeps the administration firmly in control. Should be a group that is not only discussing the issues in the prison, but talking about the problems of America and racial struggle.[60]

A representative of the Chicano group concretely explained the political education that goes on in that group:

> At yesterday's meeting someone talked of the history of the Latin American movement, history of Cuba, Paraguay, Chile . . . and how the Chicano struggle is intimately related to the struggle of Latin-American people.[61]

Along with the feeling that groups did act to raise consciousness and awareness, there was also the feeling that on balance group activity was a good thing. Prisoners were asked whether they thought inmate groups were good, bad, or made no difference. All the group respondents thought that group activity was good and many of the nonparticipants agreed. Seventy-seven percent of the thirty nonparticipants thought that groups were good for inmates, 16 percent thought they made no difference and 7 percent maintained that group activity was bad for inmates.

Groups: The Present Situation

If one were to establish a checklist of administration's policy successes and failures, it would read something like this: Structurally, the administration has succeeded in creating a group structure that conforms to its expectations—small groups, narrowly focused along ethnic and racial lines, operating in a bureaucratic mode. The expected competition between groups has come to fruition. It is not a war of all against all, but neither are the groups a united force. Finally, certain barriers between the participating minority and the excluded majority have developed. Although there are barriers, they are neither as high, nor as impenetrable as the administration might have expected.

A clear failure of the group policy initiative is its inability to win over the majority of prisoners, ideologically speaking. The expectation of James Park and the Sacramento administration that the group structure would be seen as an arena for prisoner participation, consequently decreasing insurgent political activity, has not come to pass. Prisoners generally view the group structure as more form than content. Whatever content there happens to be is seen as closely controlled by the administration. Finally, the administration itself is seen as a partisan force actively retarding the growth of certain interests held by groups of prisoners.

Although most groups are careful to keep their politics out of public view it takes only a bit of digging to get to the political base. At least seven groups (legitimate and illegitimate) regard their work and raison d'etre as political. So while each group explicitly denies to the administration that they are political, many of them carry out political work. The associate superintendent of custody, who offered his definition of nonpolitical groups (quoted earlier) was quick to add that many of the groups in the prison go far beyond what he defines as nonpolitical activity. Thus, the administration has not been successful in stifling the political dialogue, although it has altered some of the content.

There are aspects of the administration policy that cannot be correctly described as either success or failure. The area of prisoner leadership is one of these areas. The results of the policy in this most important area are ambiguous.

The administration has been able to reach a point where it has effectively excluded most of the militant inmates from participation in group activity. The number of illegal fringe groups, generally composed of more militant prisoners, show that many political activists have moved out of the group structure. Intelligence reports, included in the *Quarterly Management Reports*, put the number of radical fringe organizations at between seven and ten. This result did not come immediately, but was slowly achieved over the four years that the policy has been in place. During the early era of group activity the majority of the leadership was militant. Slowly and methodically, through the use of a variety of means, including the official suppression of activity, the administration has reduced the number and force of militants in the group movement.

While many of the prisoners and members of prison groups are politically oriented prisoners, their ability to use the group structure to attain political objectives has severely diminished. Because many of the groups are now led by moderate, and even collusionist elements, they find themselves more and more isolated. Their isolation prevents them from working in coalitions, and forces them into a position where the issues of their particular constituency (Chicano, black, etc.) dominate their agendas. While these issues have a significant political content and are important issues to raise, they will not, by themselves, lead to collective political action. In this sense, the isolation of the radical prisoners participating in group politics forces a reversion to political issues raised prior to the insurrections of 1970—nationalist rather than class politics. A member of the Chicano group explained that the racism, backwardness, and cooptation of many group leaders prevented them from working with other groups:

> At Quentin there were members of the Polar Bear Party. Polar Bear is a group that all the ethnic groups were able to work with because they weren't racist and they understood the nature of the institutions. In the past there were groups here that we could have a political relationship with. It's almost totally impossible now. That's too bad.[62]

The Men's Advisory Council

The Men's Advisory Council (MAC) is the oldest of the inmate groups. It has existed at West Prison, under various names for about fifteen years. A similar organization exists at East Prison and at most prisons in the United States.[63] In general, these organizations are designed to provide some formal mechanism to enable the prison administration to be aware of the opinions of prisoners. Awareness does not imply any legal, moral, or political obligation of the decision maker to take these considerations into account when formulating policy decisions.

The MAC at West Prison does not differ greatly from other prison representative organizations in terms of effectiveness. Thomas Murton, who has completed a comprehensive study of schemes of inmate representation, notes that:

> Almost without exception, attempts at inmate self-government have failed to involve the inmates to any great extent in the decision-making process. The history of inmate participation has been one characterized by superficial application of the general concept of inmate self-government.[64]

While the MAC at West Prison faces many of the same obstacles as its counterparts in other institutions, particular institutional features render it less effective than other such organizations are. The most significant obstacle is the relationship between the architecture (physicial structure) and institutional governance. West Prison is divided into four quadrants, each containing 600 prisoners and each represented by one MAC unit. Consequently, within the institution there are four independent MAC units representing the four institutional quadrants. Each MAC unit conducts its meetings and transactions with the program administrator from the quadrant. This particular structure of governance presents many problems. First, the program administrators have a limited range of decision-making power. In general, they can only decide matters particular to the quadrants they govern. Consequently, many of the issues and problems raised by individual MAC units fall outside the administrator's decision-making powers. Where the suggestions of the prisoners go beyond the administrator's jurisdiction, he acts as a conduit, or mediator, between the MAC and the administrative official empowered to make the decision. Thus, even the advisory relationship between the prisoner and decision maker is mediated by the program administrator.

The second problem concerns the ability of any MAC unit at the quadrant level to offer proposals that affect the entire prison population. The administration refuses to recognize the legitimacy of any quadrant's proposals that have institution-wide ramifications. And since no institution-wide representative organization exists, the problem is a classic Catch 22.

The final problem resulting from decentralization concerns the consistency of rule interpretation at the quadrant level. Both correction officers and program administrators interpret institutional rules differently. Certain quadrants are permitted varying degrees of latitude based on the administrator's interpretation of the rules. Thus, no standards exist for the MAC to use as guides for policy recommendations and to document agreed-on procedures.

Aside from these problems created by decentralization the administration faces certain others in achieving the proper relationship with the MAC. By virtue of the fact that MAC representatives are elected by the prisoners in each quadrant, as opposed to particular constituencies within the prison body, their position in the governance system is central. As with other groups the administration must strike the proper balance in its relationship with the MAC, to give it some legitimacy in the eyes of other prisoners and still control the range of political activity within the group. The problem of balance is magnified because of the broad constituency represented by the MAC.

In accomplishing this balance the administration has used a variety of techniques similar to those used in regulating other prison groups. Prisoners claim that certain prisoners were prohibited from serving on the MAC because of their political beliefs.[65] Disagreement emerged between administrators interviewed over the question of whether the administration had removed or prohibited certain prisoners from MAC activity. The associate superintendent of inmate affairs said,

> Rebels don't get a chance to be on the MAC. Administration makes efforts to sidetrack rebels from wanting to be on MAC. Program administrators have, in the past, turned down the choice of certain inmate representatives.

Program administrators interviewed denied that they had ever prohibited anyone from serving on MAC and knew of no case where an inmate was explicitly prohibited from serving. One said that he had "searched the bylaws and found no bylaw for removing inmates from the MAC."[66] However, he added, "even if there is no statute, all that need be done is to move an inmate from one quadrant to another, and consequently he won't be able to serve."

The superintendent denied ever having intervened in the election of inmate representation. "To the best of my knowledge," he added, "no program administrator has ever taken this sort of action." Qualifying this response, he acknowledged that he does not approve interinstitutional transfers, conceding that this method could have been used without his knowledge.

Since five prisoners interviewed claimed that other prisoners had been prohibited from serving on the MAC, and supplied the names of those prisoners to bolster their contention, there is strong evidence that prisoners had been stopped from serving on the MAC. The associate superintendent of inmate affairs also supported these prisoners' claims. It appears that the administration has utilized its prerogative of transfer to prevent dissident prisoners from serving on the MAC.

Although most of the administrators maintained that the MAC effectively represents the interests of the prisoners, a vast majority of the prisoners disagreed. In interviews the prisoners were asked if "the MAC effectively represents the interests of the prisoners." Seventy-one percent of the thirty nongroup prisoners who answered the question felt that the MAC did not represent the interests of prisoners. One prisoner's response sums up the range of responses.

> There is a total and complete lack of communication between MAC and the administration. The lack of communication is to a large degree, a product of the institutional setup. There is essentially four different institutions at West Prisons. All the P.A.'s interpret the rules and regulations in their own way. The MAC representatives from different quadrants, and the chairmen are not allowed to meet with each other and discuss institutional issues of concern to all inmates.[67]

On the question of effectiveness other group members tended to be kinder to the MAC than were the prisoners at large. Four of the ten group members interviewed felt that the MAC did effectively represent the interest of prisoners.

It is evident that most prisoners did not view the MAC as an effective medium for representation. This indicates that, as with the other prisoner groups, the prison administration failed to achieve the end of giving the groups a degree of legitimacy. However, contrary to the behavior of other groups, some MAC units were involved in an active struggle against administrative control.

This struggle is typified by the wholesale resignation of a quadrant council during the period of the study. It appears that the delegitimation of the MAC became so severe within this particular quadrant that prisoners could no longer serve without completely losing face. Members of the committee told me that they could no longer play the game of representing prisoners. According to them, the MAC served the interest of the administration, not the prisoners.

The Men's Advisory Council

A reading of all the minutes of the MAC meetings reveals that the committee took up a variety of issues with the administration—food, television and leisure time, visiting, complaints concerning officers, legal assistance, and the structure of the MAC itself. Seldom, if ever, was the administration willing to make any concession that would have increased the power or scope of the MAC. A few examples of the type of suggestions and the responses of the administration should help convey a sense of the relationship.

In order to increase the amount of legal information available to prisoners, the MAC in July 1972 made the following request:

> This is a request that the institutional paper (The Communicator) make sufficient space in which a legal column can run for the inmate population. The paper is supposed to be for the inmates and such a column would provide the information needed by the men here at West Prison.[68]

On August 9 the superintendent answered,

> I am in agreement with staff who are unanimous in rejecting the proposal. We do not have personnel sufficiently versed in the law to conduct such a column. It would require a great deal of research time, time which I feel would be better spent in a program. Also, there is a matter of space in the Communicator.
>
> Our inmate legal library, which we are constantly striving to improve, should take care of this need.[70]

In November the MAC submitted another request aimed at expanding the legal services available to prisoners. The MAC requested that a legal aid program be established for prisoners who need to engage in legal research.[70] The superintendent responded on January 15, 1973:

> We are now enlarging and improving our law library. This includes purchasing of texts and minor construction and adjustments within the library; also, additional training will be provided for involved staff. At present we have no plans to furnish professional legal advice or training in the law.[71]

These responses are typical of the communication between the MAC and the administration. The administration, in most instances, steadfastly resisted almost any modifications suggested by the MAC. There seemed to be a conscious administrative initiative to limit the MAC's advisory ability.

Among the major dilemmas faced by the MAC were the problems that arose from the decentralized form of prison governance. The minutes of the MAC meetings showed that this problem was clearly understood by MAC members, who consistently attempted to move the administration to modify its structure of governance to allow greater centralization and coordination of MAC activities. The administration had refused to accede to any request for change. A few examples of the types of requests made by the prisoners and the line of argumentation adopted by the administration follow.

On April 10, 1972, the MAC proposed that "all MAC chairmen and secretaries have a monthly unified business meeting."[72] The administration responded to the proposal two days later with the following statement:

> Disapproved, as tendency to blur quad lines. I feel little would be gained through such meetings, and suggest you work out any interquad problems through your program administrators who do get together each Monday.[73]

These sorts of demands were issued several times a year for the five-year period that I reviewed. Different types of structural suggestions were offered, but all were intended to centralize the functions of the MAC. For example, the MAC proposed the following on March 12, 1975:

> Proposed: That an inmate coordinator chosen from presently active and honorably retired MAC chairmen be nominated by the associate superintendent and approved by each Quad MAC Council, term of service to be six months.

The administration responded in its usual manner. The superintendent replied that:

> Such an office would be a first step toward blurring of quad lines, which were intentionally set up so that quads would be distinct and apart. Our present system, if properly used, provides a forum for expression and dialogue with the administration.[74]

Despite five years of steadfast opposition, the administration decided in November 1975 to allow the MAC councils from the different quadrants to hold a joint quarterly meeting with the superintendent. This modification was proposed less than a month after the mass resignation of a quadrant council—a period in which the institution of the MAC was under severe attack. While this was a significant change it came at a point where the political momentum of the MAC was at a low. Members of the councils were disillusioned and cynical, and the majority of prisoners held the MAC in low esteem. Therefore, the timing of the administration's concession may have diluted some of the potential effects of the move toward a more centralized pattern of inmate representation.

The Limits of Representation

As a model of governance the MAC and other prisoner representative organizations bear intense similarities to many historical and contemporary forms of political organization. Murton equates this model of political representation with various forms appearing in neocolonial relationships.

> The self-government model is in reality patterned after colonialism in that some degree of autonomy over local affairs may be granted to a colony as a subdivision of the empire.
>
> This practice historically has been implemented at that time when demands for local rule emerge simultaneously with the realization that it would be too expensive or too impractical to exercise total control over the colonists.
>
> In this sense, prisoners are colonists in a hostile foreign environment. When "the natives get restless" it may become expedient to grant to the inmates some control over their daily lives.
>
> Self-government (then) is not synonymous with self-rule but instead a paternalistic exercise as a gesture to create the impression of government without the inherent threat to the established order such power would entail. Also, administrators can benefit from the input from the inmates . . . not as an exercise in responsibility but as a method to accomplish greater control. In this sense, prison management has been operative as military government imposed during war on foreign communities in the sense that the alien power maintains control with the assistance of collaborators.[75]

On the community level the political activities of the 1960s hatched a number of political forms whose stated purpose was to localize decision-making by including the direct participation of people in the community. Many of these community control experiments were launched in black ghettos to deal with issues like housing, education, police, and community services. On a larger scale, Jerome Skolnick views community control experiences as a result of efforts to broaden the range of participation afforded the citizens:

> A common theme, from the ghetto to the university, is the rejection of dependency and external control, a staking of new boundaries, and a demand for significant control over events within those boundaries.[76]

For the minority population, community control was envisioned by some as a means to raise citizenship status by bringing decision-making under the control of those historically excluded from political participation. Community participation, in this view, is an alternative to the full political integration of blacks:

> It is a movement to allow black people to experience majority status and to make significant decisions affecting their lives which heretofore have been

made by a majority apathetic or hostile to their aspirations. Community control would build black power by providing a basis for organization and through its concentration of resources.[77]

The result of community control should be an increase in the political efficiency of those participating, according to the view of democratic theorists, such as Robert Dahl:

Participation and political confidence evidently reinforce one another. A citizen with a high sense of political efficiency is more likely to participate in politics than a citizen pessimistic about the chances of influencing local officials. Participation in turn reinforces confidence.[78]

Although the community control projects in the community (specifically New York) are not identical to those within the prison, they are close enough to speak about them in tandem. In West Prison and East Prison evidence strongly suggests that the prisoner representative organizations have not increased the political efficacy of the participants or produced extended control over the decisions that affect the prisoners' lives.[79]

In general, the administrations of West Prison and East Prison appeared to be more responsive to the initiatives of other inmate groups than they were to those of the MAC. In a period characterized by pluralistic group representation, the MAC is the one prison organization that pushes collective demands. The issues and disbursements requested by the MAC are generally those that affect the entire prison body rather than a particular constituency. Therefore, the effect of a favorable administrative ruling in regard to issues generated by the MAC has a much wider impact than favorable decisions that affect other prisoner groups.

As a general rule, the political impact of a request made by the MAC seemed inversely proportional to the likelihood that the request would be granted. If a request had considerable political impact or content, such as the demand to make legal aid and advice more accessible, it was quite likely that the administrator would refuse the request. If a request had a limited political impact, such as changing certain foodstuffs available in the canteen, the probability that the administration would grant the request was much greater. Although other factors bore on the administration's decision, the political impact of a demand far outweighed other considerations, and could be mechanically applied to explain past decisions and predict future ones.

The potential political impact of any administrative decision concerning a MAC issue was greater because of the collective nature of the organization. Thus, controlling the range of political issues was more important in regard to the MAC than it was for other organizations.

As a result, the MAC found itself faced with the contradiction that it could be most effective, in technical terms, when it was least political. If the MAC cooperated in depoliticizing its agenda the administration would cooperate by rendering more favorable decisions.

Inmate representation organizations demonstrate that democracy in form (participatory election) will not necessarily result in democracy in practice. Several conditions must obtain before a democratic form can conceivably produce a democratic output. Two of these conditions are worth a brief mention.[80]

First, there must be a willingness on the part of the institution or agent of power to cede some portion of its decision-making powers to the participants. There must be a genuine willingness to participate in a power-sharing arrangement. This includes a willingness to make available the resources and instruments necessary for effective decision-making. In the case of West Prison these conditions were not met. There was no serious effort to allow prisoners to obtain the resources and instruments necessary for them to act even in an advisory capacity. Participation within West Prison was a showpiece, to be dusted off and displayed to interested outside parties, then put back on the shelf again to atrophy.

Second, the decisions that reach the agenda must be of some consequence.[81] If the participants can only act on decisions that have little bearing on the direction of institutional power, participation matters little. Participation inside the prison contains built-in filters to dilute its political content. When political stakes are involved, this form of participation does not produce even the smallest opportunity to win.

Like the community control experiments, such as the New York City school project, the representative schemes within the prison lack muscle. These models have failed to provide any real measure of political control, or significantly alter the feelings of political competence held by community participants and their constituencies. It is safe to conclude that these participatory mechanisms were designed to preserve institutional power relations rather than transform them. To this end, these programs have been most effective.

Individual Rights

One of the three major areas of prisoners' grievances concerned individual rights. Although the areas of collective and individual rights are closely related, they can be treated as separate entities. Individual rights are entitlements associated with governance processes in the institution, or with quality of life issues. In the governance process individual rights include due process protections in disciplinary procedures, rights associated with First

Amendment guarantees, such as freedom to read desired publications and correspond freely, and the right to have input and redress procedures in administrative decisions. Quality of life issues are those which affect personal choices, such as the right to wear one's own clothes rather than institutional garb.

To examine the wide-ranging area of individual rights it was necessary to isolate particular areas of prison governance and examine changes in procedure since the prisoners' movement, and the attitudes of the prisoners concerning these changes. The questionnaire examined the areas of treatment, training, classification and discipline. Of these, discipline was the most important. Disciplinary procedures are in many ways the hallmark of the prison governance system. For the prisoner, the potential for harm as a result of a disciplinary hearing makes this area crucial.

The questions dealing with treatment, training, and classification were broadly phrased to capture the open-endedness of these procedures. The demands in the area of individual rights, at the institutional level, were aimed at providing the prisoner with a means of having some formal way of appealing administrative decisions. The prisoner wanted to find a means of participating in important administrative decisions.

Respondents were asked "How much say should the prisoner have in treatment and training programs?" They could choose among five responses: no say; very little; some say; as much as the administration; more than the administration. This question is designed to measure the levels of participation that prisoners think they should be accorded. This is followed by the question: "Do prisoners have a say in treatment and training programs?" Respondents could choose among four answers: a lot of say; some; little; none. Respondents were encouraged to elaborate on their responses to both questions.

Most of the administrators thought that prisoners should have "as much say as the administration" in deciding the appropriate treatment and training program for the prisoner. Prisoners generally agreed that an equal role in deciding treatment and training programs was a proper decisional balance, although a significant percentage thought it should have more than the administration, and a small percentage thought it should have less.[82] There was a general feeling that the prisoner was a worthy judge of what he wants to do and what he is capable of doing. This was the rationale usually offered by the prisoners to justify their claim that they should equally share in the decision-making process.

The consensus on the appropriate role in the decision-making process for the prisoner is shattered when the terrain is shifted from the theoretical to the actual. When asked how much of a say prisoners actually have in training and treatment allocations and decisions, there is much divergence between prisoners and the administration. Most of the administrators maintained that prisoners had either "some say" or "a lot of say" in decisions. Most of the prisoners, however, claimed to have very little or no say in decisions. Thirty-two percent of the thirty-four prisoner respondents answered the question with "very little say" and half answered "no say". The remaining 18 percent replied "some say" or "a lot of say".

The same pattern emerged in questions relating to the role of prisoners in influencing job and custody assignment. Prisoners felt that although they had the right to some formal input, their input was not effective in influencing administration decisions.

Although pressures generated by the prisoners' movement, externally through the courts and outside groups, and internally by protest actions had the effect of establishing mechanisms for prisoners to have some input into classification, custody and treatment decisions, most prisoners feel that that right is meaningless in practice.[83]

In California, much of the early prison litigation concerned disciplinary procedures. Before this, adjudication of disciplinary charges was totally controlled by the administration; the prisoner had little opportunity to intervene in his own behalf.

Before the prisoners' movement, there were three types of charges that could be filed against prisoners accused of rule infractions, known as CDC 115s and subdivided into "administration," "disturbance" and "major" categories. A hearing officer decided on the category. The various categories of charges were heard by different institutional disciplinary boards.

Each housing unit within the institution had three officers who sat on the disciplinary committee. Nothing prohibited officers involved in the incident from sitting on the committee. The instructions involving adjudication stated that the committee "inform the inmate of the charges against him, receive his plea of guilty or not guilty".[84]

Inmates were neither given copies, nor permitted to see the 115 form lodged against them. The author of the disciplinary charge was not present during the hearing. A prisoner was neither entitled to call witnesses nor confront his accuser, nor was he entitled to the assistance of a lawyer, a staff member, or other inmates who might help in his defense. There were absolutely no standards to determine what evidence was admissible and what basis (reasonable doubt, substantial evidence) should be used to judge guilt or innocence. There was no right of appeal. Prisoners could receive sentences of thirty days or more in isolation cells. Records of all offenses and sentences were maintained for the paroling authority.

The first major court case concerning discipline in California was *Clutchette* v. *Procunier* (1971). Plaintiff Clutchette charged that disciplinary procedures "by which charges of violation of prison rules are adjudicated do not contain sufficient due process safeguards, consistent with the nature of the potential punishment, to meet the standards of the Fourteenth Amendment.[85] Citing the case of *Goldberg* v. *Kelly*, the court held that prisoners must be given procedural due process protection when subject to "grievous loss" at the hands of the state.[86] The court described a minimum set of punishments to be considered "grievous loss." These included:

1. Violations punishable by indefinite confinement in the adjustment center or segregation.
2. Violations, the punishment for which may tend to increase a prisoner's sentence; that is, those which must be referred to the Adult Authority.
3. Violations which may result in a fine or forfeiture.
4. Violations which may result in any type of isolation confinement longer than ten days.
5. Violations which are referred to the district attorney for criminal prosecution.

The court ruled that the prison administration must provide the prisoner with a variety of due process protections. Prisoners, according to the decision, are entitled to written notice of the charges and "sufficient time and information to prepare any defense on the merits."[87] The decision gives prisoners the right to appropriate counsel:

> While only counsel is acceptable in the case of an offense which will be referred to the district attorney, in all other cases prisoners should not be precluded from providing an adequate counsel substitute.[88]

Additionally, the decision mandates disciplinary committees to establish some "evidentiary criteria" to guide their decisions and that committees must be composed of "unbiased fact finders." Finally, the court ordered the establishment of a uniform appeal procedure.[89]

The ruling in *Clutchette* v. *Procunier* was a significant victory for the prisoners' movement. It appeared to move the prisoner into closer proximity with rights enjoyed by members of the outside political community.

Administrative Reaction

Clutchette v. *Procunier* and subsequent court decisions mandated procedures for changing the disciplinary process. As a result, the state developed system-wide policies to meet what it interpreted to be the meaning of the court's ruling. Disciplinary procedures at West Prison were representative of the changes thus mandated by the state.

Under the new procedures, amended several times, two types of disciplinary 115s can be issued; an administrative 115 for "infractions which pose no threat to the safety or security of the staff, inmates, or the institution,"[90] or serious "violations which constitute a misdemeanor or a felony, or violation of the rules or regulations which pose a threat to the safety of staff or inmate."[91] Prisoners are entitled to a copy of the charge. A program administrator decides whether the charge should be classified as "administrative" or "serious." Although there are some criteria to determine categories, similar charges often bring dissimilar decisions.

Except for some "serious" violations, adjudicated by the institutional disciplinary board, hearings are generally conducted at the quadrant level. The composition of the hearing board depends on the classification of the charge.

For example, the state contends that all administrative charges are not subject to the conditions set forth in *Clutchette* v. *Procunier*. Although some of the remedies for administration rule violation fit within those categories established by the court, the administration regards an "administrative 115" as posing an insufficient potential injury to the inmate to warrant due process protection. An example of an injury that could result from administrative 115 charges, anticipated by the court and circumvented by state policy, concerns the effect of a disciplinary decision on the prisoner's chance of release. The director's rules state:

> When an inmate is held responsible for the act charged, all documents prepared by the reporting employee and other officials and employees of the department will be placed in the inmate's central file.[92]

This central file provides the only written evidence for evaluation by the paroling authority.

Thus, prisoners charged with "administrative" violations and subject to "grievous loss" as a result of disciplinary hearings are afforded few due process protections. The director's rules state, "The inmate does not have the right to call witnesses, or to have an investigative officer assigned." Prisoners do have the right to be present at the hearing, state their defense, and appeal the decision.[93]

In the case of serious violations, prisoners are afforded a larger complement of rights, including the right to substitute counsel, an investigating officer, witnesses, and appeal. However, these rights are often specious. For example, all investigation officers are members of the corrections staff, who are surely not unbiased fact finders. Other rights are not automatically operative, but can only be asserted with agreement from a member of the administration or custody staff serving as a hearing officer. The director's rules state:

> The inmate may request witnesses to attend the hearing, and they will be called unless the person conducting the hearing has specific reasons to deny this request. Such reasons may include: danger to the safety of the witness, lack of relevant information or the unavailability of witnesses. If an inmate's request for a witness is denied, the reasons will be documented on the CDC Form 115. The reporting employee with relevant information will be expected to attend if requested by the inmate. Under the direction of the person conducting the hearing, the inmate has the right to ask questions of all witnesses.[94]

It is highly unlikely that democratic procedures, such as due process, can be effectively executed in an institution like the prison without the active, enthusiastic, and genuine support of the officials. In order to provide a genuine democratic procedure there must be more than a willingness, there must be an active and total commitment. If such a commitment is not present, thousands of avenues of sabotage exist. This holds for most institutions, but is particularly pertinent to clientist institutional procedures such as welfare and prison hearings where the individual cannot easily garner resources for redress. Successful reform is always contingent on the willingness of an institution's personnel to be reformed.

What is even more important, officials at West Prison do not demonstrate any desire to be reformed, especially by the court, which they view with skepticism and often with fierce hostility. When the associate superintendent for Custody, the official charged with responsibility for disciplinary procedures, was questioned about the importance of rights for prisoners in disciplinary procedures he said,

> I don't believe that the staff are out to screw inmates. The staff goes out of their way to be fair . . . Recent decisions of the court have come about from pressure by people on the outside, who don't know what is going on inside the institution, who don't know what it is like, who think we are totalitarians, or that the institution is like a James Cagney movie.[95]

In regard to the efficacy of particular procedures (investigative officers) he expressed similar hostility:

> Investigators are sometimes assigned to serious 115s . . . but investigators are useless, it's a waste of time, they simply do mechanical investigations, it's not worth it.[96]

A program administrator expressed similar sentiments when the same question was posed. Referring to inmate rights he responded this way:

> The rights that the inmates have presently, they don't know how to use them, so it doesn't matter whether they are given them or not.
>
> The public doesn't want inmates to have rights. I am supposed to serve the interests of the public, so I don't think inmates should have rights.[97]

The sentiments of a senior correction officer interviewed are very close to those of the administrators cited. On the subject of rights, the officer, who is in charge of a quadrant, and, like the program administrator, one of the chief disciplinary officers in the quadrant, related the following:

> Inmates have too many rights now, it creates a tremendous workload for the staff, very few officers ever write bad beefs. *If an inmate has a beef he has it coming*. We should have more inmates who are willing to admit that they broke a rule and are willing to take their punishment. Most of the inmates want to fight anything.[98] (Emphasis mine.)

Only one administrator interviewed agreed with the premise of the court, that the rights of prisoners should match the gravity of the proceedings. Other administrators stated differing qualifications concerning prison rights, but the general consensus pointed toward decreasing or eliminating prisoners' rights rather than expansion or acceptance.

The administration's resistance to the expansion of prisoners' rights has severe effects on the manner in which rights mandated by the court are instituted. Since the prisoners are dependent on the administrator for information, their knowledge of rights that are available for use depends on the administration's willingness to make such information public. Although prisoners can obtain certain information from the community, the administration is the only conduit of information for the entire institution.

Given the administration's skepticism about prisoners' rights it is not surprising that it has made only limited efforts to inform prisoners of their legal and procedural rights. The superintendent's response to the MAC's request for permission to run a legal column in the prison newspaper is indicative of the resistance to the development of autonomous channels of information. That response is worth quoting again.

> I am in agreement with staff who are unanimous in rejecting the proposal. We do not have personnel sufficiently versed in the law to conduct such a column. It would require a great deal of research time, time which I feel would be better spent in a program. Also, there is a matter of space in the Communicator.[99]

A program administrator described the manner in which changes in legal rights for prisoners are brought to the attention of the prisoners. The procedure involves "hanging up a paper on the bulletin board for the clerks to read, and to tell the other people that they have these rights.[100]

As a consequence of these methods few prisoners in the institution fully know what rights they have in disciplinary proceedings. Only three out of thirty-five prisoners questioned were able to recall fully the rights available to them in disciplinary proceedings. Others knew some rights, but only a minute percentage knew all their rights. Consequently, even those rights mandated by the court have not fully reached, or are likely to reach, their intended recipients.

Although the knowledge concerning disciplinary rights was not extensive, prisoners did realize that they had certain rights. Most prisoners knew they had the right to plead guilty or not guilty, appeal a decision and have an investigating officer. Therefore, there was a basis for prisoners to answer questions concerning the effectiveness of the rights they recognized having.

When asked whether the rights they had at disciplinary hearings were important, or made any difference, approximately 65 percent of the thirty prisoners answered in the negative—rights don't make any difference. Many prisoners contended that the administration was so opposed to providing hearings with a full complement of rights that they often dropped charges from serious to administrative to avoid a full hearing.

A negative answer concerning the importance of rights does not mean that prisoners do not attempt to use those rights they know of. Nor does it mean they would not care if rights were revoked. Instead, a negative response seemed most often to indicate a feeling that the court decisions affecting disciplinary hearings have not significantly changed the legal or political status of the prisoner. Coupled with this is a widespread feeling that rights have neither increased the efficacy of the prisoner or significantly altered the chances of conviction. Finally, there was a wide consensus that disciplinary hearings were basically unfair in the past and are equally unfair now.

A comparison between the conviction rate before and after the Sacramento-ordered changes in disciplinary procedures could not be made because statistics were unavailable. Thus it was not possible to prove whether the rights have made a difference in the conviction rate.

Information was available, however, concerning the appeals procedure; it is possible to determine the extent to which prisoners availed themselves of this particular right and the final outcome of these procedures.

Data for a nine-month period in 1975 indicate that the appeal procedures for disciplinary determinations is rarely used by the prisoners. In one quarter of 1975, 599 disciplinary charges, 371 administrative charges and 228 serious charges were issued. Of the 599 determinations, 73 were appealed. Of 73 first-level appeals, 1 was upheld. Thirty prisoners undertook second-level appeals to the superintendent, where 4 appeals were upheld.[101]

In the next quarter there were 493 disciplinary determinations of which 38 were appealed. At the first level of appeal none was upheld. At the second level of appeal, 1 appeal out of 17 was upheld. In the third quarter, there were 535 disciplinary determinations. These brought 25 appeals, none of which was upheld at the first or second levels. *In total, out of 1,627 disciplinary determinations, only 136 were appealed, with only a total of 6 appeals resulting in a finding for the prisoner.*[102] (Emphasis mine.)

These staggering figures reveal empirically what the prisoners had expressed intuitively—the rights given to the prisoner in disciplinary hearings don't make much difference. The hope that the rulings of the court would significantly raise the status of the prisoner to somewhere near that of the member of the outside political community is quickly vanishing.

Notes

1. Herbert Marcuse, *One Dimensional Man*, p. 12.

2. Although the market is the primary means of distributing resources in the outside community, the state has great leverage in controlling the distribution and use of these resources. Thus, the role of the state and prison officials in maintaining and using the unequal distribution of resources within the pluralist arena, and the society as a whole, are very similar. For an elaboration of the role of the state in the pluralist network, see Herbert Marcuse, Robert Paul Wolfe and Barrington Moore, *A Critique of Pure Tolerance* (Boston: Beacon Press, 1971), especially the Wolfe essay.

3. Peter Bachrach and Morton S. Baratz, *Power and Poverty* (London: Oxford University Press, 1970), p. 44. Although Bachrach and Baratz are credited with developing an analysis of the role of nondecision, it is not a particularly new finding. The effect of the shaping of the political arena to conform to existing biases is eloquently formulated in George Lukac, *History and Class Consciousness*, in the essay entitled "Reification and the Consciousness of the Proletariat."

4. Bachrach and Baratz, *Power and Poverty*, p. 44.

5. The whole area of the use of force by the correction staff in institutions has been given little attention in this study. Ignoring the prime importance of force and repression is necessary in order to focus on the other more subtle modes of political and social control exercised in prisons. While the sparse attention devoted to the use of force is a conscious omission, it is nevertheless, a significant missing part. I can only compensate by calling attention to the fact that a great deal of good work has already been done on this aspect of institutionalization, while little work has been done on the concerns addressed in this study. A good beginning point for information concerning the use of police force could include a reading of Jackson, *Soledad Brother*, Wright, ed. *The Politics of Punishment*, Browning, *Prison Life*, Leo Carroll, *Hacks, Blacks and Cons.*

6. Bachrach and Baratz, *Power and Poverty*, p. 44.

7. Quoted in Bachrach and Baratz, *Power and Poverty*, p. 45. This is an important idea to keep in mind, since we will discuss the participatory system in the prison. At West Prison, the inmate representation body is called

the MAC (Men's Advisory Council) and at East Prison the PRC, (Prisoners Representation Committee).

8. Bachrach and Baratz, *Power and Poverty*, p. 45.

9. Ibid., p. 45.

10. Ibid., p. 45.

11. California Department of Corrections, Management Review Questionnaire, October 17, 1975, "Inmate Groups." The figures regarding inmate participation are probably unreliable because of the vast variability in numbers from quarter to quarter. For example, in the last quarter of 1974-75 the administration listed the number of prisoners involved in group activity as 859. A drop of 357 prisoners from groups in six months is highly unlikely. Other quarterly reports reveal the same pattern of highly erratic estimates. The number 400 represents the mean number of all the estimates that I saw and represents if not the exact number, a good ball-park estimate.

12. Richard H. McCleery, "Communication Patterns as Bases of Authority and Power," in G. Grosser, ed. *Theoretical Studies in Social Organization of the Prison*, p. 53.

13. Ibid. McCleery notes that a similar shift occurred when a new warden was appointed and a policy reformulation commenced.

14. The fact that guidelines are formalized shows a significant administration shift from the period where custody controlled the communication system. In this period, according to McCleery, few formal written procedures and guidelines existed. McCleery, "Communication Patterns as Bases of Authority and Power," in Grosser, *Theoretical Studies*.

15. California Department of Corrections, *Administration Manual*, September 3, 1974, Section 323.04.

16. Interview with associate superintendent for inmate affairs.

17. California Department of Corrections, *Administration Manual*, September 3, 1974, Section 323.05.

18. Ibid., Section 323.06, added December 1973.

19. Ibid.

20. Harry Braverman, *Labor and Monopoly Capital* (New York: Monthly Review Press, 1974), p. 90.

21. Interview with associate superintendent for Classification and Treatment.

22. Ibid.

23. California Department of Corrections, "Task Force on Violence," p. 9.

24. "Assigned duties," is meant to imply that the "other element" of the administration has hampered their ability to function by intruding on their terrain.

25. Interview with quadrant administrator.

26. Interview with correctional lieutenant.

27. Interview with associate superintendent of custody.

28. Interview with superintendent.

29. The associate superintendent for classification and treatment informed me that "the director's office has discouraged big groups. Big groups are much harder to handle." In both East and West Prisons various administration policies kept groups, especially groups with any social, ethnic or political orientation, from expanding their membership.

30. I should note at this point that much of what I have described so far and much of what will follow implicitly contradicts much of the literature that has appeared on the subject of the politization of prisoners. I believe that all of the current work that I have read on this subject suffers from many deficiencies, and possibly, some wishful thinking. Two recent studies that have attempted to delve into the area of politization are Steven Woolpert, "*The Political Attitudes of Prison Inmates*." This study was funded by Law Enforcement Assistance Administration, U.S. Department of Justice. Also, Erika Schmidt Fairchild, *Crime and Politics: A Study of Prisons*, Ph.D. dissertation, University of Washington, 1974. Each of these studies follows different methodological and analytic streams; and each has serious flaws in both methodology and analysis. In appendix D these flaws are discussed at some length.

31. This is not to say that all prisoners would engage in group activities if the structure permitted. What is important is that the structure does not permit it, and consequently establishes a barrier between large aggregates of prisoners. Whether the barrier is artificial or real is less important than the fact that a barrier exists. This is crucial, since the group process is not only aimed at maximizing control of those directly involved in group activity but also of the entire prison population.

32. The bargaining process, where correction officers grant certain favors to powerful prisoners who in return help the correction staff maintain "surface order" in the institution, has been thought to have operated for many years. One of the interesting results of the period of politization was a decrease in the quantity and quality of the bargaining. After the period of politization it was more difficult to get many of the powerful prisoners to participate in bargaining. The associate superintendent of East Prison confirmed this trend in an interview. The powerful prisoners would not bargain with correction officers any longer. Correction officers attempted to recruit some less powerful prisoners to fill the void, but were relatively unsuccessful. The expected result of group activity would be a formalization of the bargaining procedure with one major variation. Instead of correction officers being the major bargaining party, much of the bargaining would be done by the administration itself. For a good article on prison bargaining, see Robert Reich, "Bargaining in Correctional Institutions:

Restructuring the Relations between the Inmate and Prison Authority," *Yale Law Review*, March 1972.

33. The questionnaire is reproduced as appendix B.

34. Interview with Chicano group.

35. I did not delve into what might be the differences between a "popularity contest" and an election, nor did I make a systematic attempt to ascertain who was telling the truth.

36. The associate superintendent for inmate affairs designated learning to work in a bureaucracy as one of the prime objectives of the prison group structure. Interview.

37. Interview with quad MAC chairman—32-year-old white inmate.

38. Interview with quad MAC chairman—26-year-old white inmate.

39. Interview with a 30-year-old black prisoner.

40. Group members' failure to mention these contributions to disunity does not mean that they do not recognize that they make such a contribution. It could not be ascertained whether such a recognition does or does not exist. What is important is that membership in the group structure apparently means giving higher priority, or top priority, to the administration role.

41. Appendix B, question 1, (Administration section). Although directions say to probe answers other than 'neutral', in reality all answers were probed.

42. The two groups I spoke with who did not have official status (one officially disbanded and the other group whose status was uncertain) not unexpectedly described the administration's attitude as hostile. Although the question specifically asked about the administration's attitude toward all groups, it is entirely possible that some of the responses reflected perceptions of fact about the administration's attitude toward the group from which the respondent came. Although this question might have profitably been asked in two parts (particular and general), the responses elicited from the one question still seem relatively pure. Since it is always difficult, if not impossible, to differentiate a response based on personal experience from a response based on objective fact, the possibility of this sort of contamination always looms large. Therefore, I assume that this particular question, which could have admittedly been better broken up into two questions, and come closer to differentiating between types of responses, is not significantly more contaminated than other questions that were posed.

43. Interview with a white prisoner in his late fifties.

44. Judging the responses from these two questions, it could be maintained that the administration's expectation that group leaders could be coopted has not been realized. In fact, the opposite seems to be occurring.

45. Some of the prisoners who thought the administration policy differed based on the group involved, characterized the administration's

general attitude as helpful. The prisoners explained their answer by saying that since the administration had disbanded the groups it didn't like, its attitude toward the remaining groups was generally helpful.

46. The answers of the administration are curious. During the course of most interviews the administration consistently referred to group opinions that should not have representation. The case of the Black History group, mentioned earlier, is a good example. The associate superintendent of custody during an interview, pointed out several groups he was presently watching: "I'm concerned with the Humanist group, which developed as agnostics and have been taken over by a group of blacks who are using their facilities to meet. This is an organization that has revolutionary potential, and I'm watching it closely." The administration will usually characterize opinions that it feels shouldn't be represented as revolutionary.

47. Interview with 45-year-old black inmate.

48. Although it is impossible to be sure what the switch meant, it could mean that the group tends to blame prisoners themselves rather than the administration for the lack of certain viewpoint representation.

49. Once again there is no precise explanation for the switch. It could mean that the prisoner thought that certain viewpoints were being represented in spite of the administration's desire not to have them represented. It could also mean that these opinions are based on representation outside the group structure and that the administration has not been able to eradicate them completely.

50. In the previous question, 39 percent of the nonparticipants thought that groups represented all major viewpoints. In this question only 10 percent thought that the administration is in favor of all opinions being represented. Obviously, there are prisoners who feel that opinions are being represented that the administration is not in favor of. However, the number of prisoners is not large; most feel that the groups do not represent major viewpoints (61 percent) and that the administration is not in favor of opinions being represented (90 percent).

51. This explains the disparity between the 39 percent who thought that major viewpoints were represented and the 90 percent who thought that the administration was not in favor of the views being represented.

52. Quoted in Marilyn Gittell et al., *Local Control in Education*, p. 47.

53. Alan H. Altshuler, *Community Control* (New York: Pegasus, 1970), p. 19.

54. Gittell, *Local Control in Education*. Gittell's study was done during the first two years of the control project. Her observations relate only to her experiences during that period. It is not clear how the patterns changed (or did not change) in subsequent years. The group structure at West Prison is about five years old. I would suggest that the length of the period of interaction between community participants and bureaucracy could significantly affect attitudes.

55. Of course, when the leadership from underground political groups, or those who function on the margin is added in, considerably more than half of the leadership fits into this category of independent leaders.

56. Among these were the humanist group, mentioned by the associate superintendent, and the Black Muslims, mentioned by the correctional lieutenant. The Chicano group in the institution was viewed with considerable hostility by many administrators.

57. Admitting that the compromise served the interests of the administration, several members of the Chicano group felt the solution came at the expense of the group. One officer blamed the president, whom he accused of acting opportunistically to avoid repercussions that could affect his imminent release date. In sum, the members I spoke with saw the compromise as a zero-sum game—with the administration the winner.

58. This only pertains to a portion of the group respondents, in most cases 50 percent of the respondents. The discussion that follows also concerns only a portion of all group members interviewed.

59. Interview with a 30-year-old black inmate.

60. Interview with a 32-year-old white inmate.

61. Interview with a 28-year-old Chicano inmate.

62. Inmate interview.

63. For a good survey of mechanisms for the representation of inmate opinion throughout the United States see J.E. Baker, *The Right to Participate.*

64. Thomas A. Murton and Phyllis Jo Baunach, *Shared Decision-making as a Treatment Tool in Prison Management* (Murton Foundation, Minnesota, 1974), p. 12.

65. Prisoners who made these claims supplied the names of other prisoners who they claimed were prohibited from serving on the MAC.

66. Interview with program administrator.

67. Interview with 37-year-old white inmate (ex-member of Hell's Angels).

68. Minutes of the July 5, 1972 meeting of the Men's Advisory Council.

69. Minutes of the August 9, 1972 meeting of the Men's Advisory Council.

70. Ibid., November 29, 1972.

71. Ibid., January 15, 1973.

72. Ibid., April 12, 1972.

73. Ibid., May 10, 1972.

74. Ibid., April 12, 1975.

75. Murton and Baunach, *Shared Decision-making*, p. 17.

76. Jerome Skolnick, *The Politics of Protest* p. 10.

77. William F. Mullen, "Community Control and Black Political Participation" in Cook and Morgan, *Participatory Democracy*, p. 264.

78. Robert Dahl, "The City in the Future of Democracy" in Cook and Morgan, *Participatory Democracy*, p. 95.

79. These conclusions are upheld with regard to community control of education projects. See Gittell et al., *Local Control* and Rhody McCoy, "The Year of the Dragon" in *Confrontation at Ocean Hill-Brownsville*, ed., Maurice Berube and Marilyn Gittell (New York: Praeger, 1969), p. 52.

80. For a complete and penetrating discussion of democratic decision making in and out of the prison environment, see McCleery, "Power, Communication and the Social Order," chapters 4 and 5.

81. This point is made by Peter Bachrach and Morton Baritz, "Two Faces of Power," *American Political Science Review* 56 (December 1972), pp. 947-952. Bachrach and Baritz's criticism was aimed at pluralists who they charge with failing to provide an independent definition of "key political decision" but can be adjusted for use in this case. Interestingly, McCleery raised the issue of "key political decisions" in his dissertation sixteen years before the Bachrach-Baritz article appeared.

82. How much say should inmates have in treatment and training programs?

Response	Non-group (%)	Group (%)	Cumulative Total (%)
No say	3.6	0	2.8
Very little	0	0	0
Some say	14.2	12.5	13.9
As much as administration	53.6	75.0	58.3
More than administration	28.6	12.5	25.0
Total	100.0	100.0	100.0
	(N=28)	(N=8)	(N=36)

83. In classification hearings a prisoner is given the right to attend those hearings, submit written documentation to the committee, present his case in person, and appeal the decision.

84. This description of disciplinary procedures is taken from the decision in *Clutchette* v. *Procunier*, 328 F.Supp. 767 (N.D. Calif. 1971) and California Department of Corrections, *Director's Rules*, chapter 4.

85. *Clutchette* v. *Procunier*, Krantz, *The Law of Corrections*, p. 642.

86. Krantz, *The Law of Corrections*, p. 648.

87. Ibid., p. 650.

88. Ibid., p. 650.

89. Ibid., p. 651.

90. California Department of Corrections, *Director's Rules* (Revision No. DF/7-Policy), p. 4505, October 6, 1975.

91. Ibid., Policy, p. 4506.

92. *Director's Rules* (Revision-DR/7-DP-4516) Article 2B, October 6, 1975.

93. Ibid., Section DP-4505.
94. Ibid., Section DP-4506.
95. Interview with associate superintendent of custody.
96. Ibid.
97. Interview with program administrator.
98. Ibid.
99. Minutes of the August 9, 1972 meeting of the Men's Advisory Council. Recently a legal column has appeared in the paper which is permitted to report on Supreme Court decisions only. These decisions usually bear little on institutional procedures. The editor of the Communicator showed me guidelines from Sacramento which prohibit inmate newspapers from reporting legal decisions that do, or could, affect institutional governance or procedures.
100. Interview. There are two or three clerks in each unit of 600 prisoners. These clerks are assigned to functions associated with unit record keeping.
101. All data from the *Quarterly Management Report*, fiscal year 1975-1976.
102. Totals are based on three quarters (nine months).

Conclusions

This book has had a dual purpose. It has been designed to recount the history of a political movement within certain prisons in the United States. At the same time, the book has attempted to show the reader how the movement affected the institutions and individual prisoners.

Through this microscopic study of political activity it is possible to learn a great deal about larger processes of political change in the society. This book has discussed pluralism, democratic rights, bureaucracy, race relations and several of the important political movements that were prominent during the sixties and early seventies. It is now time to pull this material together and extract some important lessons from it.

The political activities of the sixties have changed the prisoners' conception of political authority. This is an important part of the process of politization. Gresham Sykes had found in his 1958 study that prisoners viewed the administration as a legitimate agent of state power. Consequently, there was a political obligation to obey. From what I was able to learn, this no longer holds true. Prisoners generally regard the administration as a lawless body unwilling to follow legal rules and procedures and unprepared to yield any portion of its power. The administration is seen as a force resisting court-ordered changes and concealing its activities from the court and the public.

In the absence of any moral or legal obligation to obey, compliance is secured (and often it is not secured) through the use of threats, intimidation, and policies of social control used to divide the prisoners. The compelling force behind the prisoners compliance is power—the administrative monopoly of the power market. Realizing that the exercise of administrative power can bring a variety of adverse consequences, prisoners comply because there appears to be no rational alternative.

The prisoners' fear of reprisals also accounts for the diminution of political activity, or more precisely, the change in the type of activities. When prisoners were asked the question, "How active should prisoners be in the political problems and issues inside the institution?" there was an overwhelming feeling that prisoners should be deeply involved. However, when prisoners were asked "How active is the prisoner in the problems and issues in the institution?" the chasm between normative belief and reality became evident. Respondents said that most prisoners were not involved. They were not involved because they felt that the administration would act in a lawless manner if that was necessary to blunt the challenge and punish the participants. One prisoner put it this way:

> In order for the prisoners to be involved, they got to believe it is going to do some good. They could stop all the violence. The violence is a reaction to powerlessness.[1]

In this context politization has meant a change in the obligation to obey on the part of the prisoner and a more realistic, although sometimes overly pessimistic, assessment of the possibilities for change.

Prisoners have also critically examined, and often transformed many feelings about themselves. They have begun a process of redefinition, a prerequisite to any sustained political activity. A prisoner who described the manner in which he experienced political change spoke to a pattern experienced by many prisoners:

> I was illiterate when I came to this institution at the age of 27. I couldn't read and I couldn't write. I educated myself. School here doesn't teach anything. You become quickly discouraged. I learned more by myself. Now I'm more interested in politics. I've read about life. I know a great deal more now.[2]

As a result of political learning, the prisoner's conception of himself, the prison, and the society that incarcerated him is radically altered. There is greater understanding of the use of racism in and out of the institution. Prisoners have begun to overcome the feeling that incarceration signals a pathological disorder. Also, there is growing class consciousness. Prisoners realize that only a certain stratum of society is incarcerated, despite people of all classes being involved in criminal activity. There is widespread feeling that if a prisoner were not poor, he would not be a prisoner. Finally, there is little hope that society will accept the prisoner and provide an opportunity for him or her to be productive. When contrasted with George Jackson's view of prisoners as a solidly conservative class in the fifties, the present level of political development is put in very sharp relief.

The problems of translating these feelings into a political position (left-right spectrum) are no different from translating the feelings of others on society's margins, or even those involved in productive activity, into standardized criteria. To ask Americans whether they consider themselves on the left or the right, or radical, liberal or conservative, does not make a lot of sense. These political attributions are generally unintelligible to many Americans, or heavily influenced by ideological pressures. Thus, the desire to see meaningful social change cannot be gauged by referring to political categories associated with different ideological persuasions. This is especially true for prisoners and others in the clientist sphere where formal political education is lacking. Of course, there are many within prison who consider themselves socialists and look toward societies like China and Cuba for theories of organization. But there are others who deeply feel the need for change, without fully knowing what to call it and where to place it.

Having spoken of some general effects of the prisoners movement, it is necessary to give attention to some specific organizational and political changes the movement occasioned inside the walls.

Political Development

Political activity was a relatively new phenomenon to most prisoners as it was to many students who participated in the antiwar movement. Political activity can be thought of as activity designed to change a prevailing balance of power or institute policies favorable to achieving particular political ends. Because of the relative inexperience of the actors, and the hostility of power agents, it is amazing that anything even approaching the dimensions of the prisoners' movement got off the ground.

Considering the extreme prohibitions on activity, organizing prisoners is a difficult and dangerous task. Many prisoners risked serving additional time to attempt to form collective organizations among a constituency historically fragmented by racial divisions, graded privileges, and an ideology which elevated the maxim "do your own time," to a biblical truth.

An ideological combination of racial division and extreme individualism made the prison body a poor candidate for organization. Trust among prisoners was very low; everyone suspected everyone else of being an informer. Prisoners were conditioned to view themselves as inadequate in some fundamental way. This led to astonishingly low levels of personal and political efficacy. These sorts of emotions were powerful tools of administration control and sizable obstacles to collective organization.

Despite these obstacles the prisoners' movement made a visible dent in the institutional armor. Many of its ideas and programs were transformed by prison officials to serve administrative ends, but many survived intact. Many prisoners learned much about themselves and society through their experience with the movement, while others became disillusioned as a result of the movement's inability to produce what they saw as meaningful change. But none of the prisoners I spoke with expressed anything but praise and admiration for the movement's ideals and respect for its leadership.

Group Activity

Much of the collective organization started by the prisoners' movement has been channeled into more narrow ethnic, racial, social, or religious associations in the group movement. Changing the base of the movement from one chiefly concerned with the collective needs of the prison body to one organized around particular constituencies must be considered an administrative policy success. Despite the fact that the base of organization has temporarily changed, the realization that collective organization is necessary has not been tarnished.

The most serious problem facing the groups now is the lack of credibility they have with many prisoners. Groups have lost the support of a good percentage of their fellow prisoners because they are viewed as collaborators with the administration. In some cases this perception is accurate. But for several groups this characterization is inappropriate.

Maintaining a stable group structure faced with an administrative strategy that seeks to maximize cooptation and disunity is a very difficult task. Faced with the hostility of their fellow prisoners and an administrative wing which cooperates only when cooperation serves its interests, the group movement has lost much of its original power to muster prisoner and outside support. As a result of these difficulties most groups have fallen away from collective projects into more constituency-oriented work. Moreover, many groups have moved away from public functions and become quasi-private organizations. Both of these tactics have seemed to further isolate the groups. This has occurred because of the widespread realization that collective organization is essential.

Without an independent resource base—support from the community or administrative cooperation—the group movement has entered a period of partial paralysis. This paralysis is made more acute since most of the prisoners see the groups themselves, rather than administration, as the agent of disease. Only a small number of groups, approximately 30 of those functioning at West Prison are seen as aggressive and principled organizations willing to fight for their constituencies. If there is no intervention in the near future, it is unlikely that even those groups can independently carry on the struggle.

In order to permeate the administrative strategy of keeping the groups isolated, the groups must attempt to forge and strengthen relations with outside organizations. Of course, this is difficult to accomplish without administrative approval. If contacts between prison and the outside could be improved and citizen groups linked closely to inside groups, some administrative discretion might be eliminated. Given somewhat more space to operate, groups then might be able to deal with internal problems more effectively.

The most significant internal problem is the groups' lack of legitimacy. This can only be overcome by taking on a more public and visible role within the prison. Groups could conceivably publish newsletters reviewing the history of the group, its objectives and its relationship with the administration. Attempts to enlarge and broaden group membership should be a primary objective. A more active education program could provide a mechanism to reach out to other prisoners. Groups must become involved in cooperative activity to work on issues in the interest of all prisoners. A greater degree of autonomy is necessary to break the linkage between the administration and the groups.

While the group movement currently faces a severe crisis and may be producing certain negative results, it has been an important mechanism in aiding the political development of prisoners. Before the sanctioning of group activity, no form of collective prisoner organization was possible. There were no resources for prisoners to attempt to reach out to their fellow prisoners or to the outside community. As a result of the development of groups, more information was available and probably somewhat more trust, at least among certain constituencies, was built. Whatever the final fate of prisoner groups turns out to be, the decision to demand the right to organize collectively and build prisoner groups seems the correct one. For the time being the group movement will probably remain in its present state of partial paralysis.

The need for change in the group structure, including more concrete organizing and public activity, must be weighed against the possibility that agitation could result in either administration concessions or actions to further circumscribe group activity. There is evidence, such as the mass resignation of the MAC from B quad, that the notion of change is beginning to build. An important ingredient to speed and sustain the movement for change is an increase in mass political energy of the type generated during the early years of the prisoners' movement. To a great degree political motion within the prison is dependent on political motion in the community.

Labor

In the area of prison labor the administration finds itself in a more vulnerable position than it does in relation to inmate groups. It is more vulnerable because of the centrality of the labor systems. The administration must depend on the prison labor force to accomplish vital tasks associated with commodity production and institutional maintenance.

Because of this dependency, the administration has adopted a variety of strategies for dealing with opposition in the prison labor force. As a result of the potential political power of the prison work force the administration has refused to agree to any form of collective organization of the work forces, or any mechanism that would like the work force to any other prisoner organization, such as the Men's Advisory Council. While resisting collective organization the administration (state-use) has sought to create incentive programs to reward the prison labor force and bolster productivity

Without similar resources the prison administration has been unable to provide similar incentives.

Difficulties in formulating policy to deal with prison labor are magnified because of the bifurcation in control between state-use industries and institutional workers. The prison administration must enforce policies it has no part in fashioning and must recruit and discipline a work force often at the expense of its own institutional work force and labor requirements. As a result of this power arrangement, consistent and effective policy is harder to arrive at and more difficult to enforce. This leaves the prisoners in a somewhat stronger position than their counterparts in the group movement.

While administrative policy has reaped certain dividends in the area of group politics, administration policy has totally failed to create the desired results in the work area. At present the administration relies on individual work incentives, repression, and the use of labor from prisoners ready for release. If a return to the days of acceptable productivity and the disciplined work force is in the cards, the administration of state-use industries and the prison are going to have to close ranks and submit to the demands for competitive wages, "real" training and some form of industrial unionism. This is not likely to occur quickly, but if resistance persists, there seems no alternative. Once again, political energy is vitally needed to turn the individualist protest of the labor force into a collective statement.

Collective organization in the workplace would positively affect the group movement and other political forces in the prison if a way could be found to link them together. Labor is without doubt the most effective political weapon in the prisoner's repertoire. If it is used correctly it could change the face of prison governance. Consequently, the next wave of prison political activity will almost certainly bring the labor issue to the forefront.

Aside from meeting the demands of the labor force one other administrative option seems available. If the administration could soften the total regimen of institutional life, the work force might be more willing to cooperate. This would entail restructuring the governance system to provide more freedom for prisoners, more rights, more access, and more power. However, the administration shows no signs of following this course.

Individual Rights

From a position of considering anything approaching a right to be a privilege, prisoners have come to see constitutional rights as an entitlement. This change could not have been possible without the ideological interventions of the prisoners' movement, fueled by the larger civil rights struggle. The civil rights struggle clearly demonstrated that a stratum of American society was systematically deprived of its rights because of race, ethnicity, economic and social position. Prisoners, first blacks and then whites, came to see their position as intimately tied to other groups deprived of rights.

The main agency of redress for prisoners seeking the expansion of rights was the court. In some areas the court responded favorably to the litigations brought by prisoners. The court response was a product of the times, responding to the external pressure of masses of people organized for political action. Although the courts' rulings have expanded the rights of prisoners, the expansion was not nearly as great as many expected. There was even a further constricture when administrators and correction officers fiercely resisted court-ordered change.

While the court was willing to expand prisoners' rights in certain areas, it never provided the mechanism necessary to ensure that the prison authorities would comply. While on paper there was a growth in the legal rights of prisoners, in reality, prisoners have great difficulties availing themselves of their rights. The failure of legal rights to significantly change the governance system of the prison led to mass disillusionment with established channels of change.

Although many prisoners view the court with great skepticism, it still remains the only governmental agency that prisoners can look toward for change. Presently, the court has retreated from the activism that characterized many decisions in the sixties and early seventies. Prison litigation continues, but relief is rare. Even for those who see the court as a possible agency for relief, there is the knowledge that rights do not exist in a vacuum, but are only as effective as the power of the group or individual who seeks to utilize them.

The Birth of a Movement

Both the gains and losses of the prisoners' movement must be considered in the context of the movement's age and maturity, plus the special circumstances attached to conducting political activity within a prison. The prisoners' movement was the first organized political expression of prisoners. It attempted to formulate a program to change the balance of power in the institutional governance system.

Ideologically the movement had a tremendous impact. The prisoners' ideological growth may be the most lasting contribution made by the movement in its early stages. The movement offered definitions of the offender which sharply contrasted with the way the prisoners defined themselves and the prevailing societal definition attached to the offender. It sought to broaden the prisoners' focus to include an examination of the society that incarcerated them and the conditions attached to exile. As a result of the political activity associated with the prisoners' movement, prisoners began to experiment in actions designed to affect the political conditions attached to incarceration. They began stridently to challenge the absolute authority of the governing force.

The prisoners' movement set a process in motion. It developed the conditions necessary to sustain political activity. The next stage of the movement will be considerably stronger as a result of this beginning.

Notes

1. Interview with a 40-year-old white prisoner.
2. Interview with a 41-year-old Chicano prisoner.

Appendix A
Methodology

West Prison

At West Prison I interviewed three groups of inmates. Different questionnaires were used for each group, although most of the same questions appeared in each questionnaire. I also interviewed certain key administrative and corrections officers, repeating some of the questions asked of the prisoners.

The first group of prisoners interviewed were those who held leadership positions in recognized aboveground groups, called "TIPS" by the prisoners. The questions probed the effectiveness of the group; the relationship to other groups; the group's goals; the group's relationship with the administration; the group's relations with nonparticipating prisoners and other areas of activity. Besides questions concerning the individual's member group, there were questions that inquired into perceptions about the institution in general. The purpose was to note if leaders (or group members) perceived the institution differently than nonparticipants, which in fact turned out to be the case.

The second group of prisoners was randomly selected, excluding anyone who currently held a leadership position in an organization. Prisoners could be members of organizations now or in the past, as long as they did not hold any significant decision-making spot. It turned out that less than 25 percent of those interviewed had ever belonged to a group. Inmates selected as part of this group had to meet two additional criteria. They had to have been in the institution for at least one year, and could not have a parole date within three months of the date they were interviewed. Prisoners who had spent less than a year in the institution might not yet be well enought acquainted with diverse aspects of prison life covered in the questionnaire, while those who had a parole date in three months or less might be excessively biased by the thought of soon returning to the streets.

Prisoners in the third group interviewed were required to meet the criteria of the second group with the additional stipulation that they had previously been incarcerated at one of the three other California prisons chosen for purposes of conformity. The purpose of interviewing this group was to add some general knowledge about activities in other institutions to particular information gained at West Prison. The questionnaire of the transfer group was exactly the same as the second group, except that it asked the prisoner to make a number of comparisons between West Prison and the prison he had transferred from.

The total number of prisoners interviewed was sixty-five, although forty-one were included in the final sample. I interviewed the additional twenty-four prisoners because they were either directly involved in the prisoners' movement during the height of the activity (1965-1972) or had a reputation among the prison body as experienced and politically knowledgeable. A good part of the historical information came from these prisoners. Their attitudes concerning the political system of the prison are not included in this sample because of the tendency of a category of prisoners such as this to severely bias the sample.

Of the forty-one prisoners included in the sample, ten were leaders of prisoners' organizations. Often the leader was the chairman or president of the group, but several groups sent other officers. The groups themselves were asked to select an individual who they felt was knowledgeable about the history and present activities of the group to represent the group at the interview.

The remaining 31 prisoners were picked at random from a possible group of 450 that met the criteria. Fifteen of these prisoners had served a sentence at another California prison and 16 were prisoners who served the majority of their time at West Prison. Although the prisoners who had served sentences at other institutions were asked to contrast the two institutions, they were lumped together with the 16 nontransfer prisoners when the survey was tabulated. All of these prisoners were asked exactly the same questions, which allowed the groups to be combined. Since there was almost no variation between the responses of the two groups, and since both had been chosen at random, using essentially the same criteria, it was both easy and practical to combine them.

Additionally, I interviewed every top administrator at the institution, including two members of the correctional hierarchy. These included the superintendent, three associate superintendents, two quadrant administrators from the sample quadrants and the chief correctional officer assigned to those quadrants—a total of eight administrators.

There are some difficulties. First, the group members I interviewed were all in the leadership elements of the groups. This begs the question of the possibility that members hold significantly different opinions than leaders do. Probably there are differences between leaders and members, but my experience leads me to believe that they are not highly significant. The groups are fairly small cohesive units that do not differ greatly on most issues. As a rule, group members tend to be closer on issues with others in the group than with non-members.[a]

---

[a]In the course of using several interviewing techniques a pattern of consistently corresponding answers emerged in the same inmate group. This was especially true when members were interviewed collectively. Having discovered this tendency before I even embarked on this study, I never interviewed group members in a collective situation. All my subsequent experience has strengthened my feeling that there is at least, a greater cohesion between group members than between a group member and a nonparticipant.

The other apparent difficulty is the size of the sample. No doubt the reliability of the findings could have been increased by enlarging the number of prisoners interviewed. However, this was neither possible or necessary. The questionnaire was only one mechanism to probe questions about the prison governance system. It provided some quantitative measure of attitudes, but acted more as a roadmap to assure that I was covering the same ground with all prisoners. While I believe that the attitudes elicited from the forty-one prisoners formally interviewed do reflect many of the attitudes of the prison body at large, I do not claim that the sample meets the rigors of statistical reliability.

East Prison

At East Prison the interviews were more free-form. No standardized set of questions was used, although I did construct a set of topics that I sought to cover with all the prisoners and administrators I spoke with. Usually, I took copious notes during the interview and dictated them for typing immediately after returning from the prison.

I spoke with two aggregates of prisoners—those belonging and not belonging to groups. This conforms with the clusters of prisoners I interviewed in California. Eight inmate groups and ten inmates not belonging to groups were interviewed, as well as several key administrators. Besides these interviews, which I later transcribed, I conducted many conversations with prisoners that were never transcribed. In total, I spoke with approximately thirty-five prisoners at East Prison.

Appendix B Participant Questionnaire

Member Groups

1. How did your group first begin?
2. What kinds of activities is the group involved in?
3. How is the leadership of your group determined?
4. Are there any requirements for membership in your group? Yes ____ No ____ If yes: What are the requirements?
5. Does your group actively seek new members? Yes ____ No ____ If yes: How is that recruiting done?
6. Can you tell me what you think makes a good group member and a bad group member?
7. How does a group come to know the interests of its group members?
8. Generally, would you say that inmates within a group agree with each other on: all issues; most issues; some issues; few issues; no issues.
9. Do most inmate groups cooperate and work with each other? Yes ____ No____
10. How would you describe the relationship between group members? Would you say that inmates in a group are closer with each other than with other nongroup members? Yes ____ No ____
11. Does your group have a relationship with, or receive support from, some outside group, organization, or individual? Yes ____ No ____
12. In what ways do the outside groups assist you?
13. How important is this outside help to your group?
14. Why do some inmates join groups while other inmates don't?

Men's Advisory Council (MAC)

1. Do you think MAC effectively represents the interests of the inmates? Yes ____ No ____ If No: Why Not?

2. Suppose the administration wanted to make a new rule restricting the length of hair, beards, etc., and the inmates were against it. What do you think MAC would do? Do you think they would be effective?
3. How much authority should MAC have over inmate discipline and other prison rules?
4. Generally, do you think MAC is: good for inmates; bad for inmates; makes no difference. Why?

Groups in General

1. Would you say that groups generally represent the interests of their members? Yes ____ No ____. If No: Why not?
2. Do you think that groups within the prison are representative of the major viewpoints held by the prisoners? Yes ____ No ____. If No: Which views are not represented? Why are they not represented?
3. Would you say that groups represent those within the population who have the same interests, but are not members? Yes ____ No ____. If No: Why not?
4. Would you say that most groups in the prison have: exactly the same interests; most of the same interests; some of the same interests; few of the same interests; none of the same interests.
5. Are there any areas in which MAC or other inmate groups have had an important say in changing things? Yes ____ No ____. If Yes: What are those areas?
6. Do you think that groups have acted to increase or decrease the political awareness of inmates? How?
7. Would you say that most groups in the prison have: exactly the same values/beliefs; most of the same values/beliefs; some of the same values/beliefs; few of the same values/beliefs; none of the same values/beliefs.
8. Would you say that groups in general should have: more power; less power; about the same. Why? (what groups more, what groups less.)
9. Do you think that inmate groups are: good for inmates; bad for inmates; makes no difference. Why do you say that?

Administration

1. What is your group's relationship with the administration? Would you say the administration is: hostile; neutral; helpful/supportive.
2. What is your group's relationship with the correction officers? Would you say that the corrections officers are: hostile; neutral; helpful/supportive.
3. Was there a time when the administration's attitude towards your group changed? Yes ____ No ____. If Yes: Can you tell me why the administration changed its attitude?
4. If your group wanted to achieve a goal that you felt would be helpful or important to your group members, and that goal involved administration approval or consent, how would you go about it?
5. Suppose the administration refused your request? What would you do?
6. Do you think that all inmate opinions should be represented? Yes ____ No ____. If No: Why not?
7. Do you think the administration is in favor of all opinions being represented? Yes ____ No ____. If No: Which opinions don't they want represented?
8. Suppose you came back to your cell after work and found that it had been searched while you were gone. Your belongings were tossed all over the place and a personal letter that you had been writing was missing. What would you do? What do you think would happen if you did that?
9. Suppose that the officers wanted to cut down on the visiting hours for inmates and the inmates were against it. Do you think that the administration would make a decision: favorable to the officers; favorable to the inmates; a compromise would be made.

Underground Groups

1. Are there any underground groups in this prison? Yes ____ No ____. If Yes: What are the differences between the aboveground groups and the underground groups: (Probe; ideology, tactics, values, interests, violence).
2. Have underground groups resulted from administration suppression of

certain groups of inmates which they felt were undesirable? Yes ____ No ____. Please explain.

3. What reasons do you think the administration has for labeling a group undesirable?
4. Do you think there is a relationship between group activity and the amount of violence within the institution? Yes ____ No ____. If Yes: Why?
5. What would be the result if underground groups were allowed to function openly?

Background (optional)

1 Were you employed at the time of your arrest? Yes ____ No ____. If Yes: What type of job did you have? If No: Were you receiving welfare or unemployment at the time of your arrest?
2. Were you working previous to your arrest? For how long?
3. Did you ever belong to a trade union?
4. Did any member of your family ever belong to a trade union?
5. When you were on the street, how active was your interest in political affairs and community activity?

Unions

1. Do you think inmates should have the right to organize unions? Yes ____ No ____.
2. Do you think a union should represent a group of inmates (like those working in the knitting mill) or all inmates? Why?
3. Suppose unions were allowed to be organized. Do you think they would be: good for inmates; bad for inmates; make no difference.
4. Do you think that unions would make the administration's job: more difficult; less difficult; about the same.

Appendix C
Official Description of Stress-Assessment Unit

California Men's Colony Stress-Assessment Unit (SAU)

Due to an increase in the number of violent offenders within the department and a growing waiting list for the Stress-Assessment Unit at Vacaville, an additional SAU has been established at CMC. As stated in the Classification Manual, this unit observes and evaluates inmates selected by the Adult Authority who have a history of aggressive behavior and who have served enough time and completed enough correctional treatment to be considered for parole, but need further clinical clearance.

1. Criteria for Placement

All inmates placed in the SAU are assigned on the basis of Adult Authority order with the inmate agreeing to comply with the order. Cases selected for the unit usually follow the below criteria:

a. Crime of unsual violence, bizarre behavior, or history showing potential for unusual violence in or out of prison.
b. Suitable time served where release would be feasible.
c. One "favorable" psychiatric report if no previous "unfavorable" psychiatric reports. Two recent favorable psychiatric reports if the file contains any unfavorable psychiatric reports.
d. The inmate must have two or more years remaining before reaching maximum sentence.
e. The inmate must be capable of adjusting in a medium custody general population setting.

2. SAU Inmate Housing

Inmates placed in the CMC Stress-Assessment Unit are housed in B Quad, Building 3, 2nd floor left. Maximum capacity is 50 inmates. Normal institution rules and regulations are applicable.

3. Program Description

The SAU program is divided into three phases. The first and second phase total approximately six months. If the inmate successfully completes the second phase, he then makes his Adult Authority appearance while still assigned to the unit.

Phase I is an orientation and initial evaluation lasting eight weeks. All Phase I inmates are assigned to the B Quad dining room. In hard confrontation groups four times per week, the Phase I inmates meet together with the unit CC II, CC III and/or SAU Housing Officer. It is in these groups that the significance of the program is driven home and the initial steps of evaluation are taken. The goal is to develop group unity and free the inmate to talk about himself. While each inmate is clearly informed that the program is voluntary, each is required to confront his criminality and is not allowed to hide or evade the issue. Phase I inmates also attend community groups twice per week during evening hours, complete various written tests, and are viewed in numerous formal and informal contacts with unit staff. At the end of eight weeks each inmate is reviewed by the unit classification committee for advancement to Phase II. If his overall performance has been unsatisfactory, the inmate may be retained in Phase I for two weeks. If performance is unsatisfactory at that time, the inmate will be removed from the program, a termination report submitted, and the inmate recommended for transfer to an appropriate institution.

Phase II is composed of those inmates who survive Phase I. Phase II inmates will usually be assigned minimum custody and outside work assignment on a SAU outside crew. Phase II confrontation groups meet twice per week during evening hours as a continuation of the evaluative process. These inmates will also attend community groups twice per week.

Phase III is composed of those inmates who gain release. Effort will be made to assist each in the transition from long-term confinement to release. When possible, work assignments comparable to release employment will be made. Parole obligations will be carefully reviewed with emphasis on individual responsibility.

4. Program Philosophy

The SAU program is based upon the idea that inmates with a history of violence may be most adequately evaluated when observed under ongoing stressful situations. During initial exposure to SAU, each inmate is questioned as to why he thinks he was sent to SAU. Contrary to their initial belief, all are clearly informed that SAU staff are not directed toward aiding them in gaining release nor are the staff interested in "treating" them. Inmates are told that it is our job to keep them in prison unless they can "get across" and provide assurance that they are a safe risk and deserve the opportunity of parole. Another factor which is emphasized is that it is not what is known, but what is not known that is keeping the inmate in prison. Emphasis is placed on exposing this secret by creating a feeling that he has nothing to lose by doing so.

Thoughout the first and second phases of the program, staff remains intentionally detached but not necessarily impersonal. Information is gathered and the inmate repeatedly confronted; the inmate is never informed of staff evaluations unless he is failing to the extent that removal is considered.

An air of uncertainty is intentionally maintained so as to encourage each inmate to make a concentrated effort to get himself across. Much attention is given each inmate to determine whether he remains unduly sensitive and if so in what area. SAU evaluation is based upon the intentional provoking of conflict during group encounters and by maintaining the atmosphere of uncertainty and ambivalence. This atmosphere is maintained by displaying concern and interest in each inmate while at the same time being critical and provocative.

While SAU inmates live, work, and group together, they have access to the general population. Much of the time the inmates are under close observation by staff. However, during many hours, they have more freedom than much of the inmate population, for example open door and hallway visiting. This is done not to reward them, but to give them greater latitude to succeed or fail, again testing their responsibility.

Based upon the above process, the SAU inmates are evaluated. After the reports by all staff have been completed, the inmate appears before a psychiatric council composed of the SAU CC III, CC II, and a psychiatrist. The purpose of psychiatric council is to review each case and verify the psychiatric report written by the CC II.

The day prior to the inmate's Adult Authority appearance, he is informed whether his evaluation is positive or negative. After making the Board appearance, each is informed of staff evaluations. The purpose for this is to enable each to see how they are viewed by the staff and then either accept or reject the observations. For the inmates denied parole, it focuses on problem areas for them to work on and provides a guideline for future staff evaluation. For the inmate granted parole, the reports clarify staff opinions, point to existing problem areas as we see them, and act as a reward for his efforts.

Prepared by:

R.H. GARVIS, CC III
Supervisor
Stress-Assessment Unit

J.W. HUSKEY, CC II
Assistant Supervisor
Stress-Assessment Unit

Appendix D
A Review of Current Studies

Of the literature that deals with questions concerning the process of politization in prison, two studies are close to this one and deserve some attention. Both these studies suffer from methodological and substantive problems. By examining these studies, it is possible to begin to isolate some methodological requisites necessary for investigating political activity and attitudes within a prison or related within a prison or other complex social institutions (mental hospitals, schools, welfare systems, etc.)

The first study is a doctoral dissertation by Erika Schmidt Fairchild. It is a study of the problem of crime, within a study of the political attitudes of prisoners. The study was done at Washington State institutions for male, female and young offenders, respectively.[1]

Fairchild's study shows a good sense of many of the sociological and political currents that run through the prison. The study is deeply influenced by the sociological model applied to institutional investigations. The approach is centrally concerned with the manner in which roles, expectations, values, and perceptions within institutions form a cultural complex or social system. It is concerned with the "system" within the "system."

At the same time, Fairchild recognizes the importance of getting past this sort of investigation and into the realm of political relations. Thus, much of the dissertation deals with the process of politization among prisoners. But much of the political analysis is in terms of political roles, rather than real political relations within institutions. The most important political concern is the way in which the prisoner subjectively sees his political role in and out of the prison.

Because the scope of the term "political" is not defined, everyone emerges as highly eclectic. To be sure prisoners do exhibit a high degree of eclecticism, but this is, in and of itself, not a compelling finding. One needs to make some sort of an attempt to localize the concerns of a political investigation of the prison in order to extricate oneself from that eclecticism—to take it apart. This is what the Fairchild study fails to do.

So the tension between the political and sociological tracts of the study is never resolved or connected. The relationship between the prisoner and the prison system of governance is consequently given scant attention.

There is insufficient attention to how the prisoners politically relate to, or understand, the prison system of governance and its component parts (officers, administrators, prison groups, etc.). A substitute for this sort of analysis is a great deal of information about how the prisoner views his own political beliefs and those of his fellow prisoners. Once again, political belief refers to a wide spectrum of perceptions.

Although the study is quite informative, it fails to present a coherent picture of what it means to be political, or the range of political activities that occur daily within the prison, some of which may not be considered political, even by the prisoners themselves. Starting with the premise that all prisoners are equally informed or involved in the power distribution within the prison, Fairchild makes no attempt to identify or speak with prisoners involved in the broad range of political, ethnic, religious, cultural, or legal activities that constantly occur within the institutions, or analyze the kind of interaction between administrators and prisoners that is occasioned by these activities. Consequently, it is very difficult to draw parallels between, or even identify, relationships between the political ideologies and political activities of the prisoners and administrators.

In addition to the problem of emphasis there are certain methodological difficulties. There are problems with the manner of selecting the prisoners to be interviewed and the number of prisoners that were chosen.

Only twenty-four prisoners were interviewed by Fairchild. These prisoners were chosen by the administration and said to represent a good cross-section of the prison population. Although a small sample can afford the opportunity for indepth interviews, the information they yield cannot be generalized to draw conclusions about the prison population. Also, allowing the administration to pick the sample has many obvious, but also some less obvious, disadvantages. Specifically, my experience showed that the administration is not in touch with many of the political and social currents within the institution. Therefore, even if the administration had the desire to pick a representative cross-section, they do not have the information to do it.

The difficulties caused by the manner of choosing the sample and the lack of concrete political questioning about the prison governance system leaves the Fairchild study a much less powerful work than it might have been. Curiously, Fairchild notes the problem when she remarks that the administration considers the real radical a prisoner who is concerned with changing conditions within the institution. Unfortunately, Fairchild's work does not concern this area of struggle.

The second study worth mentioning was done by Stephen Woolpert as a part of a larger program of study funded by the Law Enforcement Assistance Administration. Woolpert's study is quantitative. Prisoners were asked to compile a questionnaire whose results were tabulated and presented as the attitudes of prisoners. Essentially, the study is an opinion poll of prisoners and a correlation between their opinions and those of a nonprisoner group. The method is more precise than Fairchild's but also has many deficiencies.

While Fairchild chose a format that was highly informal and unstructured Woolpert chose a method that because of its formality screened out much vital material.

Woolpert is concerned with arriving at some measurement of the "political militancy" of prisoners. In order to get such a measure, Woolpert must use a definition of militancy. He defines militancy as a "willingness to support political violence."[2] Political militancy has a much broader meaning than Woolpert suggests. Creating a container that lends itself to quantification leads Woolpert into the error of attempting to capture a process in the form of a moment. This is the opposite of the Fairchild error—leaving all terms open-ended and undefined.

Woolpert chooses to examine political activity outside of the prison. This leads to the same problem of emphasis seen in the Fairchild study. Woolpert makes politics mean what you do when you are on the street or how you define yourself on a continuum. The context of the examinations (outside political activity) leads Woolpert onto terrain very difficult to traverse.

For example, Woolpert asks prisoners to identify their partisan political affiliations (Democrat, Republican, Independent) and then place themselves in an appropriate slot on a Left-Right continuum. Not unexpectedly, prisoners exhibit some difficulties in placing themselves on a continuum. Woolpert takes this as an indication of political apathy, and then must square these findings with the interest in political militancy expressed by prisoners answering the questionnaire.

Woolpert found that political militancy cannot be dismissed as the action of a small handful of dissenters "in a population of allegiant prisoners."[3] So Woolpert needs to provide an explanation of why prisoners don't identify themselves as leftist or radicals but show a preference for political militancy. Woolpert resolves this contradiction by relating political militancy to activities in the "criminal sub-culture." He argues that violent modes of behavior, frequent in the life of the criminal, are transplanted into the political realm to form the bases for political militancy. This finding is as facile as Woolpert's definition of political militancy. So each step of the study further increases the confusion, until explanations become nothing more than tools to provide rationalizations for disconnected premises. All this results from the original problem of examining political activity and attitudes by using ineffective indices.

The stress or starting point for an examination of the political attitudes of the prisoner must be the prison itself, since almost all of the political life of the prisoner occurs within the walls. The prison is the most immediate political frame of reference. Political activity associated with the prison governance systems (disciplinary procedures, work, group activity) is the most immediate form of political behavior and attitude formation the prisoner experiences. Skipping over the political life of the prison in favor of broader or more identifiable forms of allegiance and behavior is analogous to skipping over the factory life of a worker. Of course, political science has traditionally ignored the realm of work as a political "substance," so it is not surprising that prison studies, done by political scientists, exhibit the same tendencies.

In order to make any sense out of second level political abstractions, such as ones placed on a Left-Right continuum or party allegiance, one must ascertain the attitudes and behaviors in the institutions (factory, prison, welfare system, city government) where the individual resides, works or interacts. Thus, the first question must concern the political perception and behavior of the individual in the "proximate political context." After establishing these relations, it is possible to attempt to associate them with wider political currents.

Yet, often there is a close relationship between political programs and ideologies developed in other political contexts. For example, there was a close relationship between the political activities of the sixties and the development of the prisoners' movement. Rather than treat the relationship between these forces on a philosophical or sociological level, I attempted to translate the relationship into what concrete political forms and programs it produced. This is the stage that Fairchild and Woolpert skip, leaving a sizable omission at the core of these studies.

Notes

1. Erika Schmidt Fairchild, *Crime and Politics: A Study of Prisons*, Ph.D. dissertation, University of Washington, 1974.
2. Stephen Woolpert, "The Political Attitudes of Prison Inmates." Paper read at the American Political Science Association 1976 annual meeting, p. 21.
3. Ibid., p. 33.

Appendix E
The Folsom Manifesto of Demands (1970)

1. *We demand* the constitutional rights of legal representation at the time of all Adult Authority hearings, and the protection from the procedures of the Adult Authority whereby they permit no procedural safeguards such as an attorney for cross examination of witnesses, witnesses in behalf of the parolee, at parole revocation hearings.

2. *We demand* a change in medical staff and medical policy and procedure. The Folsom Prison Hospital is totally inadequate, understaffed, prejudicial in the treatment of inmates. There are numerous "mistakes" made many times, improper and erroneous medication is given by untrained personnel. The emergency procedures for serious injury are totally absent in that they have no emergency room whatsoever; no recovery room following surgery which is performed by practitioners rather than board member surgeons. They are assisted by inmate help neither qualified, licensed, nor certified to function in operating rooms. Several instances have occurred where multiple injuries have happened to a number of inmates at the same time. A random decision was made by the M.D. in charge as to which patient was the most serious and needed the one surgical room available. Results were fatal to one of the men waiting to be operated upon. This is virtually a death sentence to such a man who might have lived otherwise.

3. *We demand* adequate visiting conditions and facilities for the inmates and families of Folsom prisoners. The visiting facilities at this prison are such as to preclude adequate visiting for the inmates and their families. As a result the inmates are permitted two hours, two times per month to visit with family and friends, which of course has to be divided between these people. We ask for additional officers to man the visiting room five days per week, so that everyone may have at least four hours visiting per month. The administration has refused to provide or consider this request in prior appeals using the grounds of denial that they cannot afford the cost of the (extra) officers needed for such change. However, they have been able to provide twelve new correctional officers to walk the gun rails of this prison, armed with rifles and shotguns during the daytime hours when most of the prison population is at work or attending other assignment. This is a waste of the taxpayers' money, and a totally unnecessary security precaution.

4. *We demand* that each man presently held in the Adjustment Center be given a written notice with the Warden of Custody signature on it explaining the exact reason for his placement in the severely restrictive confines of the Adjustment Center.

5. *We demand* an immediate end to indeterminate adjustment center terms to be replaced by fixed terms with the length of time served being terminated by good conduct and according to the nature of the charges, for which men are presently being warehoused indefinitely without explanation.

6. *We demand* an end to the segregation of prisoners from the mainline population because of their political beliefs. Some of the men in the Adjustment Center are confined there solely for political reasons and their segregation from other inmates is indefinite.

7. *We demand* an end to political persecution, racial persecution, and the denial of prisoners to subscribe to political papers, books or any other educational and current media periodicals that are forwarded through the United States mail.

8. *We demand* an end to the persecution and punishment of prisoners who practice the constitutional right of peaceful dissent. Prisoners at Folsom and San Questin Prisons, according to the California State Penal Code, cannot be compelled to work as these two prisons were built for the purpose of housing prisoners and there is no mention as to the prisoners being required to work on prison jobs in order to remain on the Mainline and/or be considered for release. Many prisoners believe their labor-power is being exploited in order for the state to increase its economic power and continue to expand its correctional industries which are million-dollar complexes, yet do not develop working skills acceptable for employment in the outside society, and which do not pay the prisoner more than the maximum sixteen cents per hour wage. Most prisoners never make more than six or eight cents per hour. Prisoners who refuse to work for the two-to-sixteen-cent pay rate, or who strike, are punished and segregated without the access to the privileges shared by those who work. This is class legislation; class division, and creates class hostilities within the prison.

9. *We demand* an end to the teargassing of prisoners who are locked in their cells; such action led to the death of Willie Powell in Soledad Prison in 1968 and of Fred Billinslea, on February 25, 1970 at San Quentin Prison. It is cruel and unnecessary.

10. *We demand* the passing of a minimum and maximum term bill which calls for an end to indeterminate sentences whereby a man can be warehoused indefinitely, rehabilitated or not. That all prisoners have the right to be paroled after serving their minimum term instead of the cruel and unusual punishment of being confined beyond his minimum eligibility for parole, and never knowing the reason for the extension of time, nor when his time is completed. The maximum term bill eliminates indefinite life time imprisonment where it is unnecessary and cruel. Life sentences should not confine a man for longer than ten years, as seven years is the statute for a considered lifetime out of circulation and if a man cannot be

rehabilitated after a maximum of ten years of constructive programs etc., then he belongs in a mental hygiene center, not a prison. Rescind Adult Authority Resolution 171, arbitrary fixing of prison terms.

11. *We demand* that industries be allowed to enter the institutions and employ inmates to work eight hours a day and fit into the category of workers for scale wages. The working conditions in prisons do not develop working incentives parallel to the money jobs in the outside society, and a paroled prisoner faces many contradictions on the job that add to his difficulty to adjust. Those industries outside who desire to enter prisons should be allowed to enter for the purpose of employment placement.

12. *We demand* that inmates be allowed to form or join labor unions.

13. *We demand* that inmates be granted the right to support their own families; at present thousands of welfare recipients have to divide their checks to support their imprisoned relatives who without the outside support could not even buy toilet articles or food. Men working on scale wages could support themselves and families while in prison.

14. *We demand* that correctional officers be prosecuted as a matter of law for shooting inmates, around inmates, or any act of cruel and unusual punishment where it is not a matter of life or death.

15. *We demand* that all institutions who use inmate labor be made to conform with the state and federal minimum wage laws.

16. Deleted.

17. *We demand* an end to trials being held on the premises of San Quentin Prison, or any other prison without the jury as stated in the U.S. Constitution as being picked from the county of the trial proceedings and of the peers of the accused; that being in this case, other prisoners as the selected jurors.

18. *We demand* an end to the escalating practice of physical brutality being perpetrated upon the inmates of California State Prisons at San Quentin, Folsom, and Soledad Prison in particular.

19. Deleted.

20. *We demand* appointment of three lawyers from the California Bar Association for full-time positions to provide legal assistance for inmates seeking post-conviction relief, and to act as liaison between the administration and inmates for bringing inmate complaints to the attention of the administration.

21. *We demand* updating of industry working conditions to standards as provided for under California law.

22. *We demand* establishment of inmate workers insurance plan to provide compensation for work related accidents.

23. *We demand* establishment of a unionized vocational training program comparable to that of the federal prison system which provides for union instructors, union pay scale, and union membership upon completion of the vocational training course.

24. *We demand* annual accounting of the Inmate Welfare Fund and formulation of an inmate committee to give inmates a voice as to how such funds are used.

25. *We demand* that the Adult Authority Board appointed by the governor be eradicated and replaced by a parole board elected by popular vote of the people. In a world where many crimes are punished by indeterminate sentences; where authority acts within secrecy and within vast discretion and gives heavy weight to accusations by prison employees against inmates, inmates feel trapped unless they are willing to abandon their desire to be independent men.

26. *We strongly demand* that the state and prison authorities conform to recommendation 1 of the "Soledad Caucus Report," to wit,

"That the State Legislature create a full-time salaried board of overseers for the state prisons. The board would be responsible for evaluating allegations made by inmates, their families, friends, and lawyers, against employees charged with acting inhumanely, illegally or unreasonably. The board should include people nominated by a psychological or psychiatric association, by the state bar association or by the Public Defenders Association, and by groups of concerned, involving laymen."

27. *We demand* that prison authorities conform to the conditional requirements and needs as described in the recent released manifesto from the Folsom Adjustment Center.

28. *We demand* an immediate end to the agitation of race relations by the prison administrations of this state.

29. *We demand* that the California prison system furnish Folsom prison with the services of ethnic counselors for the needed special services of brown and black population of this prison.

30. *We demand* an end to the discrimination in the judgment and quota of parole for black and brown people.

31. *We demand* that all prisoners be present at the time that their cells and property are being searched by the correctional officers of state prisons.

Bibliography

Books

Altshuler, Alan, H. *Community Control.* New York: Pegasus, 1970.

American Friends Service Committee. *Struggle for Justice.* New York: Hill & Wang, 1971.

Andrews, Frank Earl and Dickens, Albert. *Voices From the Big House.* New York: Pyramid Books, 1972.

Atkins, Burton, and Glick, Henry, eds. *Prisons, Protest and Politics.* Englewood Cliffs, N.J.: Prentice-Hall, 1972.

Bachrach, Peter, and Baratz, Morton. *Power and Poverty: Theory and Practice.* New York: Oxford University Press, 1970.

Baker, J.E. *The Right to Participate.* Metuchen, N.J.: Scarecrow Press, 1974.

Barry, Brian. *Sociologists, Economists, and Democracy.* London: Macmillan Company, 1970.

Blackburn, Robin, ed. *Ideology in the Social Sciences.* New York: Vintage Books, 1972.

Blassingame, John W. *The Slave Community.* London: Oxford University Press, 1972.

Breitman, George. *The Last Year of Malcolm X.* New York: Pathfinder Press, 1970.

Browning, Frank, and *Ramparts*, eds. *Prison Life.* New York: Harper & Row, 1972.

Carroll, Leo. *Hacks, Blacks, and Cons.* Lexington, Mass.: Lexington Books, D.C. Heath, 1974.

Casper, Jonathan. *American Criminal Justice.* Englewood Cliffs, N.J.: Prentice-Hall, 1972.

Clark, Ramsey. *Crime in America.* New York: Simon & Schuster, 1971.

Cleaver, Eldridge. *Soul on Ice.* New York: Dell Publishing, 1968.

Clemmer, Donald. *The Prison Community.* New York: Christopher Publishing, 1940.

Cressey, Donald, ed. *The Prison: Studies in Institutional Organization and Change.* New York: Holt, Rinehart and Winston, 1961.

Dahl, Robert. *Pluralist Democracy in the United States.* Chicago: Rand McNally, 1967.

Davis, Angela Y., ed. *If They Come in the Morning.* New York: Third Press, 1971.

Durkheim, Emile. *The Division of Labor in Society.* New York: Free Press, 1964.

Emerson, Thomas. *The System of Freedom of Expression.* New York: Vintage Books, 1970.

Essien-Udom, E.U. *Black Nationalism*. New York: Dell, 1962.
Fanon, Franz. *The Wretched of the Earth*. New York: Grove Press, 1963.
Fogel, David. *"We Are the Living Proof"* Cincinnati, Ohio: W.H. Anderson Company, 1975.
Frankel, Marvin. *Criminal Sentences: Law without Order*. New York: Hill & Wang, 1973.
Gittell, Marilyn and Berube, R. *Local Control in Education*. New York: Praeger Publishing, 1972.
Goldfarb, Ronald, and Singer, Linda. *After Conviction*. New York: Simon & Schuster, 1973.
Goffman, Erving. *Asylums: Essays on the Social Situation of Mental Patients*. New York: Doubleday Anchor, 1961.
Grosser, George, ed. *Theoretical Studies in Social Organization of the Prison*. New York: Social Science Research Council, 1960.
Haft, Marilyn, and Hermann, Michele. *Prisoners' Rights Source Book*. New York: Clark Boardman, 1973.
Hart, H.L.A. *The Concept of Law*. London: Oxford University Press, 1961.
Hazelrigg, Lawrence, ed. *Prison within Society*. Garden City, N.Y.: Doubleday, 1969.
Irwin, John. *The Felon*. Englewood Cliffs, N.J.: Prentice-Hall, 1970.
Jackson, George. *Soledad Brother*. New York: Bantam Books, 1970.
Johnson, Elmer Hubert. *Crime, Correction and Society*. Homewood, Ill.: Dorsey Press, 1964.
Johnston, Norman; Savitz, Leonard; and Wolfgang, Marvin, eds. *The Sociology of Punishment and Corrections*. 2nd ed. New York: John Wiley and Sons, 1971.
Kassenbaum, Gene; Ward, David N.; and Wilner, Daniel. *Prison Treatment and Parole Survival*. New York: John Wiley and Sons, 1971.
Krantz, Sheldon. *The Law of Corrections and Prisoners Rights*. St. Paul, Minn.: West Publishing, 1973.
Leiby, James. *Charity and Corrections in New Jersey*. New Brunswick, N.J.: Rutgers University Press, 1967.
Leighton, Alexander. *The Governing of Men*. Princeton, N.J.: Princeton University Press, 1968.
Lincoln, Eric C. *The Black Muslims in America*. Boston: Beacon Press, 1961.
Lopez-Rey, Manuel. *Crime*. New York: Praeger, 1970.
Lukac, George. *History and Class Consciousness*. Cambridge: MIT Press, 1971.
MacIver, R.M. *The Modern State*. Oxford: Clarendon Press, 1926.
Mandel, Ernest. *The Marxist Theory of the State*. New York: Merit Publishers, 1971.
Marcuse, Herbert. *One Dimensional Man*. Boston: Beacon Press, 1964.
Mathiesen, Thomas. *The Politics of Abolition*. New York: John Wiley and Sons, 1974.

Matles, James, and Higgins, James. *Them and Us*. New York: McGraw-Hill, 1973.

McCleery, Richard H. "Power, Communication and The Social Order: A Study of Prison Government." Ph.D. dissertation. University of North Carolina, 1956.

Menninger, Karl. *The Crime of Punishment*. New York: Viking Press, 1966.

Messinger, Sheldon. "Strategies of Control." Ph.D. dissertation. University of California, Los Angeles, 1958.

Messinger, Sheldon; Studt, Eliot; and Wilson, Thomas. *C: Unit: A Search for Community in Prison*. New York: Russell Sage Foundation, 1968.

Miliband, Ralph. *The State in Capitalist Society*. New York: Basic Books, 1969.

Minton, Robert J., ed. *Inside: Prison American Style*. New York: Random House, 1971.

Mitford, Jessica. *Kind and Usual Punishment*. New York: Alfred A. Knopf, 1973.

Morris, Norval, and Hawkins, Gordon. *The Honest Politician's Guide to Crime Control*. Chicago: University of Chicago Press, 1970.

New York State Commission on Attica. *Attica*. New York: Bantam Books, 1972.

O'Connor, James. *Fiscal Crisis of the State*. Boston: St. Martin's Press, 1973.

Ohlin, Lloyd E., ed. *Prisoners in America*. Englewood Cliffs, N.J.: Prentice-Hall, 1973.

Orland, Leonard. *Justice, Punishment, Treatment*. New York: Free Press, 1973.

Oswald, Russell. *Attica, My Story*. Garden City, N.Y.: Doubleday, 1970.

Packer, Herbert. *The Limits of the Criminal Sanction*. Stanford: Stanford University Press, 1968.

Parker, Tony. *The Frying Pan*. New York: Harper, 1970.

Piven, Frances Fox and Cloward, Richard. *Regulating the Poor*. New York: Vintage Books, 1971.

Quinney, Richard. *Critique of the Legal Order*. Boston: Little, Brown, 1973.

Quinney, Richard. *The Social Reality of Crime*. Boston: Little, Brown, 1970.

Radzinowicz, Leon. *Ideology and Crime*. New York: Columbia University Press, 1966.

Rubin, Sol. *Law of Criminal Correction*. St. Paul, Minn.: West Publishing, 1973.

Rudovsky, David. *The Rights of Prisoners*. New York: Avon Books, 1973.

Seale, Bobby. *Seize the Time*. New York: Vintage Books, 1970.

Selznick, Phillip. *Law, Society and Industrial Justice*. New York: Russell Sage Foundation: 1969.

Skolnick, Jerome H., *Justice Without Trial.* New York: John Wiley and Sons, 1975.

Skolnick, Jerome. *The Politics of Protest.* New York: Ballantine Books, 1969.

Sykes, Gresham. *The Society of Captives.* Princeton, N.J.: Princeton University Press, 1958.

Title, Charles R. *Society of Subordinates.* Bloomington, Ind.: Indiana University Press, 1972.

Wolin, Sheldon. *Politics and Vision.* Boston: Little, Brown, 1960.

Wright, Erik Ohlin, ed. *The Politics of Punishment.* New York: Harper & Row, 1973.

X, Malcolm. *The Autobiography of Malcolm X.* New York: Grove Press, 1966.

Yee, Min S. *The Melancholy History of Soledad Prison.* New York: Harper Magazine Press, 1970.

Articles

Berk, Bernard. "Organizational Goals and Inmate Organizations." In *Correctional Institutions*, ed. Carter, Robert, Glaser, Daniel and Wilkins, Leslie. New York: J.P. Lippincott, 1972.

Bram, Jonathan. "Prison Disciplinary Procedures: Creating Rules." *Cleveland State Law Review*, May 21, 1972.

Browning, Frank. "Organizing Behind Bars." In *Prisons, Protest and Politics*, ed. Burton Atkins and Henry Glick. Englewood Cliffs, N.J.: Prentice-Hall, 1972.

Cleaver, Eldridge. "The Muslims Decline." In *Prison Life*, ed. Browning. New York: Harper & Row, 1972.

Coons, William. "An Attica Graduate Tells His Story." *New York Times Magazine*, October 10, 1971.

Glaser, Daniel. "Disciplinary Action and Counseling." In *Correctional Institutions*, ed. Daniel Glaser, Carter and Wilkins. New York: J.P. Lippincott, 1972.

Glick, Brian. "Change through the Courts." In *Politics and Punishment*, ed. Erik Ohlin Wright. New York: Harper & Row, 1973.

Lamott, Kenneth. "San Quentin." *New York Times Magazine*, May 2, 1971.

Leeke, William. "Some Aspects of the Effects of Inmate Suits on Correctional Systems." *EBI Law Enforcement Bulletin*, July, 1974.

McCleery, Richard. "Policy Change in Prison Management." Governmental Research Bureau, East Lansing, Mich., 1957.

McCleery, Richard. "The Governmental Process and Informal Social Control." In *The Prison: Studies in Institutional Organization and Change*. ed. Donald Cressey. New York: Holt, Rinehart and Winston, 1961.

Minton, Robert and Rice, Stephen. "Race War at San Quentin." *Ramparts Magazine*. January 1970.

Minton, Robert and Rice, Stephen. "Using Racism at San Quentin." In *Prison Life*, ed. Browning. New York: Harper & Row, 1970.

Mullen, William F. "Community Control and Black Political Participation" in *Participatory Democracy*, ed. Terrence Cook and Patrick Morgan. San Francisco: Canfield Press, 1971.

Murton, Thomas. "Too Good for Arkansas." *Prisons, Protest and Politics*, ed. Burton Atkins and Henry Glick. Englewood Cliffs, N.J.:Prentice-Hall, 1972.

Pallas, John and Barber, Robert. "From Riot to Revolution." In *Politics and Punishment*, ed. Erik Ohlin Wright. New York: Harper & Row, 1973.

Polansky, Norman. "The Prison as an Authority." *Journal of Criminal Law and Criminology* 33 (1942).

Reich, Robert B. "Bargaining in Correctional Institutions: Restructuring the Relations between the Inmate and the Prison Authority." *Yale Law Review*, vol. 81, no. 4 (March 1972).

Rothman, David J. "Decarcerating Prisoners and Patients." *Civil Liberties Review*, vol. I., no. 1 (1973).

Schrag, Clarence. "Leadership Among Prison Inmates." In *The Sociology of Punishment and Corrections*, 2nd ed., ed. Norman Johnson, Leonard Savitz, and Marvin Wolfgang. New York: John Wiley and Sons, 1971.

Schrag, Clarence. "Some Foundations for a Theory of Corrections." *The Prison: Studies in Institutional Organization and Change*, ed. Donald Cressey, New York: Holt, Rinehart and Winston, 1961.

Stanford, Phil. "A Model Clockwork-Orange Prison." *The New York Times Magazine*, September 17, 1972.

Szulz, Ted. "George Jackson Radicalizes the Brothers in San Quentin and Soledad." *New York Times Magazine*, August 1, 1971.

Tappen, Paul. "The Legal Rights of Prisoners." *The Annals*, May 1954.

Weather Underground Organization. "Break the Chains." *Osawatomie*, Autumn 1975.

Woolpert, Steven. "The Political Attitudes of Prison Inmates." Paper read at the American Political Science Association 1976 annual meeting.

Government and Organizational Sources

Bennet, L.A. "Crime and Violence on the Streets and in Prisons." *California Department of Corrections*, January 1974.

California Department of Corrections. *Administration Manual.* Sacramento, Calif., 1974, 1975.

California Department of Corrections. *Director's Rules.* Sacramento, Calif., 1975.

California Department of Corrections. "Characteristics of Felon Population in California State Prisons by Institution." June 30, 1975.

California Department of Corrections. *Management Review Questionnaire.* West Prison, 1974-75.

California Department of Corrections. *Master Plan.* Sacramento, Calif., August 16, 1968.

California Department of Corrections. "Working Papers of the Task Force to Study Violence," March 22, 1974.

California Prison Task Force. "Correctional Systems Study." Sacramento, Calif., July 1971.

California Senate. Black Caucus Report on California Prisons. July 15, 1970.

California State Employees' Association. "California Prisons in Crises." Sacramento, Calif., September 24, 1971.

East Prison. *Minutes of the Meetings Between PRC and Administration.* 1956-1975.

National Association of Attorneys General. "Special Report of Corrections" January 18, 1974.

New Jersey Governor's Negotiating Committee. "Report of Prison Riot." December 18, 1972.

New Jersey, Rahway State Prison, Inmate Committee. "Response of Administration to Issues Developed between Governor's Committee and Inmates' Committee." July, 1972.

West Prison. *Minutes of Meetings Between MAC and Administration,* 1965-75.

Newspapers and Pamphlets

Center for Prison Services, "Forum Bridge," Trenton N.J. State Prison.

Fortune Society. *Fortune News.*

Inmate newspapers. East and West Prisons.

People's Court. "Free Popeye": *A Report on the Assassination of Popeye Jackson.* San Francisco, California. Undated.

Prisoners' Representative Committee *News.* Trenton N.J. State Prison.

Prisoners' Union, *The Outlaw.* San Francisco, Calif. 1974-1976.

Transitions to Freedom, *Your Rights as a Free Convicted Citizen.* San Francisco, 1975.

Universal Fellowship of Metropolitan Community Churches. *The Cellmate.* 1975.

Court Cases

Abernathy v. Cunningham, 393 F.2nd 775 (4th Cir. 1968).
Clutchette v. Procunier, 328 F.Supp. 767 (N.D. Calif., 1971).
Coffin v. Reichard, 143 F.2nd 443 (6th Cir. 1944).
Cooper v. Pate, 84 SCt. 1733 (1964).
Cruz v. Beto, 405 U.S. 319, 321 (1972).
Evans v. Mosley, 445 F.2nd 1084, 1086 (10th Cir. 1972).
Goldberg v. Kelly, 397 U.S. 254, 90 SCt. 1011, 25 F.2nd 287 (1969).
Morales v. Schmidt, F.2nd (7th Cir. 1973).
Morales v. Schmidt, 340 F.Supp. (W.D.Wis. 1972).
National Prisoners Reform Association v. Sharkey, 347 F.Supp. 1234 (DRI 1972).
Palmigiano v. Travisone, 317 F.Supp.776 (1970).
Pierce v. Lavalee, 293 F.2nd 233 (2nd Cir. 1961).
Procunier v. Martinez, 945 St.1800 40 1.Ed. 2nd 224 (1974).
Rowland v. Jones, 452 F.2nd 1005 (8th Cir. 1971).
Ruffin v. Commonwealth, 62 Va. 790 (1871).
Sostre v. McGinnis, 334 F.2nd 906 (2nd Cir. 1964).
Sostre v. Rockefeller, 312 F.Supp. 863 (N.Y. 1970).
Theriault v. Carlson, 339 F.Supp. 375 (N.D. Ga. 1972).
Walker v. Blackwell, 411 F.2nd 23 (5th Cir. 1969).

Index

About the Author

Ronald Berkman is assistant professor of political science at Brooklyn College-City University of New York. He received the B.A. from William Paterson College and the M.A. and Ph.D. from Princeton University. He has taught at the Woodrow Wilson School of Public and International Affairs at Princeton and has been the recipient of a Guggenheim Foundation grant. He is presently writing a book about the question of legitimacy in American politics and doing research on the political economy of the city.